AFTER THE HONEYMOON

HOW CONFLICT CAN IMPROVE YOUR RELATIONSHIP

REVISED EDITION

DANIEL B. WILE

CONTENTS

Preface

After the honeymoon. The very words carry a burden of sadness, as if for a short while we lived in a golden trance of love, and now we've been jolted awake. The fog of early infatuation has lifted and we see our partners for who they are. Behavior that seemed cute now becomes annoying. "Does she have to smile that way all the time?" Differences that seemed minor now appear glaring. "Doesn't he ever want to go out?" Habits that were irritating now become infuriating. "Does she have to turn on the radio every time she comes into the room?" The negative side of what originally attracted us slides into view. "I love her energy, but can't she ever sit down for a second?" "His steadiness is calming, but doesn't he get excited about anything?" "I love her honesty, but does she have to be so brutal about me?"

Immediately comes the thought, "Oh no! Is this the person I'm supposed to spend the rest of my life with?" followed by a frantic internal debate:

> **YOU**: Okay, no relationship is perfect. I've got to accept the bad with the good.

> **PANICKY YOU**: But right now it's hard to remember much that is good. Is there any way out of this?

> **YOU**: Yes, by remembering that a deeper, more satisfying love will emerge over time.

> **PANICKY YOU**: But how do I know that it will? And how long will it take? Can I wait that long? And in the meantime, how do I deal with the annoying behavior, the glaring differences between us, and the negative side of what originally attracted me?

YOU: You deal with them by bringing these things out into the open.

PANICKY YOU: That's easy to say. The last time I tried that, I ended up sleeping on the couch.

This book is about finding a way to avoid that couch. How? By creating a non-accusing vantage point above the fray—ideally a platform from which we can talk about the relationship without getting into fights; more practically, a way to recover from those fights we do get into. Operating from such a platform, we will be able to commiserate with our partners about these fights and turn them into occasions for intimacy.

That's what I want to do—create intimacy—and I'm going to start by turning your partner into a better person. I'm going to do this without your partner having to do anything and without you having to do anything except read this book. This may seem like a lot to promise. We've all been told that we shouldn't try to change our partners; if we are dissatisfied, we should concentrate on changing ourselves. But don't we all secretly wish that we *could* change our partners?

So here's my recommendation. Read the first six or seven chapters, and then look at your partner. (Let's say that you are a woman, and your partner is a man.) If I'm right, he won't appear quite so unloving, neglectful, demanding, insensitive, withholding, controlling, selfish, self-righteous, or afraid of intimacy. Then read another six or seven chapters, and look at him again. By this time, like a werewolf in reverse, he should actually have begun sprouting signs of nobility. And that's because you'll begin to see that:

1. What appears as his defensiveness and excessive arguing may actually be the result of an inability to present his case in a way that you can appreciate and understand.
2. What appears as his angry tantrums or unrealistic fantasies may actually be useful clues to important hidden issues in the relationship.
3. What appears as his unwillingness to meet you halfway may actually be the result of his over-compromising and giving in

too much. For example, in preparing for a vacation, he may have left all the arranging and packing to you. But that may be because he has already over-compromised. In an effort to be agreeable and accommodating, he may not have sufficiently stood up for the kind of vacation he really wanted.

He probably won't do anything differently while you read this book; in fact, he could be asleep on the couch the whole time. But somehow he will have changed—or your view of him will have changed. In your eyes, he will have turned into a more vulnerable, more struggling, more caring, and, in short, better person.

This book enables us to view our partners more empathically by counteracting our usual tendency, which is to view our partners— and ourselves—accusingly. At the heart of our difficulties is this focus on laying blame. We don't realize how much this hidden blame— especially self-blame—interferes with our ability to think and talk effectively about problems. In particular, we believe that:

- Our relationship problems arise from our character defects (for example, our selfishness or dependency).
- These problems are the result of emotional baggage from childhood that we're carrying into the present.
- These problems are the result of our failure to accept reality, give up unreasonable expectations, and make compromises.
- We really want our problems. We are getting too much out of them to want to give them up.

You may be surprised that I'm describing such ways of thinking as blaming. People use them all the time. They think of them not as blaming but simply as *true.* Neighbors talking over a cup of coffee use them. Hairdressers and bartenders chatting with their customers use them. Characters on sitcoms use them. Therapists use them. I use them.

And to a large extent they are true. In fact, they seem so true that they can easily preclude all other interpretations. There is no doubt, for example, that couple problems do go back to childhood.

But once we track a problem to childhood and, for example, trace a man's outbursts at his wife to his being spoiled as a child, all that we now see when we look at him is a spoiled little boy who has tantrums if he doesn't immediately get his way. It becomes difficult to consider the possibility that he might have a real reason right now for being upset.

I want to show that behavior that appears on the surface to be irrational, childish, or pathological has a hidden rationality—it makes sense in terms of the present situation and not just as a carryover from childhood. People do have emotional baggage from childhood, but this baggage may enable them to detect subtle difficulties that are actually occurring in their present relationship. A wife's childhood-based special sensitivity to being ignored—she felt rejected by her mother—can enable her to detect the subtle ways in which she is actually being ignored by her husband right now.

Imagine the difference it would make if we were to find the hidden reasonableness in our own and our partner's behavior. This is what I mean when I say that reading this book will enable you to look at your partner and at yourself in a new way. The goal is to develop a platform, a non-blaming vantage point, from which people can recognize the ways in which their partner's (as well as their own) behavior makes sense.

The ideas in this book apply to heterosexual couples, to gay and lesbian couples, and to some extent, to people in nonromantic relationships: business colleagues, roommates, friends, relatives and tennis partners.

At various points in the book, I have a hypothetical skeptical reader breaking in with an objection. He is your stand-in—my effort to engage you in conversation by imagining reactions you might have. He berates me and abuses me. He calls me to task for being simplistic, belaboring the obvious, beating many a dead horse, engaging in psychobabble, and simply being wrongheaded. His comments are flip at times, as are some of my responses, but by the end of the book we're getting along pretty well.

Whatever the situation in your relationship, there's a way of thinking about it—and a conversation you can have with your partner—that can make a difference. It's just difficult to figure out what this conversation is. This book is an attempt to help you figure it out.

This book comes out of my thirty years as a couples therapist and is built on ideas of Bernard Apfelbaum, a psychologist who practices in Berkeley, California, who developed a way of thinking about people and their problems that I find extremely compelling. To learn more about Apfelbaum, please visit his Web site at http://www. bapfelbaumphd.com.

Acknowledgments

The revised edition

Thanks to Susan Weiss, Penny Kramer, Carol Carr, Peggy Karp, Alan Plum, and Bernard Apfelbaum for their editorial help.

The original 1988 edition

Carolyn Pape Cowan, Philip A. Cowan, Betty J. Wenz, Eleanor Bulova, Daniel Berman, Robert Epstein, Norman Livson, Ronald Spinka, and Carol Swanson thoroughly read the manuscript and made valuable suggestions. Howard P. Wile, Margery B. Wile, Patricia Blanche, Philip Blanche, and Peg Kemper made important comments on specific sections of the book. Joanne R. Wile, Bernard Apfelbaum, Nan Narboe, Carol Carr, Alan Rinzler, Diana Weinstock, and Dean Delis read several drafts of the book and, in addition to their invaluable detailed comments, made useful suggestions about the book's overall style, tone, and organization.

Grateful acknowledgment is made to Alfred A. Knopf, Inc., for permission to reprint passages from *Heartburn* by Nora Ephron. Copyright © 1983 by Nora Ephron.

Part I

USING YOUR RELATIONSHIP TO SOLVE YOUR PROBLEMS

Chapter 1
Blending the Problem into the Relationship

What we all want to do with our problems, of course, is to solve them. In fact, we expect to solve them, and we feel like failures if we don't. But certain problems are *un*solvable. And while each relationship has its own special set of satisfactions, it appears also to have its own special set of unsolvable problems. You and your partner are pretty unusual—and pretty lucky—if you can't immediately think of a number of problems that you've worn yourselves out trying to make go away.

Imagine another thirty years of struggling with the same problems from which you've been suffering since the beginning of the relationship. It's enough to make a person want to separate or divorce or simply commit adultery with a TV set. And that's what a lot of people do. A lot of other people resign themselves to a second-class relationship. And a lot of other people just try not to think about it.

But there is something else you can do; you can blend these problems into the relationship. And by so doing, you will (1) reduce their destructive effect, (2) eliminate some of them entirely (they turn out not to be so unsolvable after all), and (3) turn them into opportunities for intimacy.

> SKEPTIC: That sounds like psychobabble to me. If you have a problem, you should solve it and, failing that, try not to mind it so much.

> WILE: Well yes, but that doesn't always work. Think of the last

time you tried not to mind something that upset you about your wife. Let's say that she doesn't talk much to you, or doesn't want to have sex often enough, or wants to stay home when you want to go out. Since bringing it up would just start an argument, you keep your mouth shut. If you're lucky, your resentment passes: You satisfy your need to talk by calling a friend, or your wife surprises you with a drink and a suggestive remark, or you discover that you're content to stay at home with a good book

SKEPTIC: You're making my case for me. If you don't go around all the time having to express every little resentment, things will take care of themselves.

WILE: Sometimes. But the rest of the time, your resentment won't pass. Calling the friend just makes you more aware of how you miss being able to talk to your wife. Or by the time you get into bed, the drink has worked to put your wife to sleep. Or the book turns out to be disappointing, and so does the evening

SKEPTIC: Something like that happened to me just last night.

WILE: Yes, and if you're like most people, you probably made the complaint you would have made two hours before, but now with greater force since your resentment about the matter has had time to gain heat, volume, and a few thorns. And the resulting fight is likely to be worse than if you had stated your complaint in the first place.

SKEPTIC: Yes, I know. I should have just kept my mouth shut.

Yes, this is where people usually decide it would have been best to keep their mouths shut. But for most people having to do so for any length of time will demoralize them. It will sap their spirit. Soon they'll feel less like talking, having sex, going out, or anything. And the wall between them and their partners will thicken.

This is why I suggest blending the problem into the relationship. You can do this by:

1. Holding an ongoing conversation about the problem rather than doing what you have been doing, which is to smolder silently until you erupt into angry exchanges that sometimes escalate into war;

2. Expecting the problem to recur, and in fact planning for its recurrence, rather than simply hoping that it will go away; and

3. Turning the problem to whatever positive use you can, rather than simply trying to put up with it.

But Doesn't Talking about the Problem Make Matters Worse?

Blending a problem into the relationship requires developing an effective ongoing way of talking about the problem. Of course, partners have good reason *not* to talk about their problems, since the attempt to do so often turn into arguments that make matters worse, as the following example shows.

Paul and Alice are a couple in their late twenties who have been married for five years. Paul is upset at the way Alice acts at parties. Driving home one night, he tries to talk with her about it.

PAUL: Listen, I have to tell you this. You talked too loud all night and laughed like a fool at every dumb joke. Everyone was looking at you.

ALICE: (*feeling accused—no wonder—and fighting back*) That's ridiculous! I didn't talk louder than anyone else. In fact, you're the one who looked peculiar, glued to the couch and never opening your mouth.

PAUL: (*defending himself*) I talked to plenty of people. And if I was quiet at times, it was only because I was so embarrassed by the way you were acting. I just wanted to hide.

ALICE: In a book? At a party?

PAUL: Better than listening for the umpteenth time to how you

were raised on a farm. I'd like to go somewhere where you
didn't bore everyone to tears with the story of your life.

The argument rages for twenty minutes after which neither speaks
to the other for two days. Paul vows to himself never to go to another
party with Alice, ever.

Eventually the whole thing blows over. Paul forgets his vow, and
they start socializing with their friends again. Everything is okay the
first few times they go out. Then they go to a picnic where they hardly
know anybody. Not surprisingly:

- Alice feels self-conscious.
- She talks loudly and laughs nervously.
- Paul gets quiet.
- They argue on the way home.
- Paul vows never again to go to another party with Alice.
- It's two days before they start talking.
- They start talking.
- They go out again.
- Three months later, they have the same fight.

It's easy to imagine Alice and Paul going though this cycle forever.
But let's try to imagine how it might be possible for them to talk
effectively about the problem.

Let's start by having them do something they rarely do: bring up
the issue when they aren't fighting. They rarely do it because they're
afraid that this would just restart the fight.

When one finally gets the nerve up, it can go like this. "Paul
sweetie," Alice says tentatively, "I'm really tired of how your always
picking fights with me when we come home from parties." Paul,
tensing up, responds, "Well I'm tired of the way you get so gushy at
them."

How did the conversation go from zero to sixty in five seconds?
Simple. Alice led off with an accusation, which turned Paul into an
enemy, so he accused her right back. To start a useful discussion,
Alice would need to lead off with something conciliatory and, for
example, admit her role in the problem. But when she even thinks

about the problem at parties, she becomes flooded with resentment and loses the ability to admit anything.

The situation seems hopeless.

But Alice and Paul have the possibility of talking usefully about the issue, which we can see by tapping into their inner dialogues. What we find is a whirr of reproaches, self-reproaches, self-justifications—and, carefully hidden, the makings of a conversation.

Alice's Inner Dialogue

BLAME: Damn! I want to kill him. Why does he always have to get so defensive when I try to talk to him?

IMPULSE: I'll go back and tell him that right now. Where is he?

DOUBT: No, it will just start another round, and I still have a headache from the first one.

BLAME: Why does he have to keep doing things like that? If it wasn't for the kids, I'd …

IMPULSE: Okay, I'll tell him that.

DOUBT: But I promised him I'd stop threatening divorce all the time … and for stuff that's so minor.

IMPULSE: But it's not minor. Maybe I should stop threatening and just do it.

BLAME: Not to mention that he should promise me a few things—like not attacking me all the time. There I am finally relaxing—the ordeal is over—and he has to start in on me. And it is an ordeal. Parties ought to be banned. They're like junior high school all over again.

ADMISSION: Okay, Paul's right, I do get gushy … the same way I acted all through junior high.

SELF-BLAME: I can't stand myself sometimes.

BLAME: Though where does he get off thinking he's so perfect?

Alice deals with her sense of helpless frustration by imagining various responses she might make. She recognizes that Paul isn't totally wrong (she does get gushy) but she quickly returns to blaming him. Our look into Alice's thinking shows little room for conciliation, which, as we will find, is also true of Paul's thinking.

Paul's Inner Dialogue

> **FRUSTRATION:** I can't stand how Alice always gets so defensive when I'm just telling her what she needs to know—what a total fool she makes of herself.
>
> **PLAN:** Maybe she'd get it if I sent it all in an E-mail.
>
> **DOUBT:** But I tried that last year, and she sent back a ten-page diatribe as an attachment.
>
> **GRIM HUMOR:** Skywriting! That's an idea.
>
> **REPROACH:** How can she be so totally oblivious to what other people think?
>
> **SELF-REPROACH:** Why do I have to care so much what other people think?
>
> **SELF-JUSTIFICATION:** It's not me. Anyone would be embarrassed if their partner acted that way.
>
> **SELF-REPROACH:** Especially me. It makes me want to dig a hole and bury myself in it. I hate how self-conscious I get.
>
> **SELF-JUSTIFICATION:** Though none of that would happen if Alice didn't act like such a total fool.
>
> **SELF-REPROACH:** Of course, I had the problem long before I met her.
>
> **SELF-JUSTIFICATION:** But not nearly as bad. It's now ten times worse. And that's her fault.

Alice's principle inner struggle is between what she wants to do (tell Paul off) and sees as prudent to do (avoid provoking him). Paul's major struggle is between self-reproach and self-justification; he fights off his doubts about the justice of his complaint. Each finds each other's accusations hard to bear because they reinforce self-accusations.

If it were earlier in the relationship, Alice and Paul would spend the rest of the evening in angry silence. But over the years they have developed knowledge—about themselves, each other, and what happens between them—that provides at least the possibility of working things out. Couples often become entrenched in their counterproductive patterns, but they may also develop a relationship wisdom that may enable them to escape these patterns. Our tap into Alice and Paul's thinking enables us to detect this new knowledge, this relationship wisdom, which I've indicated with an asterisk

Paul's Inner Dialogue

> **REPROACH:** Alice isn't talking. That's just like her to give me the silent treatment. She's so immature.
>
> **PLAN:** I won't talk, either. Let her stew in her own juice.

So far there is no new knowledge here. Paul has been engaged in this kind of thinking from the first year of the relationship. But starting in the second year, the following element crept into his inner dialogue:

> ***ARGUMENT AGAINST THIS PLAN:** Except I'm the one doing the stewing. She can go on like this forever, and I'm sitting here devastated.
>
> **RESOLUTION:** I don't care. I won't be the first to talk.

This new knowledge—Paul's realization that he is operating at a disadvantage—doesn't lead to a change of behavior; he still refuses to talk. But in his third year with Alice, a further new element crept into his thinking.

> ***FURTHER ARGUMENT AGAINST:** And when we go to bed, she'll fall asleep, leaving me up all night eating ice cream.
>
> **DECISION:** Her arrogance is disgusting. No way will I go first.

This further bit of new knowledge—Paul's anticipation that he will have a bad night—*still* doesn't lead to a change of behavior. But now comes an element, added just last year, that does.

> ***RECOGNITION**: But hey, this may be one of those times that Alice sees me as her father who was always telling her, "I'm not going to talk to you until you apologize."

What's new isn't Paul's realization that Alice can see him as her father, since she told him about this tendency years ago. What's new is the shift of this information from the periphery of his mind into his working consciousness. What was just a random bit of data has now been applied where it counts.

> **NEW PLAN:** I don't want her to think I'm like her father, and I've got to show her that.

Paul's recalling what Alice said about her father enables him to glimpse the vulnerability behind her arrogance, a glimpse that dispels his sense of helpless frustration. He realizes that he is having an effect on her, more than he even wants, and this leads him to revise his plan. He now *wants* to talk, to prove that he's not like her father.

> **NEW PROBLEM:** But what do I say? I'm not going to apologize. There's nothing to apologize for.
>
> **PLAN:** I'll act as if nothing has happened and hope that she'll do the same.
>
> **ARGUMENT AGAINST:** It's risky. She might take advantage to lash out at me.
>
> **DECISION:** I'll chance it. I'm not going to stay up all night eating saturated fat and letting her think I'm her father.
>
> **MOBILIZING COURAGE:** Here goes.

Paul says, "Just thought I'd let you know—I love the way you were reading to the kids just now."

Alice's Inner Dialogue

> **EVALUATION:** So he's trying to be nice now after all that meanness.
>
> **PLAN:** I'll tell him, "Oh, you don't think I was reading too gushily?"
>
> **GOAL:** That'll show him how hurt I was and how angry I still am.
>
> **ARGUMENT AGAINST:** No, I can't say that. The poor guy is trying to patch things up.
>
> **ARGUMENT FOR:** This may be my last chance to show him how angry I still am.
>
> **ARGUMENT AGAINST:** I'll be sorry as soon as I say it. He'll go through the whole gallon of ice cream and be up the whole rest of the night sulking.
>
> **DECISION:** Who cares? It's too good to pass up.

Alice says, "Oh, you don't think I was too gushy?" Less than a second passed between Paul's "I love the way you were reading to the kids just now" and this sarcastic response by Alice. But that was long enough for her to conduct this inner debate. Alice's mind—everyone's mind—ratchets through chains of reasoning with computer-like speed. I've slowed it down and put it in the form of discrete sentences so that we can get a good look. Paul now holds an inner debate of his own.

Paul's Inner Dialogue

> **EVALUATION:** Uh-oh. She's still angry.
>
> **REPROACH:** Bitch!
>
> **PLAN:** I'll tell her that.
>
> **ARGUMENT AGAINST:** I can't. It's over the line.
>
> **ARGUMENT FOR:** No, it isn't. She is a bitch.
>
> **ARGUMENT AGAINST:** But I don't want to start a war.

> **COMPROMISE:** I'll say it under my breath.

If it were early in the marriage, Paul would mutter "bitch." But the following recent addition to his inner dialogue prevents him from doing that:

> ***ARGUMENT AGAINST:** But that's the coward's way. I'll feel like such a jerk.

Paul is anticipating the shame he would feel were he to call Alice a bitch, which contrasts with earlier in the marriage when he would become aware of the shame only after he spoke.

> **PROBLEM:** But I've got to say something. I can't let her sarcasm go unanswered.
>
> **PROBLEM:** But what? I can't think of anything.
>
> **PLAN:** I'll storm out and slam the door behind me.
>
> **ARGUMENT AGAINST:** Childish.
>
> **NEW PLAN:** I'll break the cup I gave her that she likes so much.
>
> **ARGUMENT AGAINST:** Even more childish.
>
> ***NEW PLAN:** I'll glare at her.
>
> **EVALUATION OF PLAN:** Totally inadequate, but better than spending the rest of the evening kicking myself for doing something that makes me look like an idiot.

Glaring at Alice is the outcome of Paul's search for a way to express to his rage without violating his sense of dignity.

Alice's Inner Dialogue

> ***PERCEPTION:** There's that look.
>
> **EVALUATION:** He's not happy.

Alice is the only one in the world who could understand what Paul's look meant—or even detect that he *had* a look. But its meaning is as clear to her as if it were flashing in neon lights. Our ability to read our partners develops naturally as a part of relationship wisdom.

> **SELF-CRITICISM:** Of course, he's not happy. What I said was mean.

> **SELF-JUSTIFICATION:** He brought it on himself.

Our tap into Alice and Paul's inner dialogues reveals that each confronted a series of problems. Paul dealt with his sense of help-less frustration by vowing not to talk, until he realized that his silence reminded Alice of her father, at which point he decided that he *had* to talk. He feared that Alice might take advantage of what he said to get in a dig, but he concluded that he had no choice. When she *did* take advantage, he tried to come up with a response that he wouldn't be sorry for later.

Alice simultaneously engaged in her own problem-solving. She knew that what she wanted to say ("Oh, you don't think I was too gushy?") was provocative, but she decided that it was too good to pass up. When she saw Paul's unhappy look, she felt self-reproach ("What I said was mean"), which she dealt with by self-justification ("He brought it on himself").

> **ALICE'S NEXT PROBLEM:** Yes, but now I'm stuck with a zombie, and I'm certainly not going to get him to fix the toilet tonight.

> **SOLUTION:** Well, I can be a zombie, too. We'll see how much he likes it.

If it were earlier in the marriage, Alice would give up talking at this point and go off and try to fix the toilet by herself. She wouldn't be able to think of anything to say that wouldn't just make matters worse. But she has made a friend recently.

> ***NEW THOUGHT:** Evelyn would know what to do. She can think of something good to say in any situation.

> **QUESTION:** What would she say?

ANSWER: Something like what she said to me the other day.

ALICE: (*to Paul*) Oops. That was mean. I shouldn't have said that. I just couldn't resist.

Alice is confiding to Paul the doubts she has about whether she should have said what she did. She is bringing Paul in on her inner debate, which is something that she learned from Evelyn. Although much of our relationship wisdom comes from spending time with our partners, some of it comes from friends, books, and so on.

Paul's Inner Dialogue

EVALUATION: It was mean.

REALIZATION: No wonder I felt bad.

If it were earlier in the relationship, Paul would have told Alice, "Yes, so why did you have to say it? I'm tired of you always doing things like that." Alice's conciliatory effort would have triggered this angry reaction, which would have made her sorry she'd said anything at all. But before he can blurt this out, he has the following thoughts.

*ARGUMENT IN ALICE'S DEFENSE:** Of course, it was nice that she admitted it.

*ARGUMENT IN ALICE'S DEFENSE:** And she *does* seem sorry.

ARGUMENT AGAINST ALICE: Of course, if she were serious about being sorry, she wouldn't have said it in the first place.

ARGUMENT IN ALICE'S DEFENSE: Although I can see why she did. It had to be irresistible.

VERDICT IN ALICE'S FAVOR: Hell, I would have said it, too.

Paul is looking at things from Alice's point of view—and he is feeling better about her—which enables him suddenly to see the hurt behind her anger.

> **REVISED VIEW:** That was really harsh of me to criticize Alice for gushing.
>
> **REGRET:** I'm really sorry I did that.
>
> **SELF-REPROACH:** Why did I have to do that?

Earlier Paul was frustrated at Alice over her unwillingness to admit that she gushes. Now he feels bad that he raised the issue at all.

> **PAUL:** I feel bad about what I said—you know, about your gushing.

Alice's admitting that she said something mean has led Paul to admit that he did too.

Alice's Inner Dialogue

> **REPROACH:** He should feel bad.
>
> **SATISFACTION:** I'm glad he does.
>
> **APPRECIATION:** But at least he admitted it.
>
> **COMPASSION:** And that hangdog look—he does seem sorry.
>
> **FORGIVENESS:** He's not such a bad guy.
>
> **AFFECTION:** In fact, he's sweet.
>
> **ADMISSION:** And he's not entirely wrong.

Alice's thoughts form a natural progression. She begins by feeling vindicated ("He should feel bad. I'm glad he does"), which puts her in position to forgive Paul ("But at least he admitted it. And that hangdog look—he does seem sorry"), which leads, in turn, to a resumption of warm feelings toward him ("He's not such a bad guy. In fact, he's sweet"), which then makes it possible for her to consider what he has been saying ("And he's not entirely wrong").

She says, "Well you know you're right—I do get gushy, particularly when I'm around people I don't know." But immediately she has a worry.

Alice's Inner Dialogue

> SECOND THOUGHTS: Uh-oh. Paul could say, "More than just with them."
>
> PLAN: I'll nuke him if he does.

Paul's Inner Dialogue

> *REALIZATION: I forgot that she already knew that she gushes, and what I said just rubbed it in.
>
> DISTRESS: I feel horrible about that.
>
> VOW: I'll make it up to her.
>
> PLAN: I'll tell her that she isn't really that gushy.
>
> ARGUMENT AGAINST: She won't buy it, not after I made such a deal about it.
>
> NEW PLAN: Okay, I'll tell her that I like her gushiness—when it's about the kids or me.
>
> ARGUMENT AGAINST: Small comfort that.
>
> NEW PLAN: Okay, I'll tell that her "No one's perfect."
>
> ARGUMENT AGAINST: She'll roll her eyes. I wouldn't blame her.
>
> NEW PLAN: I'll tell her how I'm not perfect.
>
> ARGUMENT FOR: Well, there's something she can agree with.

When we try to comfort our partners, we search our minds looking for how best to do it.

*PAUL: You know, you're not the only one who gets nervous around strangers. I do too.

ALICE: You're just saying that, right?

*PAUL: No, really. Except I express it by getting quiet.

Paul generally feels too embarrassed about his social awkwardness to discuss it. He does so now only because it serves the more pressing need of comforting Alice. For the moment he is *glad* for his social awkwardness because it gives him a way to make up for what he feels was his insensitive criticism of her.

As long as Alice and Paul continue in this vein—admitting, confiding, and comforting in response to the other doing the same—they will be able to talk usefully about their problem at parties.

> **SKEPTIC:** But how long do you think it's going to last? It was touch and go from the very beginning. One false step and they'll be back in the fight.
>
> **WILE:** Yes, the whole thing is in delicate balance.
>
> **SKEPTIC:** Again, you're making my case for me. You're showing how *hard* it is to talk.
>
> **WILE:** But I'm also showing that a wisdom develops that might make it possible to talk. The greater this wisdom, the greater the chance that Alice and Paul will be able to avoid false steps and to recover from those that they do make. The purpose of this book is to provide information that can increase a reader's relationship wisdom.

Holding an Ongoing Conversation about the Problem

The problem is clear. It isn't just that Alice gets loud and awkward when she gets nervous. And it isn't just that Paul gets shy and self-conscious. It's that Alice's way of getting nervous exacerbates Paul's way. It's a joint problem, and, for a moment at least, that's how they see it. They are talking together about it compassionately. The angry tone is gone and, with it, much of the problem.

A relationship problem is typically really two problems:

1. *The problem itself* (e.g., the interaction between the different ways that Alice and Paul get nervous at parties)
2. *The way partners talk (or don't talk) about the problem* (e.g., the way

Alice and Paul deal with the problem—keeping quiet about it and then getting into angry arguments over it—is the bigger part of the problem and largely responsible for the difficulties between them.

Changing how Alice and Paul *talk* about the problem could go a long way toward detoxifying it and blending it into the relationship. Alice and Paul would be talking together about how their problem at parties drives them apart. They would no longer be cut off from one another. They would no longer be privately preoccupied, each with his or her own particular troubled thoughts about the matter.

The goal is for Alice and Paul to be able to talk about the problem, not just this once, but in an ongoing way. Just as people in the Midwest need to keep in constant contact about the possibility of tornadoes, so couples need to keep in contact about their relationship problems. Each couple has its own set of private tornadoes to keep watch on.

Planning for the Problem

The first step in blending a problem into the relationship sets the stage for the second. To the extent that partners have established an ongoing way of talking about the problem, they can then make joint plans about it.

The following illustrates how Alice and Paul might make such plans. It's an idealized version. It leaves out all the blowups, false starts, dead ends, and conversation breakdowns that typically occur. For the moment, though, let's just focus on what emerges at the end of the process.

Alice and Paul sit down together to decide how they want to handle their recurring problem about parties. They decide that they don't have to worry about every occasion. It's only those where they don't know many people that give them trouble. But that's exactly what's facing them this coming weekend at the Collins's house.

What are they going to do about it? The strategy up to now has been to adopt a "positive attitude." If you go expecting problems, they felt, that's exactly what you'll find.

A positive attitude sounds like a good idea, but it may have serious drawbacks. If you're not expecting problems, you may be unprepared to deal with them. There's a certain advantage, accordingly, in adopting a negative attitude. There's the power of negative thinking just as there's the power of positive thinking. If you expect something to go wrong, you'll be prepared if it does.

So Alice and Paul go off to the Collins's having adopted a negative attitude. They jointly predict that Alice is going to get loud and that Paul is going to withdraw. They further predict that Paul will get embarrassed by Alice's loudness and that Alice will get embarrassed by Paul's withdrawal.

These anticipations give them a joint platform—a shared, non-blaming vantage point—from which to view their behavior. It provides them a way to get outside of and be less affected by the problem.

And now that they have predicted that they might have their usual problem, Alice and Paul make plans to deal with it. They agree to:

1. Check with one another during the party to see if what they fear is happening (Compared to previous parties at which they had ended up enemies, they will now be allies.)
2. Leave the party early if they begin to feel too uncomfortable (Compared to previous parties at which they felt trapped, they will now have an escape hatch.)
3. Help each other out (Alice, who doesn't realize when she begins to get loud and awkward, asks Paul to point out when she does. Paul, who can get silent and moody at a party, asks Alice to notice when he is and help pull him out of it. Compared to previous parties at which they were left to deal with their problems alone, they will now be appealing to one another as resources.)

There are many things that partners can do once they begin to blend the problem into their relationship. When they get home, Alice and Paul know that they'll be able to (a) commiserate with one another if, as may be the case, just what they'd feared might happen did happen or (b) celebrate the fact, if this is the case, that what they feared might happen did not happen.

I recommend that partners deal with couple problems in the same way that people deal with the flu. People are careful to avoid conditions that might lead to the flu, but they also keep on hand a supply of aspirin, and they are alert to the first signs of symptoms. When a child in the family gets a fever, everyone snaps into action. No one calls this negative thinking.

So Alice and Paul go to the Collins's party, and here is what happens: Alice is loud, but only for a short time. Paul, to his surprise, is less bothered by it. Paul does get self-conscious, and Alice, as planned, comes to talk with him about it. The option to tell Alice that he wants to go home and Alice's pre-stated willingness to do so make a difference. Paul no longer feels as trapped, alone, or self-conscious and no longer wants to go home.

Jointly anticipating a problem makes it (1) less likely to occur and (2) less distressing and easier to deal with if it does.

> **SKEPTIC:** Yes, but suppose that Paul's telling Alice that he wanted to go home *doesn't* make him feel better about the party. He *still* wants to go home.

> **WILE:** Well then, Alice may need a chance to express how she feels about *that*, after which she might …

> **SKEPTIC:** Why don't they just take two cars?

> **WILE:** Yes, that might be the simple solution.

> **SKEPTIC:** It's too simple; it's *all* too simple. You haven't talked about really difficult problems—like when one partner wants to have a baby and the other doesn't.

> **WILE:** Well sure, some problems are deal breakers.

> **SKEPTIC:** But even just with Alice and Paul, I can't help thinking that they're simply poorly matched and would be better off married to someone else.

> **WILE:** Maybe, but problems would arise no matter who they

married. There are always points in any relationship where the sensitivities of one partner grate against the sensitivities of the other.

Choosing a Partner Is Choosing a Set of Problems

True, if Paul had married Susan or Gail, his previous two girlfriends, he wouldn't have had the particular problem at parties that he has with Alice. Neither of these women got loud and awkward when nervous, and neither objected when Paul got quiet.

- But if Paul had married Susan, he and Susan would have gotten into a fight before they even arrived at the party. That's because Paul, who is rarely on time, would have kept Susan waiting. Susan would have felt taken for granted, which is something she is sensitive about. And Paul would have taken her complaint about his always being late as her wanting to control him, which is something *he* is sensitive about.
- If Paul had married Gail, he and Gail wouldn't have gotten out the door, period. That's because they would have been too upset about an argument earlier that day about Paul's not helping with the housework. Gail would have experienced his not helping as abandonment, which is something she is sensitive about, and Paul would have experienced Gail's insistence that he help as a way of controlling him, which, as I just said, is one of his sensitivities.

Each potential relationship has its own particular set of inescapable recurring problems. If Alice had married Steve or Lou, her previous two boyfriends, she wouldn't have had the particular problem at parties that she had with Paul.

- If she had married Steve, she'd have had the opposite problem. Steve gets louder at parties than she does. He would have gotten drunk; she would have gotten angry about it; and they would have gotten into a fight.

- If she had married Lou, both would have enjoyed the party since it would have provided momentary relief from the disconnection that generally developed between them on weekends. But they would have had have trouble when they got home and Lou wanted sex. Lou responds to disconnection by wanting sex. It's his way of reestablishing closeness. Alice responds by not wanting sex. Sex is something she wants only when she already feels close.

There is value, when choosing a long-term partner, in realizing that you will be choosing, along with that person, a particular set of irresolvable problems that you'll be grappling with for the next ten, twenty, or even fifty years. (If you get divorced and remarry, you are in essence exchanging one set of irresolvable problems for another. Your hope is that the new set may be easier to deal with than the old.)

It is like having an old car that you really loved but that you knew had a temperamental carburetor. You'd become an expert in adjusting carburetors. And whenever you went driving, you would take along a set of tools and a manual. In a couple relationship, partners need to become joint experts, and they need to have a joint set of tools.

Each relationship has its own set of unsolvable problems that can best be dealt with by developing a shared nonjudgmental vantage point from which to view them. As time goes on, the couple problem may become less of a problem and more something partners may even be able to laugh at. A few months later, Alice and Paul had the following exchange:

ALICE: I've been saving my voice so I can be really loud tonight.

PAUL: Won't worry me a bit; I'm bringing *War and Peace.*

People who can share a joke like this have gone a long way toward blending the problem into the relationship.

Chapter 2
Building a Relationship on a Problem

"Blending your problems into your relationship" isn't just learning to live with them. It's also turning them to advantage. Problems have two particularly powerful advantages. They can be used as:

1. Pathways to intimacy
2. Clues to important issues in the relationship

These are significant benefits. It's possible in some cases to turn your problems (the things that most distress you) into the things that most help you. Partners who are able to do this are using their problems to help build their relationship.

Using Problems as Pathways to Intimacy

Intimacy is what everyone seeks in relationships—everyone, that is, except those who have given up hope of ever getting it or who never knew it was possible in the first place.

As I see it, intimacy comes from telling your partner the most important things on your mind and hearing the most important things on your partner's mind.

Intimacy is the contact partners make with one another about their hopes, fears, and problems, especially those about the relationship.

Everyone knows that problems can lead to a loss of closeness. But closeness can be regained by the way people talk about these problems. Here's an example.

Mary and Dennis are a married couple in their early thirties. Mary feels resentful that Dennis doesn't do more around the house.

MARY: We've got a great division of labor here. You mess the house, and I clean it.

DENNIS: (*defending himself*) What are you talking about? I do a lot around here. And speaking of messes, take a look at your desk sometime.

MARY: Take a look at your *own* desk. It's messier than mine. And don't change the subject.

And they get into a fight. So far, that is not new. That's what people typically do when talking about a difficult issue. One partner attacks, the other retaliates, and they get into a fight.

But then Mary and Dennis do something that *is* new. After they have the fight, they use it as an entry point into an intimate conversation. The next day, when both have cooled off, Dennis goes to Mary and says that he's upset with himself because he hasn't done as much around the house as he had promised to do. His willingness to acknowledge the truth of what Mary was saying makes her feel like acknowledging the truth of what he was saying.

MARY: Well, actually, you *have* been doing more.

This mutual admitting creates a friendly atmosphere that enables Mary to discover more about how she really feels.

MARY: I guess it's just … when I was vacuuming this afternoon, I felt … I felt such loneliness.

Dennis's Inner Dialogue

QUESTION: Oh-oh, is she blaming me for it?

ANSWER: Sure sounds like it.

DEFENSE: But I didn't do anything wrong.

If it were early in the relationship, Dennis would say, "Why do you always have to be such a drama queen?"—an accusation that would leave Mary feeling misunderstood and enraged. But before he can say this, he has the following *additional* thought.

> *REALIZATION: But there's a sadness in her voice.

> *RECONSIDERATION: Maybe she isn't blaming me.

> *FURTHER RECONSIDERATION: And if she feels lonely, I can believe it, because that's how I feel, too.

These additional thoughts completely change Dennis's feelings about the matter. Instead of accusing Mary of being a drama queen, he says, "I know what you mean. I feel that way, too."

And now Mary and Dennis are no longer just talking about the problem of who does housework. They have used this problem to uncover the loneliness that has crept into their relationship. They now talk about how each has his or her own separate interests and how they have been living parallel lives. They feel a shared sadness and, in a strange way, feel closer than they have in a long time.

> SKEPTIC: That's very sweet, but how often are Mary and Dennis going to be able to have such a good conversation? It was only by chance that it didn't turn into an argument *this* time.

> WILE: Yes, but if they *are* able to have such a conversation, it can create a sense of intimacy.

> SKEPTIC: I don't see the intimacy. Mary and Dennis are talking about living parallel lives.

That's what Mary and Dennis are concerned about too. They believe that intimacy means spending a lot of time together, enjoying the same things, having the same interests. They worry that they are incompatible and that getting married might have been a mistake. Their conversation is likely to bog down at this point. They don't feel there's anything more to say. And each is likely to go away feeling discouraged.

But if they had the view of intimacy that I have, they'd recognize that talking about feeling lonely can itself be an intimate act. Confiding about feeling unconnected can be connecting. For the moment at least, Mary and Dennis would be in it together.

A relationship is a busy place. It's like an airport with lots of things going on and scheduled and unscheduled feelings arriving and departing.

If a relationship is an airport, then intimacy is the traffic control conversation—the dialogue between the partners about whatever is going on. Intimacy is created by the way partners talk about what's happening in their lives and, in particular, what's happening between them. It's a consequence of their ability to be mutual confidants.

Conflicting work schedules may limit partners' time together to five minutes a day. Business travel may limit their contact to a phone call a day. But a phone call or a five-minute talk may be enough to reestablish a powerful sense of connection. Partners who, in such a phone call or talk, are able to get across how they feel will experience greater intimacy than partners who, although spending a lot of time together, are unable to do so. Among the major things that partners need to get across, and in a way that doesn't merely lead to arguments, are feelings, worries, and dissatisfactions about the relationship.

Without such talks, long periods of time together may be difficult. A wife may think that she'd love to spend more time with her husband, that it would help them grow closer together. When he retires, however, and spends much of the day at home, she discovers she doesn't like it. He is underfoot and interferes with her schedule. Neither partner has a way of letting the other in on what he or she is thinking and feeling. The wife can't tell her husband about her difficulty having him home without it leading to a fight. If she could, she might discover more pleasure in his company. And her sense of liberation, of freedom from festering resentments, might make her more able to connect in a host of situations and ways in which she could not before.

Depending on how partners talk or don't talk about them, problems can lead to either an increase or a decrease in intimacy.

Using Problems as Clues

Couples can use their problems in another way: as relationship barometers for detecting moment-to-moment fluctuations in the relationship atmosphere. Partners have certain unwanted feelings that keep coming up. Many people are preoccupied with perceived imperfections in their partners, such as an unattractive physical feature, a nervous habit, sloppiness, excessive neatness, and so on. Many have repeated periods in which they are preoccupied with jealous thoughts about their partners' past romantic relationships, worries about suspected current ones, or envious thoughts about their partners' greater professional achievement or closer relationship with their children. Many have recurrent episodes of resentment about their partners' perceived:

- Lack of affection or excessive need for it
- Unwillingness to talk or inability to shut up
- Failure to initiate activities together or inability to be alone
- Low desire for sex or excessive desire for it
- Unwillingness to help with the housework or inability to stop cleaning up
- Excessive TV watching or unwillingness to relax
- Overzealous involvement with the kids or lack of involvement with them
- Extravagance with money or stinginess

Recurring feelings such as these may reflect general ongoing problems that need to be dealt with on their own terms. But they may have hidden potential uses. A recurring relationship problem is like a trick knee. No one would ever want to have one. But it does have a side benefit. You'll know when it s going to rain. In a similar way, a recurrent relationship problem can be used to measure the current relationship climate.

The following is an interchange in which Mary and Dennis do just that. Later that evening, Mary finds herself stewing again about having to do all the housework. She complains about Dennis's not doing his part, and they get into the following fight.

MARY: You never do anything around here.

DENNIS: I'd do more if you weren't such a nag.

MARY: I didn't used to be a nag. You've turned me into one.

DENNIS: No, you managed to find a way to do that all on your own.

Mary and Dennis are caught in an angry cycle in which each automatically refutes what the other just said in response to the other doing the same.

MARY: And *you've* managed to find a way to avoid doing anything around here.

DENNIS: Because you always have to be in control. You don't like the way I do things, so I've given up trying.

MARY: What a convenient excuse.

DENNIS: You've got your way of doing things, and I've got mine.

MARY: Yes, I know your way. It's to leave it for *me* to do.

No matter what either partner says, the other always has a comeback.

DENNIS: I do *lots* around here, and I've been trying to do even more. Of course, you'd never notice that.

MARY: Exactly what "even more" have you done? Can you name one thing?

DENNIS: The dishes.

MARY: You wash two spoons and expect a medal.

SKEPTIC: This is all too painfully familiar.

WILE: Yes, each partner feels too stung by what the other has just said to do anything other than sting back.

The fight is self-fueling, much like a hurricane gaining strength over warm waters. To stop the fight—for this hurricane to move onto dry land—something needs to happen to interrupt the self-refueling. The doorbell rings, which provides the needed interruption. It is the next door neighbor asking them to feed his cat while he is away. He stays for only a few minutes, but that is long enough for Mary to regain her perspective.

Mary's Inner Dialogue

> **SELF-APPRECIATION:** "Two spoons and you expect a medal"—not bad, not bad at all.
>
> **SATISFACTION:** And it really makes the point.
>
> **SECOND THOUGHTS:** But it was also sarcastic. It's something my father could have said. And I don't want to be like him.
>
> **DETERMINATION:** I'll make amends.

MARY: (*softly*) I don't know how we're going to solve the housework problem, but I shouldn't attack you like that.

Dennis's Inner Dialogue

> **AGREEMENT:** No, she shouldn't.
>
> **APPRECIATION:** But at least she admits it.
>
> **FORGIVENESS:** And she does seem sorry.
>
> **RECOGNITION:** And she wasn't entirely wrong in what she was trying to say.

DENNIS: Well, you had reason. I should be doing more.

Dennis is admitting what he had denied in the fight, which inspires Mary to do the same.

MARY: Well, actually, you *have* been doing more.

Mary and Dennis are in a collaborative cycle, in which each makes a conciliatory comment in response to the other doing the same.

DENNIS: But not as much as I could.

MARY: You help in other ways.

Since Mary is no longer criticizing Dennis, he has room to criticize himself.

DENNIS: (*sadly*) But I don't want to be like Dad, who left all the housework to Mom. I don't think he ever washed even *two* spoons.

By this time, Mary has forgotten her anger about housework, which demonstrates the power of the collaborative cycle: that it can temporarily dissolve grudges.

MARY: I know I make it difficult. I know I'm a perfectionist.

Mary may live to regret this admission, since Dennis may use it against her in a fight. But at the moment, she can't imagine his possibly doing this. And Dennis can't imagine Mary using what he is about to say against him.

DENNIS: Well, actually, I wish *I* were more of a perfectionist.

MARY: (*surprised*) Huh?

DENNIS: I've been sort of screwing up at work lately. The boss called me in today.

MARY: (*quietly*) Oh.

DENNIS: He may send me back to my old desk job. I worked so hard to get on the survey team, and now I'm totally blowing it.

Dennis's shame about what his boss had said that day had kept him from telling Mary about it when he first came home, which again demonstrates the power of the collaborative cycle: that it can enable people to talk about things that they had been holding back because of shame.

MARY: Oh, poor baby.

The quickness with which Mary jumps to Dennis's side warms his heart.

DENNIS: I know I haven't been very good company tonight.

MARY: Oh, so that's what it was?

Mary had sensed that something was up when Dennis first walked in the door, but it was only when she was vacuuming that it emerged into consciousness—as a surge of loneliness that she was the only one doing the housework. This surge of loneliness (or, rather, the anger that followed it) was her way of registering Dennis's preoccupation with work and his disengagement from her. Her anger about the housework served as her trick knee informing her about this shift in the relationship climate. Ideally, she will be able, in the future, to use her anger to signal such a shift.

> **SKEPTIC:** But wait a minute. Mary is still doing most of the housework. That is the real problem, isn't in? Shouldn't they be talking about that?
>
> **WILE:** Yes, but another real problem is the ways in which she and Dennis disconnect—for which her feelings about the housework can serve as a clue.

And people often need such a clue. Many of the most important feelings in a relationship are such under-the-radar feelings, as we'll see in the following examples.

Building Your Relationship On Your Negative Feelings

People hope to build their relationships on their positive feelings and their good times. I recommend that they also build them on their negative exchanges and their bad times. The following are examples of how to do that.

Jane and Tony have been married for twelve years. They have the following slightly disagreeable conversation that couples often have. They are in bed reading. Jane slowly puts down her book.

JANE: Do you love me?

TONY: (*keeping his eye on the page*) You know I do.

JANE: Yes, but sometimes it's nice to hear you say it.

TONY: You know I'm not very good with words. I express it in other ways.

JANE: What other ways?

TONY: Lots of ways. Don't I tell you how good you look? Don't I bring you flowers?

JANE: It's not the same.

TONY: (*sighing*) Well, I don't know what to do, then.

JANE: I just told you what to do. You could say it in words.

TONY: Okay, I love you.

JANE: Well, it wouldn't hurt if next time you say it as if you mean it.

Jane and Tony are caught in a discussion neither of them wants. Jane doesn't like the role of the beseeching wife. Tony doesn't like the role of the withholding husband. They worry that Jane is just too needy, Tony is just too closed off, and maybe it was a mistake to marry.

How could they have avoided this disagreeable exchange? And, now that they are in it, how can they get out of it?

The answer is to recognize Jane's "Do you love me?" as a clue, rather than as just a question that Tony should answer. Feeling unloved is Jane's relationship barometer. It is her way of registering any of a number of possible disruptions in the relationship. Feeling unloved is a rough measure, however. It indicates that something is wrong, but not exactly what. Jane and Tony need a conversation in which:

1.   Instead of simply getting Tony to say he loves Jane, they jointly recognize that she feels *unloved.*
2.   They jointly find out what her feeling unloved is about.

Here is a conversation in which Jane and Tony do just that. It is an idealized conversation because it omits all the false starts and breakdowns that generally occur. And it assumes an ability on the part of Jane and Tony to stand back calmly and appreciate the situation they are in—an ability that it is hard to imagine people having when they are filled with emotion.

In the original conversation, Jane began with, "Do you love me?" Tony felt criticized for not having spontaneously thought to say it. He got defensive and said in a beleaguered tone of voice, "You know I do." But in this idealized conversation, Jane's approach is different.

JANE: (*putting down her book*) Tony, I just caught myself about to ask, "Do you love me?"

Instead of asking for reassurance, Jane is expressing puzzlement over her *wish* to ask for it. She is standing back from and confiding in Tony about her struggle—and in a way that doesn't accuse him of anything. She has climbed up on the platform, this non-blaming vantage point from which she can view what is happening in the relationship. Since Tony isn't feeling accused, he is able to respond empathically.

TONY: Oh, are you feeling *un*loved?

Jane and Tony are now in a collaborative, rather than an angry, cycle. And being in this cycle, they are able to access the underlying tender feelings.

JANE: Yes, it's lonely over here on my side of the bed.

TONY: (*moving over next to her*) Well, we can change that.

JANE: (*putting her arms around him*) I usually like reading in bed together. But tonight … I don't know … it's like we're in different worlds.

In the earlier discussion, Jane and Tony argued about his reluctance to say "I love you." But it isn't about love, but about being in different worlds.

TONY: Yes, I know. What world have you been in?

JANE: I've been worrying about my mother's health. I've kept it to myself because I don't want to sound like a broken record.

TONY: I know what you mean. I've been stewing again about my dead-end job, but I knew you were concerned about your mother, and I didn't want you to worry about me too.

Jane and Tony kept their worries to themselves and, in so doing, shut each other out because neither wanted to be tiresome to the other. Jane's response to this mutual shutting out was to feel lonely and unloved. In the discussion that they had, they argued about Tony's reluctance to say "I love you." In the ideal conversation I made up for them, they used Jane's feeling of being unloved to discover that they were shutting each other out, which was their way of letting each other back in.

SKEPTIC: Well, that paints a pretty picture, but didn't you just say that this was an idealized conversation that's hard to imagine anyone having? So why are we even talking about it?

WILE: Because realizing how such conversations ideally can occur may enable us to make tentative steps toward having them. And any such move, however small, can make a difference.

SKEPTIC: But Jane and Tony aren't even in a real fight. What about couples who have *real* fights?

Betty and Ralph have real fights, many of which, like the following, are triggered by Ralph's jealousy.

RALPH: I saw you flirting with Malcolm just now—with everyone watching. Why do you have to humiliate me like that?

BETTY: That is so totally a product of your imagination. I don't even like Malcolm. You're driving me crazy with your jealousy.

RALPH: Well, you're driving me crazy wagging your fanny in front of every guy on the planet.

BETTY: I'll wag my fanny in front of any guy on all nine planets if I feel like it. I certainly wouldn't bother wagging it in front of you. You wouldn't even notice. You're so busy being jealous.

RALPH: That does it. We're going home.

BETTY: Fine with me. You've completely ruined the evening.

Ralph's jealous reaction—his "I saw you flirting"—is a clue to feelings of a more tender nature. To find out what they are, we would need to go back to the moment when Ralph noticed Betty talking to that man at the party. Here is what Ralph might have whispered to her if he were able to access and confide these more tender feelings:

RALPH: (*whispering*) I can't believe how insecure I just got. A good-looking guy smiles at you, and immediately I become convinced that you wish you were married to him and that our life together is a sham. I bet you're getting tired of my insecurity; I know I am! And it's easy, since *I* sometimes have a wandering eye, to think that you must have one too.

We don't expect Ralph to be able to make such a statement. To be able to do so would require a comfort with his feelings that we know he doesn't have. Even if he were to make it, that wouldn't guarantee that Betty would respond compassionately. In fact, here is what she'd say:

BETTY: At the moment, I don't care about your insecurity. I'm still fuming about what you said at breakfast. Did you really mean it when you told me that …?

Ralph's spurt of jealousy was in response—not, as he thought, to Betty's interest in that man at the party—but to her withdrawal from him because of the hurtful comment he had made at breakfast. Ralph noticed that Betty was acting friendlier toward that man at the party than she had been toward him. But that's because she wasn't acting friendly toward Ralph at all. Jealousy is Ralph's default position. It is his way of registering disruptions in the relationship. If Betty disengages from him, he concludes that it must be because she is interested in someone else.

Ralph's jealous reaction is, of course, a problem. But is it also a clue. It can be used to signal undercurrents in the relationship. If Ralph were to talk about his jealousy in the way I just described, Betty would have brought out what was upsetting her and they would have had a chance to work it out.

> **SKEPTIC:** But Ralph's jealousy isn't *always* a clue. What about times when he's just jealous.
>
> **WILE:** It's a clue, even then, to feelings of hurt he's unable to express.
>
> **SKEPTIC:** Yes, that's the point. He's unable to express them. So why are we even talking about it?
>
> **WILE:** Because having a picture of how it would look if he *could* express these feelings might enable him to make a move toward doing so.

The goal would be for Betty and Ralph to use his jealousy as a clue to disconnections in the relationship and to feelings he is unable to express. To the extent that they can do this, they will be building their relationship on Ralph's problem of jealousy.

Chapter 3

Using the Relationship
to Fill Gaps in Your Personality

People hope that love will transfigure their lives. All that's needed, they believe, is to meet the right person and everything will change. Discontents and insecurities will drop away. Life will take on a richer meaning. Birds will sing. Everything will be better.

And people are afraid that love *won't* transfigure their lives. They are worried that what everyone is always telling them is true:

- You can't expect your relationship to solve your personal problems. In fact, you'd better solve your problems first or you'll screw up the relationship.
- You can't expect a partner to make up for what you lack in yourself.
- You've got to learn to love yourself before you'll be able to love anyone else.
- You've got to become independent before you'll be capable of a mature relationship.

These things are, indeed, true, but so is the opposite:

- You *can* expect your relationship to help solve your personal problems.
- You *can* expect your partner to help fill gaps in your personality.
- Finding someone who loves you *is* a good way to learn to love yourself.

- Forming a couple relationship *is* a good way to become independent.

SKEPTIC: I think you just enjoy disagreeing with what everyone else says.

WILE: Well, actually, it's not much fun. I'd rather have everyone agree with me so I can stop all this disagreeing. In fact, I'd like to start with you. I'd like to convince you that filling the gaps in your personality, learning to love yourself, and becoming independent are what relationships can accomplish rather than what people must achieve prior to beginning them.

SKEPTIC: That's a lot to hear about, and I'm already flooded. You know something? There are too many ideas in this book. I've already forgotten most of them.

WILE: Yes, I know—so I've tried to summarize them in the last chapter.

SKEPTIC: What makes you think I'm going to last that long? I've got a mind to stop reading right now.

WILE: I hope you don't.

A Relationship is a Good Place to Solve Your Problems

The romantics are right, but not in the way they think. Romantics think that love solves all problems. As soon as the right person comes along, they say, your troubles will be over. There are thousands of women and men out there who thought the right person had come along but who are now divorced and alone or raising children on their own or separated from their children and sweating under child support payments.

However the romantics are only partly right. Relationships can in some ways solve our problems. For example, people hesitate to complain directly to friends, bosses, or coworkers when they feel irritated by them. A man submits to abuse by his boss because he feels he has no right to complain or because he fears that his boss might fire him. And his boss might. A woman feels justified in complaining about a male coworker's smoking (since it is now more socially acceptable to do so) but not about his other disagreeable habits, such as loud talking and noisy gum chewing. She feels it's petty of her to be bothered by such things.

By the same token, we stifle many of our *positive* feelings. We feel it would be boastful and self-centered to make too much of our own successes or to gloat over our rivals' defeats. A great many of everyday feelings we have are defined by society, and by us, as inappropriate or small-minded.

So we arrive at the end of a day, a week, or a year choked with feelings that we have been unable to express. This is a major cause of the tiredness that people can feel at the end of the day. And this is a major reason why people try to get away on weekends and why they need vacations.

A major positive value of a couple relationship is the opportunity to express some of these held-back feelings. In the privacy of the couple relationship, people can sometimes let themselves engage in some boasting, gloating, and griping—that is, "self-centeredness" and "small-mindedness." Here, the usual standards about what is appropriate to say and to feel can be relaxed.

The chance to talk to our partners about what happened during the day is, for many of us, the premiere event of the evening. Some couples run through the events of the day immediately upon coming together in the evening. Others are silent at first and then spill out these events in the course of the evening, the next day, or the next month.

Such mutual confiding is a way of dealing with problems from the day by getting out into the open what has been rattling around in your head and by feeling that someone is on your side. Mutual confiding is so important that partners who don't engage in it can, by this fact alone, be considered deprived.

A Relationship is a Good Way to
Make Up for Personal Limitations

We are told not to expect relationships to fill gaps in our personalities. But that's exactly what we *can* expect.

Harry, who has been modest and reserved throughout his life, is charmed by Cathy, who is expressive and expansive. He's intrigued by someone who doesn't mind drawing a little attention to herself. She makes up for what he lacks. And a little of it begins to rub off on him. He becomes more expressive himself.

Depending on the qualities you lack and the qualities that your partner has, you can learn from your partner:

- How to have fun; how to be serious
- How to take a vacation; how to hold a job
- How to be angry; how to be unperturbed
- How to be organized; how to be spontaneous
- How to follow rules; how to bend them

Forming a relationship is like entering a new culture. And if it's broadening to travel to another culture, then it's broadening to form a new relationship. Entering a new culture or a relationship produces problems, however. The goal is to obtain the benefits of this new culture and, at the same time, to be able to deal with its problems.

Sid and Barbara, who are in their mid-twenties, have been seeing one another for six months. Sid is the head librarian at a local junior college, and Barbara is an aerobics instructor. Sid is enchanted by Barbara's spiritedness and adventurousness. She is always thinking of new unusual things to do, whereas Sid enjoys keeping to a routine.

The first months of their relationship are the most exciting in Sid's life. Barbara gets them to do all kinds of things that Sid would never think of doing—canoeing, scuba diving, flying kites, riding roller coasters. And now he is beginning to initiate such activities himself. Being with Barbara is teaching him how to be this other type of person.

Barbara is charmed by Sid's style. He talks in graceful and

engaging ways, whereas Barbara always feels awkward and self-conscious. Barbara loves being with someone who has such elegance and poise. And now, she's beginning to be more poised herself. Being with Sid is teaching her how to be this other type of person.

What Barbara and Sid most like about one another, however, can, in a moment, turn sour. Sid can worry that he's not spirited and adventurous enough for her. That is something he is sensitive about. All his life, Sid has worried about being non-spontaneous. Barbara can worry that she's not charming and smooth enough for Sid. That is something that she is sensitive about. All her life, she has worried about being awkward.

All of us are sensitive about certain failings that we see ourselves as having. All of us have critical inner voices—internal prosecutors—rebuking us for these failings.

Barbara and Sid are driving back from a backpacking trip. Sid is quiet. He didn't enjoy it as much as he did the other trips Barbara had planned. They kept getting lost. There were a lot of bugs. It rained. Their tent leaked. And Sid wasn't used to such primitive bathroom methods. He's wet, cold, tired, itchy, and constipated.

A hot shower, a good night's sleep, a flush toilet, and Sid will be as good as new. But here's the crucial added problem. Sid thinks he should have enjoyed the trip. His internal prosecutor tells him, "I can't believe it. You let a few insects and a little constipation get you down. What a wimp! Look at Barbara—covered with mosquito bites and scratches and chattering on about these three days in hell as if she had a great time."

Sid feels too ashamed about not enjoying the trip to say anything about it. That's too bad because, were he to tell Barbara, she might admit that she didn't enjoy the trip either. Sid would be relieved. They'd be able to share a new common goal: looking forward to getting home.

But Sid doesn't tell her. In fact, he doesn't say anything. His quietness worries Barbara. She sees it as confirming her worst fear: that she's an overgrown tomboy who is no match for the worldlier Sid. Her internal prosecutor tells her, "Look at how quiet Sid is. You're probably driving him crazy with your nervous chatter."

In order to cheer up Sid, Barbara suggests that they stop at a winery. Her effort to makes things better makes them worse. Sid already feels like a killjoy for hating the trip. Now he feels like a worse killjoy for not wanting to stop at the winery. He does what people often do in such a situation. He shifts from blaming himself to blaming his partner. It's not that I never want to do anything, he tells himself. It's that Barbara always has to do everything.

"Can't you sit still even for a second?" he snaps at Barbara.

Immediately, Sid wants to take it back. He has never talked to Barbara like this before. But it's too late. Barbara feels hurt and insulted. She forgets that she doesn't want to stop at the winery either and suggested it only because she thought Sid might like it.

"Your problem is that you never want to do anything," she answers, picking up the rhythm.

This is a crushing blow to Sid, since it is exactly what he's been telling himself. He goes on the offensive. "Well, I'd want to do more if you didn't drive me crazy with your mindless chatter."

This is a crushing blow to Barbara, since she's already worried about not being intelligent enough for him.

Barbara sulks.

Sid sulks.

Neither speaks for the next forty miles.

Looking at this conflagration, the Skeptic would think that Barbara and Sid are just too different, and that it's a mistake for a person to make up for a personal lack by finding a partner who has the missing quality.

But the problem isn't Sid and Barbara's differences. It's how they talk, or don't talk, *about* these differences. There were a number of points in the conversation in which Sid or Barbara could have stopped the escalation and reestablished a collaborative spirit. Driving home from the backpacking trip, Sid could have said,

SID: I'm worried about being a killjoy because I didn't enjoy the trip.

Since Sid was unable to say this and instead fell silent, Barbara was then in the position in which *she* could have said:

BARBARA: I'm worried that you're quiet because you're put off by my chattering.

Since Barbara was unable to say this and, instead, suggested stopping at the winery, Sid was then in the position in which *he* could have said:

SID: I'm really worried that this will disappoint you, but I just feel like going home. In fact, this whole weekend makes me think that I can't keep up with you. You're still bouncing, and I'm dragging.

Since Sid was unable to say this and, instead, said, "Can't you sit still for a second?" Barbara was then in the position in which *she* could have said:

BARBARA: That's hard to hear because I was already worried that my awkwardness and chattering might be getting to you.

Since Barbara was unable to say this and, instead, said, "Your problem is that you never want to do anything," Sid was then in the position in which *he* could have said:

SID: That's hard to hear because I was already worried about being a killjoy.

Since Sid was unable to say this and, instead, said "Well, I'd want to do more if you weren't driving me crazy with your mindless chatter," Barbara was then in the position in which *she* could have said:

BARBARA: Well, that's exactly what I'm worried about—that I talk too much about things that don't matter and that I'm no fun to be with. That's why I suggested the winery, to try to make it more fun for you.

Barbara and Sid wouldn't have had to say *all* these things. Any one of them might have stopped the argument. (In a way, it doesn't take much to reestablish a collaborative spirit.) The problem is that in the heat of the moment people are generally unable to think of *any* of these things. But Barbara and Sid have a chance afterward, when they are no longer angry, to bring in some of these skipped-over feelings. Sid calls Barbara the next day and says.

SID: You know, you're right about what you said. I'm a party pooper—world class.

Grateful for Sid's conciliatory comment, Barbara makes one of her own.

BARBARA: Of course, in this case, the party was already pooped. The rain did it in.

SID: (*laughing*) Well, maybe. But usually it's me. I hold you back.

BARBARA: *Someone* has to; I'm unstoppable. On the way home, I was talk, talk, talk.

SID: You were just trying to be cheerful.

BARBARA: I overdo cheerful.

Choosing a partner who has qualities that you lack can round out or expand your personality. But it can also lead to conflict. At such times, it's even more important than usual to find a way to talk about what's happening that doesn't just end in fights and hurt feelings.

A Relationship Is a Good Place to Learn to Love Yourself

We are advised not even to attempt a relationship until we have first learned to love ourselves. Of course, we don't follow this advice. Learning to love ourselves is a difficult task, and few of us are good at it. If we were to wait until we learned to love ourselves, few of us would start a relationship before the age of eighty-three.

Fortunately, we don't have to wait. Learning to love yourself is something that relationships can help accomplish rather than something that you must always do prior to beginning them. People can become more self-appreciative, self-confident, and self-respecting as a result of their relationships.

Why is it so frequently said, then, that you have to love yourself before you will be able to love anyone else? It is because some people who don't love themselves:

- Lose respect for anyone who is attracted to them (This is the relationship version of Groucho Marx's comment, "I wouldn't join any club that would have me for a member.")
- Compensate for their feelings of low self-esteem by being interested only in the most beautiful, popular, out-of-reach people
- Become clingy when people do show interest, driving them away
- Become angrily jealous in a way that erodes the other person's good will
- Become easily upset (They are sensitive to slights, which they take as confirming their belief that they are unlovable.)

But many people who don't love themselves *do* work out good relationships. Their realization that someone they really care about also cares about them makes them feel that they may be more lovable than they had thought. Feeling loved is their way to begin loving themselves—although they may be vulnerable to flair-ups of their old sense of unlovability.

Barry is vulnerable to such flair-ups. He is a shy, twenty-three-year-old computer programmer who is attracted to Patsy, a vivacious twenty-one-year-old secretary who lives in his apartment building. Encouraged by her friendliness, he asks her out. They begin seeing a lot of each other and become involved.

When Patsy first said she loved him, Barry couldn't believe it. And then he began to believe it. He was ecstatic. But it was easy for him to begin not to believe it again. One evening a month later when they met up at a coffee shop, she seemed distracted.

He thought: "Okay, that's how she really feels about me. The truth is finally out. She's not really interested in me at all."

These glum thoughts lead to still glummer ones: "Why did I ever think it would work? She's out of my league. Everybody's out of my league."

These feelings of unlovability now give way to anger: "But she doesn't have to ignore me like this. She owes me more than that. Who does she think she is, anyway?"

Anger gives way to judgment: "She's totally self-absorbed. She thinks only of herself. She hasn't the vaguest idea of how to love. She needs to grow up."

Patsy's preoccupation has triggered within Barry feelings of unlovability flipping into anger and then into character assassination. By the end, Barry is convinced that Patsy has done him wrong and needs to be told off.

BARRY: (*blurting out*) It's like I'm not even here.

PATSY: What are you talking about?

BARRY: About how you've been ignoring me all evening.

PATSY: Well, actually …

Patsy is about to admit that she *hasn't* been all there. She has been mulling over something her sister had just told her over the phone. Barry would be relieved to hear this, since it would mean that Patsy's distractedness has nothing to do with him. But before she can tell him about this, he interrupts:

BARRY: I can see now why your previous boyfriend left you.

Immediately, Patsy loses interest in admitting anything. All she wants to do is lash back.

PATSY: Yes, well, you never even had a real girlfriend, and I'm beginning to see why.

BARRY: Yes, because I always pick women like you.

The argument continues in this vein until Patsy has had enough.

PATSY: Why do you always have to get like this? I'm going home. Call me when you come to your senses.

> **SKEPTIC:** (*to Wile*) This is a strange book. You've just proved the opposite of what you said you were trying to prove. You've shown that Barry needs to learn to love himself before he'll be able to love anyone else. He needs to become less sensitive to slights. Until then, he'll just keep provoking unproductive fights like this one.

> **WILE:** What Barry *needs* is a way to talk about this sensitivity to slights.

Here is Barry attempting to do so. He calls Patsy the next morning.

BARRY: I feel bad about what I said about your previous boyfriend.

Patsy likes the sound of this, but she still feels raw.

PATSY: Well, why did you do it then?

Barry is taken aback by Patsy's less-than-conciliatory response. But he realizes that he can't expect her to come around right away

BARRY: I was worried that … that …

Barry begins to lose his nerve.

PATSY: That *what?*

BARRY: (*embarrassed*) Well, I … I thought you didn't like me anymore.

PATSY: After what you said last night, I *didn't* like you anymore.

BARRY: No, I mean from the very beginning of the evening, as soon as I walked in the door. You weren't your usual friendly self.

PATSY: Oh that! I was upset about something my sister had just told me.

BARRY: Oh.

A good way to deal with fears of unlovability is to find someone who *does* love you. But the old sensitivities can reemerge—at which point, it is important to have a way to talk things out.

Chapter 4
Becoming Skillfully Dependent

I've described three ways in which relationships can cure: by providing a live-in confidant, filling gaps in your personality, and helping you love yourself. And there is a fourth way: by helping you become more effectively dependent.

I know that sounds strange. People don't generally think of dependency as something to become effective in. "Dependency dooms relationships," they say. "You've got to stop trying to turn your partner into a parent. You need to become independent before beginning a relationship." I believe that:

- Dependency isn't a deficiency that needs to be overcome but a skill that needs to be developed.
- Learning to become independent is what relationships can help accomplish rather than what must be done prior to beginning them.

A Couple Relationship Provides a Special Opportunity for Dependency

I'm going to talk about dependency in an unusual way: as something you can be good or poor at. Since children are well known for being dependent, you might think that they'd be good at it. But they're not. Children have only crude ways for getting people to comfort them (for example, by crying) or to pay attention to them (for example, by yelling "Look at me!"). Adults have more subtle, flexible, and effective means of satisfying their needs for dependency. Adults are also freer to choose where to seek such satisfaction and, if disappointed, freer to look for it elsewhere.

Adults aren't necessarily less dependent than they were as children. What has happened is that they have developed more sophisticated ways of being dependent. We don't notice that adults are dependent because of the relatively smooth, subtle, and skillful ways in which they seek to fulfill their dependency needs. We *do* notice that children are dependent because of the relatively awkward, obvious, and unskillful ways in which they seek to fulfill these needs.

The shift from childhood to adulthood is traditionally thought to require giving up childhood dependency. I suggest, however, that a couple relationship provides a special opportunity for dependency. In a couple relationship, you have a person—your partner—who is able to respond to your needs at a time in your life (adulthood rather than childhood) when you are better able to pinpoint what you really want.

Rescuing a Ruined Idea

"Dependency" is a ruined idea. There's no way to refer to "being dependent" that's not a put-down. When people wanted to find a way to talk about dependency in a non-accusing way, they had to invent a new term: "support system." While it's bad to be dependent, it's okay to need a support system.

It's hard to think of "dependent" in any way other than just as something you shouldn't be. If a five-year-old wants to deliver a devastating blow to his three-year-old brother, he says "You big baby." No other remark will have quite the same effect. Independence is seen as good, and dependence is seen as bad. Growing up means shifting from dependence to independence. And that's all there is supposed to be to it.

But if we look at exactly how we *use* the term "dependent," we see that there is more to it. We use the term to describe people who do annoying and disagreeable things such as:

- Make whiny complaints about your neglecting them

- Shower you with long, pleading, beseeching, hurt looks
- Feel easily slighted or neglected
- Hang around waiting for you to pay attention to them rather than doing things on their own
- Have tantrums about your having avoided or rejected them
- Follow you around when you go to gathering places rather than circulating by themselves
- Wait for you to initiate activities and complain if you don't

Such behavior is generally ineffective in getting you to want to take care of them, even though you might try to force yourself to do so.

In other words, we use the word "dependent" to describe people who are *unsuccessful* at getting us to want to take care of them. They turn us off. And that's the irony. They're not good at being dependent.

People who *are* good at being dependent don't even look dependent. They just look like engaging, appreciative, responsive, and loving people whom you feel like giving things to and doing things for. They are people who are successful in getting you to want to comfort and take care of them. They make it fun to do so. They are people you'd want as friends. They are people you'd want to marry.

"How dependent is the person?" is the wrong question. I suggest that everyone is very dependent. The question is "how skillful is the person at being dependent?"

And the answer for most of us is "not very," even if we are more skillful than we were as children.

That's because it's difficult to ask for things—and it's even more difficult to complain about not getting them—without, at times, your request being experienced as a pressure and the whole thing turning into an issue. There are a number of ways people deal with this issue:

- Some people don't even try to ask for things; they don't want their request to turn into an issue. They don't want

to be seen as "dependent."
- Some people try to ask for things anyway, even though their request turns into an issue.
- Some people deal with the problem by ritualizing the kinds of things they give to and do for one another.

A wife may automatically bring her husband a can of beer when they sit down to watch television in the evenings. That could be one of their rituals. And she may get him a quart of Rocky Road whenever she goes to town. And she may prepare the house and the refreshments for his regular Monday night football game. He doesn't even have to ask. And he does things for her, and she doesn't even have to ask. He keeps her car filled with gas. He accompanies her on her weekly visits to her parents—which she *really* appreciates. And he takes care of the kids on weekends so that she can have some time to herself.

This kind of ritualistic giving can be a source of satisfaction. But it can go stale and no longer satisfy the need—both for giving and getting—that it was designed to meet.

Talking Skillfully about Being Unskillfully Dependent

So, since most of us are unskillful at being dependent, we need a way to deal with the effects of our lack of skill.

Dora is unskillful at being dependent. She stays at home taking care of her ten-year-old daughter and eight-year-old son while her husband, Ned, works as an attorney.

Dora appears to have little life of her own, although she seemed quite independent before her marriage. She spent two years in Ecuador as a Peace Corps volunteer and traveled throughout Europe by herself. When Dora and Ned go to parties, she clings to him. On weekends, when Ned has work to do, Dora hangs around waiting for him to finish. She doesn't seem able to entertain herself. Every once in a while she lashes out at him for not spending enough time with her and for being married to his work.

Ned lashes back.

NED: I'd like to come home one time without being ambushed at the door and go to one gathering where you didn't wear out the sleeves of my jacket hanging onto them.

Dora is the kind of person to whom you'd want to say, "Get a life." And that's what Dora privately tells herself.

SKEPTIC: And that's what Dora *should* tell herself. You call her unskillful. She seems plenty skillful to me. Look at all she's getting from Ned.

WILE: She's not getting very much. It's hard to enjoy the attention of a person you feel sees you as a pest. And that *is* how Ned sees her. Her hanging onto him just makes him want to get away. Her criticizing him for not spending enough time with her makes him want to spend less time with her. That's what I mean when I say that Dora is unskillful at being dependent. Ned is put off by her rather than wanting to take care of her.

What Dora needs right now is a way to deal skillfully with the effects of being unskillfully dependent. To show how this would look, I'm going to turn Dora into another person, Dora-2, who *is* skillful in this regard. Ned and Dora-2 go to a party, and she clings to him. But then she says:

DORA-2: I hate the way this party is going. I'm hanging onto you in a way I don't like; and I bet you don't care much for it either.

Ned is shocked. He's used to Dora-1, who would *never* say anything like this.

Instead of criticizing Ned (and giving him beseeching looks), she is sympathizing with him for what she imagines must be her impact on him.

DORA-2: (*continuing*) Here you are, poor guy, having to worry about me, and I'm not even getting that much out of it. Something is wrong with this picture.

Ned appreciates Dora-2's willingness to look at her clinginess from his point of view. It makes him feel a little more like looking at the situation from her point of view. Instead of feeling resentful, as he usually does, he empathizes. Dora-2 is talking skillfully about having been unskillfully dependent.

> **SKEPTIC:** Wait a minute. I've known plenty of people like Dora, and none of them could *possibly* talk in this manner.

> **WILE:** Well, that doesn't surprise me because hardly anyone talks in such a non-defensive and fully aware way. I don't do so, and I wrote this book. Dora-2 is a figment of my imagination. I'm just trying to show you how it would look if someone *were* to talk skillfully about being unskillfully dependent. Dora-2 knows and says what she wants. She does so in a way that really gets her needs across. And since she isn't criticizing Ned, he would be able to hear it.

Being able to talk with Ned in this way could accomplish in ten minutes what wouldn't be accomplished in ten years of following him around at parties. It could provide the sense of intimacy and connectedness that Dora is seeking.

And if partners could talk this way, they'd be more likely to feel like doing things for each other and taking care of each other.

> **SKEPTIC:** But if they *can't* talk this way—and isn't that what you just said?—why are we even discussing it?

> **WILE:** Because knowing the shape and form of ideal conversations may enable us to make approximations to them in our own relationships.

> **SKEPTIC:** You keep saying that.

Using Your Relationship to Become Independent

I've been talking about relationships as a way to become more effectively dependent. Now I want to talk about them as a way to become more effectively independent.

And partners can become independent as a result of feeling more securely dependent. The more people feel they can depend on their partners, the more emboldened they may feel to do things on their own. The experience of having someone on their side—a confidant with whom to debrief the day—can enable people to approach the world more boldly and self-confidently.

I will use the example of Dora and Ned to show how a relationship can undermine a partner's striving for independence and how, alternatively, it can facilitate it.

Dora has had a depressing day at home. She doesn't want to bring Ned down, however, so when he returns from work, she puts aside her feelings and talks gaily about neighborhood gossip. Dora's hollow cheerfulness gets to Ned. He tries to be patient, but he's finally had enough.

NED: (*blurting out*) Why are you telling me this boring stuff? Staying home is rotting your mind. Take some courses! Get a job! Do something!

Getting a job isn't a bad idea. Were it not for Ned's reproachful tone, he could be seen as offering a useful suggestion. But his tone has had the opposite effect. Dora is upset by it. Her confidence, already low, slips further. Instead of enjoying the possibility of getting a job, she doubts that anyone would want to hire her.

The exchange has had an undermining effect, hindering Dora's move toward greater independence. It is one of those unfortunate exchanges in which each partner's attempt to make things better makes them worse. Dora's attempt to be cheerful brings Ned down. Ned's effort to listen respectfully leads to his disrespectful outburst.

Let's take it again from the top and show how the relationship might have had an *empowering* effect. This time when Ned comes home, Dora doesn't try to be cheerful. Instead, she tells him:

DORA: I haven't felt very good today ... actually this whole month.

NED: (*glad that she has finally brought it up*) Yeah, I've been worried about you. You seem to be feeling much the way I did when I was laid up that year and couldn't work.

Dora's eyes fill with tears. She feels understood.

DORA: You know what? Being at home all day isn't such a great idea. Maybe I should get a job.

Let's look at what has happened: First, Dora has been successfully dependent. She has reached out to Ned in a way that gets him empathizing. Second, being successfully dependent (relating to Ned in this way that gets him on her side) enables Dora to feel more independent. As before, the idea of a job comes up. But now Dora feels inspired to look for one. The relationship has empowered her.

Once we stop labeling dependence as childish, we'll be able to see that dependence and independence are twin needs of adults. And these twin needs are interrelated:

- Dependence—feeling secure in a relationship—can allow a person to become more independent; that is, to deal more resourcefully with the world.
- And being able to deal more resourcefully with the world includes being able to ask for things more comfortably, less accusingly, and in a way that is more likely to get others to want to provide it. Thus, becoming more independent can lead to becoming more skillfully dependent.

"Independence" is often viewed as having no needs. But, as I suggest here, it can also be viewed as competence and resourcefulness in fulfilling your needs.

Part II

MAKING TALKING
LESS DANGEROUS

Chapter 5
Having the Conversation That's Been Missing

Practically everything I've talked about in this book so far reduces to one thing: finding a way to talk with our partners that works out. At any moment, there is a conversation you and your partner could have that would help the two of you deal with what is happening in the relationship at the moment.

The heart of a couple relationship is commonly described as sharing common interests, companionship, doing things together, raising children, trust, loyalty, commitment, sex, and love.

I disagree. The heart of a couple relationship is saying what you need to say and feeling that it has gotten across. It is having conversations that work out. And that's what makes sharing common interests, companionship, doing things together, having sex, and raising children together enjoyable and worthwhile things to do. And that's what can establish trust, loyalty, commitment, and love.

Sally, who has been a traditional wife for the ten years she's been married to Stuart, tells him that she could use a night out with her friends once a week. Here's what Stuart, who has been feeling insecure about their relationship lately, needs to be able to say:

STUART: Sure, once a week is fine, if that's all it means. But things have been rocky between us recently, and I'm worried this means you've given up on us.

If Stuart were to say this, his concern about Sally going out with friends would be seen as worry about their growing apart. But Stuart is *unable* to say this. He isn't used to talking in such terms. And he hasn't clearly pinned down in his own mind that this is what he is worried about. He knows that something about Sally's going out with friends strikes him as a bad idea, but he doesn't know why.

STUART: Why can't you just talk to your friends on the phone?

SALLY: I do talk to them on the phone. The whole point is to get out a little on my own.

STUART: I just don't like it. It's dangerous to be out alone at night.

SALLY: Don't be silly. I won't be alone. There will be three of us.

Since it looks to Stuart that there's going to be no way to talk Sally out of it, he digs in his heels.

STUART: So what do you expect me to do for dinner?

In one doltish question, Stuart has regressed fifty years in the history of male-female relationships. Any modern person hearing him would immediately side with Sally. What can be said about a man living in this day and age who insists that his wife devote herself to his needs? Stuart's problem is his inability to express what he needs to say. He experiences Sally's request for a night out as a threat, and then he does what people often do when they feel threatened and don't have a way to talk about it: he reacts in a knee-jerk way. He tells her to stay home.

People say and do doltish things when they have important feelings that they are unable to express. Until Stuart is able to tell Sally that he is worried that they are drifting apart, he may be stuck making old-fashioned claims about a husband's natural rights.

But having made these claims, Stuart is stuck having to defend them. The more he says, the worse he sounds, even to himself. People can sound ridiculous when they defend indefensible positions. Even so, Sally is unable to stand up to him. She gets twisted in her words. Later, she thinks of the responses she wishes she had made. Here's how she would have liked the conversation to have gone:

STUART: You've always made my dinners.

SALLY: Too true. Maybe it's time you made mine.

STUART: You know I'm all thumbs in the kitchen.

SALLY: You can train your thumbs to fry an egg.

STUART: Very funny. It's Sue who put you up to this, isn't it.

SALLY: Yes, she's a wise friend.

Sally has great comebacks, but thinks of them only hours later. Many people might suggest that she needs assertiveness training. Easily missed, however, is the fact that Stuart is making his point no better than Sally. He has the last word, and most of those in between, but he isn't saying what he really needs to say, which is that he's afraid that her going out with friends will be a further step in their drifting apart.

Hardly anyone looking at this interchange between Stuart and Sally would guess that the problem is Stuart's failure to express what he needs to say. It's so easy to attribute the problem to his character defects (and perhaps also to Sally's). Sally's friends tell her:

- He thinks only of himself.
- He wants to keep you under his thumb.
- He wants a mother, not a wife.
- He doesn't have a clue.
- You're worth ten of him.
- Why do you let him treat you this way?
- You must enjoy suffering.
- Get rid of him.

And it's not just Sally's friends who would talk this way. Were Sally to consult a therapist who shares this way of thinking, he or she might say (or at least think):

- Stuart's making outrageous claims of narcissistic entitlement.
- He is seeking omnipotent control.
- He's functioning at an early childhood stage in which

he's symbiotically attached to his mother.
- You're adopting the cultural role of the submissive wife
  and are repeating the sadomasochistic relationship you
  had with your father.
- You're afraid to leave him because early childhood losses
  have made you fearful of separation.
- Being dominated must serve a function for you. You
  must be getting something out of playing the victim with
  Stuart.

Stuart is seen by nearly everyone (and secretly by himself) as a spoiled, manipulative bully. Once a problem is attributed to someone's character, it is difficult to consider the possibility that his problem might be an inability to get something figured out and expressed.

But if Stuart and Sally *were* to consider such a possibility—that is, were they to consult a therapist who was sympathetic to the ideas in this book—these partners would recognize that:

- If Stuart's spoiled, he's also deprived (He's deprived of a
  basic need that people have: to be able to talk about what
  is foremost on their minds.)
- If he's manipulative, he also lacks any real control (He's
  unable to talk to Sally about what is really bothering
  him.)
- If he's a bully, he is also oppressed and up against the wall
  (He can't think of anything to say that doesn't just make
  matters worse.)

Looked at in this way, Stuart seems much less the evil, exploitive, malicious, "bad" partner. He appears more like a guy struggling against difficult odds.

> **SKEPTIC:** He still sounds like a bully to me. The problem with
> you, Dan, is that you want to forgive everybody.
>
> **WILE:** I'm not saying we, or Sally, should forgive Stuart. Just
> because she understands his behavior, it doesn't mean
> that she has to like it or put up with it.

But if Sally and Stuart *were* to understand his behavior in this new way, they might be able to talk usefully about it. Imagine what might happen, for example, if Stuart told Sally that he was worried about their drifting apart. Imagine further that he told her that he was ashamed of having these worries—that he feels that a real man wouldn't feel so insecure.

Problems often seem more manageable when discussed, particularly when discussed with the person they concern. Having aired his worries, Stuart might now feel more comfortable with the idea of Sally going out.

Even if he didn't, Sally and Stuart would at least be able to talk directly about these important feelings. In fact, talking about such feelings is what Sally has been seeking all along. That is a major reason that she wants to go out with friends: to spend time with people with whom she *can* talk about personal matters.

As paradoxical as this might seem, Stuart's confiding in Sally about his reservations about her going out could make it less important for Sally to go out and for Stuart to keep her home.

There are two problems. The first problem is a failure to have needed conversations. Difficulties occur when partners are unable to discover and express what they need to say. The second problem is that people don't know that this is the problem. It is so easy for partners to attribute their difficulties to character defects that they fail to see that the problem is missing conversations.

What People Need and What They Think They Need

Partners need to have certain types of conversations, and they need to have them all the time:

- They need to be able to talk about their gripes and worries (particularly those about the relationship).
- They need to be able to talk about their wishes and fantasies (particularly those about the relationship) and about how their wishes and fantasies are being disappointed.

- They need to be able to talk about their hesitation in bringing up their dissatisfactions in fear they might hurt or anger the other.
- They need to be able to talk about how they occasionally blurt them out anyway.
- They need to have conversations and not just arguments about all these things.
- They need a chance to talk, and to commiserate, about their particular recurrent relationship problems.

Partners need all these things, and they often get none of them. And they don't even know that they need them. It's hard for people to notice that they lack something that they didn't know they needed.

They have an entirely different idea of what they need. They think they need to have:

- *Common interests,* by which they mean things to do together
- *Common goals,* by which they mean, among other things, agreement on the number of children they are going to have, who's going to take care of these children, whether they're going to live in the country or city, and so on
- *An ability to get along,* by which they mean not having too many arguments
- *An ability to communicate,* by which they mean not having too many arguments or too many silences
- *Sexual compatibility,* by which they mean wanting sex as often as their partner does, keeping their interest in having sex, and being able to have orgasms

These are usually the grounds on which people judge whether or not their relationships are satisfying and whether or not they have a right to feel unhappy about them. Whereas partners may sense that they lack something in their relationships, they don't feel they are justified in feeling dissatisfied unless they can point to established reasons such as "lack of common interests." They don't realize that they are suffering from the lack of certain types of conversations.

Seeking out the Missing Conversation

If partners were to realize that they are deprived of conversations, they could say to themselves: What is the conversation that would take care of this problem we are having (or, at least, tell us why we are having it)?

Once you begin looking for the conversations you're missing, you'll discover that they're not difficult to find. Here are some examples:

(1) A man who had been divorced for several years called his eight-year-old daughter, who was living with his ex-wife, and asked if she wanted to go for ice cream. His ex-wife had a busy schedule; she worked full time and was planning her second marriage. The man's taking his daughter for ice cream interfered with his ex-wife's evening and violated his agreement that his visits with his daughter be prearranged. The man was puzzled himself about why he did it. He generally prided himself on sticking to arrangements and keeping things friendly between himself and his ex-wife.

Asking to take his eight-year-old daughter out for ice cream was what he was left to do because he was unable to tell his ex-wife, "I know that this is ridiculous—I was the one, after all, who wanted the divorce—but I think I always had a secret belief that we would somehow get back together. Your getting remarried makes me finally realize we'll never be a family again and that I'm permanently going to lose everyday contact with Sarah."

Since this man was unable to express this concern, or even fully realize that he had it, he had no choice but to act on it. Taking his daughter for ice cream was a desperate and ineffectual effort to maintain everyday, casual, spur-of-the-moment contact with her.

(2) In their book, *Therapy for Couples*, Billie Ables and Jeffrey Brandsma describe a wife who annoyed her husband by opening his mail. Opening his mail, the authors suggest, was what she was left to do because she couldn't tell him what she needed to say, which was something like, "We lead such separate lives. I want to be more included in your life."

Opening his mail was a desperate, although totally inadequate and counterproductive, effort to include herself more in his life.

People underestimate the power of words. It is said that:

- Actions speak louder than words.
- One picture is worth a thousand words.
- Sitting here talking about the problem all day isn't going to solve it.

But it depends on what the words are. The right words can be worth a thousand pictures. And the right words can solve problems, as the following example shows.

(3) A woman was hesitant to tell the man she had just started dating that the slippers he had bought her in Mexico were too tight. He seemed so pleased with his gift to her—they *were* a splendid pair of slippers—that she just couldn't get herself to tell him. When she did finally tell him, she found out that he really didn't mind. And here's the surprise. When she went home to try on the slippers again, they now fit.

It is not too hard to figure out how this happened. When the woman put on the slippers after just receiving them, she was *afraid* they might not fit. She took the slight pressure on her toes as confirming her fear that they were too tight. After telling her boyfriend that the slippers didn't fit, the pressure of having to like them was off. She now experienced the tightness on her toes in a new way—as indicating that the slippers were snug in the way that they ought to be.

(4) A husband resented the fact that his wife invited her sister to dinner without first checking with him. All he needed was to complain and feel that his wife understood how he felt, and he would then feel perfectly comfortable in having her sister come. In fact, he was particularly gracious toward the sister during dinner.

Let's suppose, however, that his wife had responded to his complaint by saying: "I'll invite my sister anytime I damn well please." The husband wouldn't have gotten what he needed (a chance to feel that his wife understood how he felt about the matter) to enable him to change his attitude about her sister coming to dinner. When she came, he might have been rude the whole evening.

(5) Bernard Apfelbaum, my mentor and colleague, describes how

people behave when, during sex, they find themselves unaroused. They withdraw into their heads and try to conjure up erotic scenes. An alternative is for them to tell their partners something like, "For some reason I don't feel very turned on, and I'm worried about disappointing you." People hesitate to say such things for good reason, Apfelbaum says, because doing so might completely destroy the mood for sex.

But it might also *create* the mood for sex, he continues. A common effect of telling your partner that you're not aroused is then to become aroused. By so confiding, you are breaking out of the shut-down, cut-off, struggling-in-isolation effort that is turning you off.

Everyone knows how expressing a fear, worry, or grudge can, at times, diminish or even eliminate the fear, worry, or grudge. I'm simply suggesting that this idea be raised to a major principle:

> Whenever you find yourself feeling less satisfied with, less in love with, less turned on by, more walled off from, more disgruntled with, or more bored with your partner, look for feelings, wishes, worries, or complaints that you are not telling him or her and that he or she is not telling you—and see if you can find a way to talk with your partner about them.

People start acting in crazy, confused, offensive, and desperate ways when they are unable to say important things that they need to say.

Chapter 6
Avoiding Conversational Booby Traps

SKEPTIC: But, Dan, if talking is as wonderful as you say—if it's the way to become intimate—why haven't we all figured that out long ago? If it's so great, why do we do so little of it?

WILE: Because talking is also dangerous. Here's what can happen:

1. Your partner talks about a problem and you offer advice. But instead of being grateful, your partner gets angry. You get into a fight that makes both of you wish that he or she hadn't brought up the problem in the first place.
2. Your partner tells you about his or her day. You feel bored, but you pretend not to be because you don't want to hurt your partner's feelings. But your partner senses your boredom anyway and feels hurt and angry.

As I will try to show, the best way to deal with these traps is to *expect* to fall into them and to become skillful at climbing out of them.

The Unwanted-Advice Trap

TRAP NUMBER 1: Offering advice or trying to give reassurance when your partner just wants to tell you how he or she feels.

Annie and Joel are a couple in their late twenties. Joel is an engineer for the water company. Annie, who works full time as a clerical assistant for a bank, is trying to get a college degree by going to school at night. Annie comes home one evening and they have the following conversation:

ANNIE: It's all too much for me. I've got a ten-page paper due Monday that I haven't even started.

JOEL: (*reassuring*) Don't worry. You'll get it done. You've never failed to hand in a paper in your whole life.

ANNIE: Yeah, but this time's different. And it's not just that. Two people at work are on vacation, and I have to do their work in addition to mine. I don't see how my boss can expect me to do everyone else's work and still have time for my own.

JOEL: You shouldn't put up with it. You've got to tell her that you can do only so much.

ANNIE: Well sure, I can tell her that. But she'll just tell me to work harder. You can't reason with her.

JOEL: Maybe you should talk about it to *her* boss.

ANNIE: Yeah, but I'd only get into trouble if I went over her head.

JOEL: Well, then maybe you should get another job.

ANNIE: You think it's *easy* to get another job?

Annie doesn't know why they are suddenly discussing her quitting. That isn't what she wanted to talk about. She knows that Joel's comments aren't helping, but she can't figure out why. She thinks she's being ungrateful for not appreciating his suggestions.

Joel thinks she's being ungrateful for not appreciating his suggestions also. Each time he suggests something, she comes up with a reason why it won't work. She keeps saying "yes, but." Of course, we could turn the question around and ask Joel why he has to make these suggestions. He has been talking with Annie for less than two minutes, and he has already suggested she quit her job.

Joel appears the kind of person who thinks, "If you have a

problem, you should try to solve it or learn to live with it. It doesn't help to worry about it." He feels he shouldn't be too sympathetic, since that might encourage Annie to complain more and feel sorry for herself.

The major reason he is besieging her with advice, however, is that he thinks Annie expects him to solve her problem—that that's what "being there" for your partner really means. He does what people often do when they feel it's their responsibility to solve another person's problem. He offers Annie advice, and then when she fails to take it, he blames her:

JOEL: I don't think you really want to solve your problems. You get too much out of complaining about them.

This is the kind of conversation that makes people not want to have conversations. The next time Annie has problems about work, she'll think twice about talking about them. She won't want to repeat this unpleasant conversation. Joel doesn't want to repeat it either.

Joel thinks that Annie wants him to solve her problems. What she wants, however, is for him to appreciate how she feels. She would love him to say, "Poor baby. Everything's coming down on you all at once."

What Joel says, unfortunately, makes her feel that he *doesn't* appreciate how she feels:

- By reminding her that she always finishes her papers for school, Joel is telling her, in effect, that she has no reason to be upset
- By advising her to confront her boss and, if that fails, to quit, Joel is telling her, in effect, that her problem has a straightforward solution were she only to apply it and, again, that she has no reason to be upset

Joel is trying to reassure Annie that she has no reason to be upset while Annie wants him to appreciate that she does have a reason to be upset. It's an unfortunate misunderstanding. It would be a relief for him, then, if he realized that:

- Annie doesn't expect him to solve her problem.
- She doesn't even want him to try.
- She only wants him to appreciate how she feels.
- Her problem at the moment is feeling alone in her feelings about work and her boss.
- Joel's appreciating how she feels would solve this problem, since she would no longer feel alone.

I'm not saying that Joel is wrong to try to give advice and reassurance. At other times, Annie might have been reassured by Joel's reminder that she always gets her papers written. And she might have appreciated and, in fact, felt supported by Joel's advice to confront her boss or, even, to quit her job. On this occasion, however, Annie experiences his quickness to reassure and his readiness to offer solutions as efforts to talk her out of her feelings.

Joel needs an important piece of knowledge. He needs to know that there are two very different things that Annie might want from him when she comes to him with a problem:

1. She might want him to help solve the problem and, perhaps, to reassure her that it isn't such a big problem; that is, she might want him to talk her out of her feelings.
2. Or she might want him to listen to how she feels about the problem and, perhaps, to appreciate how big and unsolvable the problem really is or, at least, how big and unsolvable it seems to her at the moment.

If Joel had known that there were these two different things that Annie might want, he might have been able to say at the end of their disagreeable interchange:

JOEL: Here I've been rushing in with all this advice and all these solutions. But maybe that's not what you want from me at all.

Annie would feel relieved. She had felt all day that no one had understood how she felt. Now she would finally have found someone who did.

There is something further that Joel needs to know. He needs to know that jumping in with reassurance or advice when the person you're talking to wants to be listened to is a common error and that both he and Annie are repeatedly going to make it. The more Joel sees the error he's making as common and unavoidable, the less of a failure he will feel for making it and the more matter-of-factly he will be able to discuss it.

And the error *is* common and unavoidable. As a couple's therapist, I make my living by showing people how they give reassurance and advice when their partners really want them to appreciate how they feel. So you'd think I would know a lot about it. And I do. But that doesn't stop me from repeatedly making the same error with my partner. So I try to correct my error. I tell my partner, "This conversation isn't going right, so maybe you're not wanting all this advice I'm giving." Or *she* might say, "I think this is a time that I just want you to understand how I feel." As long as I see my giving unwanted advice and reassurance as an error that anyone can make and not as indicating that there is something wrong with me, it is easy for me to switch gears and to start listening.

The Boredom Trap

TRAP NUMBER 2: Your partner gets bored when you say what's on your mind or talk about your day.

As I have said, telling your partner what's on your mind and hearing what's on your partner's mind is how to feel close to your partner. It's how to create intimacy. But what do you do if hearing what's on your partner's mind bores you or vice versa?

Brenda and Jack are a couple in their late forties. Jack is a pharmacist, and Brenda works in an ad agency. They have been married for twenty-three years. Brenda comes into the living room where Jack is reading the paper and tells him about her day.

She describes the ad that she designed that morning. She says that she drew it with a fine-line pen to get a special shading effect, filled it in with reds and yellows rather than the usual greens and browns, used a special script to provide elegance, and put the written copy within the art work rather than beneath it as is usually done.

Jack is bored by the details of ad design. But because he doesn't want to hurt Brenda's feelings or reveal himself as a self-centered husband who doesn't care about his wife's life, he pretends to be interested.

Brenda, however, recognizes a fake product when she sees it. She shifts to something she thinks might interest him—the surprise lunch-hour potluck that people in her office threw to celebrate her promotion to vice president. Her promotion means leaving the people she had been working with for fifteen years and moving to the tenth floor executive offices. She describes how her officemate, Carmen, brought a lobster dish that took two days to prepare. Peter, her secretary, baked a cake. Kris, her pal down the hall, brought strawberries.

Jack is even more bored by this, but now he feels justified. "Why should anyone care," he thinks, "what someone else has for lunch?"

Brenda sees the glazed look in Jack's eyes and tries to talk in a more animated way in an effort to engage his interest. She tells him about something funny that happened at the potluck:

BRENDA: You're not going to believe this. Three people made the same dish. You should have seen Edna's face, poor thing, when she walked in with her chicken and rice and saw that both Sandra and Johnnie had brought in the same thing.

Brenda laughs, hoping that Jack will too.
He doesn't.

BRENDA: I guess you had to be there.

It's an unfortunate situation. The harder Brenda tries to be interesting, the more awkward and less interesting she becomes and the more distant and bored Jack becomes.

BRENDA: (*feeling hurt and angry*) You haven't heard a word I've said.

JACK: Yes I have. First you talked about your new ad, then about the party and the three people who brought the same dish.

BRENDA: Yeah, but you weren't really interested.

JACK: Well, I don't know much about ads. And I don't know most of the people in your office. And I'm not one for office gossip.

BRENDA: Don't call it gossip. You're just not interested in people.

Between them, Brenda and Jack have three ideas of why Jack is bored:

1. They have different interests (what they have just said).
2. Jack is self-centered (their hidden fear).
3. Brenda is boring (another hidden fear).

If Brenda and Jack are to get out of this spot, they will need *different* ideas. The ones that they already have—that Brenda is boring, that Jack is selfish, and that they are incompatible—are *nightmare* ideas. These nightmare ideas completely fill their minds and make it difficult for them to consider the possibility, for example, that Jack's boredom is the result of:

1. Brenda's not saying how she feels
2. Jack's inability to make a sufficiently active response
3. Brenda's awkward attempts to reengage Jack's interest
4. Jack's failure to recognize how much it means to Brenda to be able to talk to him

Let's go over these one at a time.

> **IDEA NUMBER 1:** Brenda and Jack need to know that Brenda *is* boring. She's boring because she's leaving out the part of the story that would provide the interest: how she *feels* about what she is describing.

Jack says that he isn't interested in ads. He would be interested, however, were Brenda to tell him more:

BRENDA: That ad is the best thing I've ever done. I'm really pleased. It made me think that maybe it's possible to be an artist and work in advertising at the same time.

Jack may not care about Brenda's job in itself, but he does care what *Brenda* thinks about it. If Brenda had told Jack the major point, which is that she felt pleased with the ad, he might have wanted to hear more about it. Without hearing the major point, however, he would understandably have little interest in the details.

Details can be dull when you don't know why your partner is describing them. In discussing the surprise potluck, Brenda again omitted the most important parts, which were that: She was deeply touched. No one in the office had ever been given a party like that before. It was clear that the people at work cared for her and were unhappy that she was leaving. She also felt sad, thinking how she was going to miss them.

Jack would not be bored hearing that. Once Brenda's feeling about the potluck became clear, the reason for her describing what everyone brought to it would become clear. She was touched by how everyone tried so hard to make it special. Greta spent two days preparing a dish. Kris went clear across town to get fresh strawberries. And Peter's cake was amazing for a first attempt.

Why did Brenda leave out the most important parts—her *feelings?* Because she felt uncomfortable tooting her own horn. She felt that telling Jack that she did a super job on the ad would be too boastful. So, instead, she told him *how* she composed it. She hoped he might guess from her description how good the ad really was. And she felt it would be too boastful to describe how important she was to her colleagues. She gave details that, by themselves, were not interesting because she was shy about relating feelings that ironically *would* have been interesting.

Brenda's effort not to be boastful made her boring.

Most of us are boring when we describe events without stating our feelings about them. We become less boring as we become increasingly aware of our feelings and increasingly skillful at expressing them.

IDEA NUMBER 2: Brenda and Jack need to know that Jack's boredom is as much the result of what *he* is doing as it is the result of what she is doing. It's a consequence of Jack's inability to make a sufficiently active response to what Brenda is saying and, in general, his sense of helplessness to do anything other than to sit there and listen.

Brenda's being boring is only half the story. The other half is that Jack was unable to engage Brenda in what she was saying. He sat there helplessly, listening to Brenda, trying to be the dutiful husband. Brenda had, at times, complained that Jack didn't listen to her. At those times, Jack defended himself; he said he did listen. Privately, however, he worried that she was right. He had the nightmare view of himself as a selfish person who doesn't care about anyone but himself.

So when Brenda came into the living room to talk to him, Jack felt that anything less than full and uninterrupted attention would be further evidence that he was unwilling to listen to her. He felt that he didn't have the option to tell her that she was describing the ad in too much detail for him, and that, anyway, he wanted to read the paper and would prefer to talk after dinner.

So Jack was bored, not just because Brenda was relating details without telling him how she felt, but also because his commitment to listen patiently and uncomplainingly prevented him from doing what anyone would need to do to remain engaged.

People get bored because they don't have a good way to talk about being bored.

It's hard to tell your partner that you're bored by what he or she is saying. You think that you shouldn't be bored or, if you are, that you should at least have the decency to keep it to yourself.

Of course, not everyone feels the need to keep quiet. Jack's friend Mack wouldn't sit still for two seconds if Tammy, his wife, described the dishes people brought to a potluck that she had gone to. He'd interrupt and say one of the following:

- Please stop. You're boring me to tears.

- I don't want to hear that crap.
- I don't see why you keep going to those stupid parties.
- Hey, that reminds me of a funny story I heard today …
- What's for dinner?

Of course, Mack never has to say such things anymore because Tammy had long ago given up trying to talk to him about her day. She just feels bullied by him.

Mack's way of dealing with feeling bored is to blurt out "You're boring." Jack's way is to keep his mouth shut. Each approach has serious disadvantages. So let's try a third approach. Let's have Jack try to talk about his dilemma:

JACK: I hope you don't take this wrong, but I'm having trouble listening to the details of the ad.

Jack's being able to say this might immediately relieve his boredom. He'd be making an active response—rescuing Brenda and himself from this demoralizing exchange by talking about it.

But his comment triggers the following debate within Brenda:

- He's right. I'm boring. He's found me out.
- But wait! Other people find me interesting.
- So the problem is him.
- He's interested only in himself.
- He's selfish
- And, anyway, who's he to talk? He bores me to tears when he talks about computers.

Brenda deals with her worry about being boring by redefining the problem as Jack's inability to be interested:

BRENDA: You think you're always so interesting. You bore me to tears when you talk about computers. You're only interested if it's about you.

Brenda is making her own active response. She is expressing the anger that developed in response to the humiliation she felt. She'd feel even better were she able also to confide the humiliation. Later that evening she goes to Jack and does just that:

BRENDA: You know, I *did* take it wrong—you know, when you said you had trouble listening. I worry about being a boring person. And, yes, I did go on about the ad.

Feeling grateful for Brenda's admission, Jack returns the favor.

JACK: Well, I can go on about computers.

Jack's willingness to admit that he, too, gets caught in details enables Brenda to figure out why she did in this case.

BRENDA: I felt it was too boastful to just come out and tell you that it was the best design I'd ever done.

Now that Jack understands why Brenda was telling him about the ad, he becomes interested in the details.

JACK: How was it different from your other ads? Did you bring home a copy?

In order not to be bored, people may need a straightforward way of talking about being bored. And in order not to be boring, people may need a straightforward way of talking about being boring.

> **IDEA NUMBER 3:** Brenda and Jack need to know that being boring is a consequence, in part, of trying not to be boring.

When Jack began to show signs of boredom, Brenda tried to talk in a wittier, more expansive, more animated way in an effort to reengage his interest. Although some people are skillful at bringing their partners back from the precipice of boredom, most, like Brenda, push them over it. At such times their poise crumbles; their cleverness disappears; their charm abandons them; and they become nervous, awkward, hesitant, and self-conscious.

In other words, Brenda was boring as a consequence of trying not to be boring. Let's imagine how it would look were Brenda, instead, to talk with Jack about being boring. Let's say she goes to talk to him later in the evening:

BRENDA: You know, earlier tonight, I was afraid I was boring you. So I tried to be interesting, which, of course, made me even more boring. I keep forgetting how that happens.

Jack would not be bored hearing this. He would feel relieved. Since Brenda would be saying that she was being boring, he wouldn't have to attribute his boredom to his own self-centeredness.

Let's collect all these ideas about why Brenda was boring. She was boring because she:

- Left out her important feelings
- Was worried about being boastful
- Was worried about being boring
- Was unable to recognize and to talk with Jack about any of this

SKEPTIC: Okay sure, maybe you've explained why Brenda was boring in this particular instance. But what about people who are *always* boring? There are such people, you know.

WILE: Those are people who *always* leave out the important feelings, who *always* worry about being too boastful, who *always* worry about being too boring, and who are *always* unable to recognize and talk with their partners about any of this.

IDEA NUMBER 4: Brenda and Jack need to know that Jack becomes bored, in part, because he feels left out and unimportant. He doesn't realize how crucial a role he has. He doesn't recognize what it means to Brenda to be able to tell him about her day.

Jack felt that he didn't have a role. He thought that it didn't even matter to Brenda that she was talking to him. He thought that she was chattering away about the ad and about the party because she had nothing better to do; she could have been talking to anybody. He felt ignored and unimportant. And all this made him feel bored. He didn't realize that:

- Brenda had been looking forward all day to talking to him. No one else would really do.
- Telling him about her success with the ad would be the capping event in her celebration of it.
- Much of her pleasure in the party she was given was the prospect of being able to tell him about it.
- Telling him about her sadness at leaving the people she had been working with for fifteen years (and getting him to understand how she felt about it) was her way of trying to deal with this sadness.

Jack didn't realize any of these things, partly because Brenda didn't make it clear that she was feeling them. If he had realized it, or if Brenda had told him, he wouldn't have felt so left out and bored.

So these are some of the major booby traps that we can stumble into when we try to talk to our partners:

- Instead of doing what our partners want us to do, which is to listen to them and to appreciate how they feel, we offer solutions, which tells them that we *don't* appreciate how they feel.
- We become boring because we leave out the most important parts—our feelings—and as a result of our efforts not to be boring.
- We become bored because we don't know how to talk about being bored and because we don't realize how much our partners are getting out of talking to us.

When you think about how easy it is to fall into these booby traps, and how discouraged we get when we do, it's amazing that any of us still talk to our partners at all.

Chapter 7
Using Communication Errors as Clues

Talking is dangerous. In an effort to make it less so, communication skills trainers have developed some rules for good communication. Here are some of them:

- Make "I statements" rather than "you statements" (e.g., say "I felt hurt and angry when you came home late last night" rather than "You're completely irresponsible; you don't think about anybody but yourself").
- Don't say "always" or "never" (e.g., "You never lift a finger around here").
- Don't interrupt your partner.
- Paraphrase what your partner says so that he or she will know that you have heard (e.g., "I hear you say that you feel … Do I have it right?")
- Don't mind read; that is, don't speculate about what your partner is feeling, thinking, or trying to do (e.g. "You're trying to make me feel guilty").
- Stick to one topic.
- Don't bring up resentments from the distant past.
- Don't get sidetracked in an argument over irrelevant details (e.g., "It happened in September." "No, it was October." "No, I distinctly remember it was September").
- Don't label or name-call (e.g., "You're a wimp").
- Don't dump out stored-up complaints (e.g., "And another thing … And now that I think of it, why did you have to …?").

In the following short conversation, Nancy and Bruce violate all ten rules:

NANCY: (*making a "you statement" and using the word "never"*) You never talk to me anymore. The only time we ...

BRUCE: (*interrupting rather than listening*) What do you mean "never"? We talked the whole time we were walking in the park last weekend. We ...

NANCY: (*mind reading and interrupting*) You have a funny definition of "talking." You were trying to make me feel guilty for inviting my mother to dinner.

BRUCE: I just don't see why we have to see her so much.

NANCY: (*changing the subject*) What about all the time we spend with your brother?

BRUCE: (*bringing up an old resentment*) I didn't hear you complaining when your sister came to dinner and left three months later.

NANCY: She was having a bad time. Her husband had just left her. And, anyway, that was fifteen years ago.

BRUCE: (*getting sidetracked over an irrelevant detail*) It was only ten.

NANCY: Fifteen.

BRUCE: Ten.

NANCY: (*name-calling*) Fifteen! You know, you're a real nutcase. It's crazy to nurse a grudge so long.

BRUCE: (*changing the subject and dumping out stored-up complaints*) I'll tell you what's crazy. What's crazy is telling me over and over again to be ready to leave in time for a party and then keeping me waiting half an hour (*this happened twelve days ago*). It's worrying about a stray dog but ignoring my migraine (*this happened three days ago*). It's ...

Let's look at Nancy and Bruce's violations of these communication rules one at a time.

COMMUNICATION RULE 1: Make "I statements," not "you statements."

In starting the conversation by saying "You never talk to me anymore," Nancy thought she was just stating a fact. And in a way she was. Bruce *hadn't* been talking to her as much as he used to. But she was also accusing him. There is no way that anyone could hear, "You never talk to me anymore" without immediately feeling accused of doing something wrong. She was accusing Bruce without knowing it.

A number of years ago, a psychologist, Thomas Gordon, discovered a clever way to help people recognize when they are accusing others without knowing it. He pointed out that statements that begin with "you" or "you are" tend to be accusations and that a good way to avoid such accusing is to say, instead, "I" or "I feel."

There are exceptions, of course. Some statements that begin with a "you are" are not accusations; for example, "You are wonderful." And some statements that begin with an "I feel" are accusations; for example, "I feel you are a jerk." In general, however, Gordon's principle—make "I statements," not "you statements"—is useful. Instead of "*You* aren't listening," say "*I* feel frustrated because I feel I'm not getting my point across."

Had Nancy made an "I statement," she wouldn't have said "You never talk to me anymore." She would have said something like:

NANCY: I feel hurt and angry because I take your talking less to me these days to mean that you're less interested in me than you used to be.

There is little doubt that Nancy and Bruce would have been better off had she said this. Since her emphasis would be on what she is feeling rather than on what Bruce is doing wrong, he is less likely to have become defensive.

Nancy, however, doesn't feel like making an "I statement." She doesn't feel like saying "I feel hurt and angry." She feels like saying "You never talk to me anymore." The words "I feel hurt and angry" don't even occur to her.

As a couples therapist, I have done a lot of communication skills training, so I know the communication rules pretty well. In the heat of battle, however, the "I statement" rule can go out the window. I don't even think about it.

Everyone makes "you statements," even communication-skills trainers. Sometimes you just feel like accusing. Sometimes nothing but a good you statement will do. So I've got my own revised version of the "I-statement–you-statement" rule. In my version, it's not what you do that is important. It's what you know.

The major problem with Nancy's "You never talk to me anymore" is that she doesn't know that she's being accusing. She thinks she is just expressing her feelings. Since she doesn't know she's being accusing, she has no choice but to take Bruce's defensive and accusing response as indicating, "You can't talk to Bruce. He gets upset for no reason at all."

The biggest problem with "you statements," in other words, is not that you become accusing. And it's not that your partner becomes defensive. It's that you end up feeling that there is no way to talk to each other.

So here is my revised "I-statement–you-statement" rule:

1.   Make "you statements" if you feel like doing it, but know that you are doing it, so that you won't be surprised by the effect—namely, your partner getting defensive or angry.
2.   Know how to make "I statements," so that you will be able to make them if you want to.
3.   Recognize "you statements" as clues to hidden "I statements."

"You statements" (accusations) are not all bad. In fact, they can be useful. They are rough first approximations to I statements with a little heat added. The "you statement," "You are completely selfish and irresponsible," can be thought of as a rough first approximation of the "I statement," "I felt taken for granted when you came home late last night."

"You statements" may not reveal very clearly what's askew, but they indicate that something is. "You statements" indicate that there is something that needs to be talked about. "I statements" provide the means to do so.

The hope is to obtain full benefit from your "you statements" without suffering too much from their costs. In other words you want to be able to:

- Make "you statements" without you and your partner getting too terribly upset about it
- Use these "you statements" as stepping-stones to "I statements" in which you are really able to talk about the matter

Here is the conversation that Nancy and Bruce's argument could have been a stepping stone to:

NANCY: I know I said some pretty strong things. I was hurt and angry.

BRUCE: I knew you were angry, but I didn't know you were hurt.

NANCY: Well, maybe not so much hurt as worried.

BRUCE: Oh? About what?

NANCY: About us.

BRUCE: Well, I have been kind of quiet lately. Is that what you're talking about? I've been worrying about the bills and not making enough money to cover them.

As this brief conversation shows, the use of "I statements" changes everything. Bruce is himself bringing up the issue that Nancy had before so unsuccessfully tried to raise: that he hasn't been talking much.

COMMUNICATION RULE 2: Don't say "always" or "never."

Nancy's opening statement, "You never talk to me anymore," has another element that communication skills trainers would not approve of: her use of the word "never."

The problem with "never" is that it's an exaggeration. Nancy doesn't really mean that Bruce *never* talks to her anymore. She simply means that he doesn't talk to her as much as he used to and that she misses it. The problem with such an exaggeration is that it gets the other person angry.

Another problem is that it makes your charge easier to refute. All Bruce has to do is to point to an exception, which he does. He says, "What do you mean, *never*? We talked the whole time we were walking in the park last weekend.

The terms "never" and "always" are too powerful. They provoke the other person unnecessarily. And they are too weak and easy to counter.

Because of these hazards, communication skills trainers have established the rule: Don't say "always" and "never." But there is a problem with this as with all the other communication rules. Communication errors are clues to use rather than just mistakes to correct. Rather than telling people not to violate communication rules, I would want them to expect to violate them and then to use their violations as clues. When people say "always" or "never," they do it for a reason. It is a means of emphasis and an expression of frustration. Nancy's saying "never" is:

- An expression of how frustrated she feels about Bruce's silence
- A consequence of having previously held back her complaint (Now that it is finally coming out, it is doing so in this dam-breaking form.)
- An attempt to be emphatic enough to get Bruce's attention

Nancy wouldn't have to say "never" if she had a more direct way of expressing herself. Since she doesn't, it's a good thing that she can at least take this exaggerated and indirect route.

When Nancy says "never," it isn't just a communication error. It's a stand-in for, and thus a clue to, what she is feeling. Instead of telling Nancy, "Don't say 'never,' " I would want to help her discover and express the feelings for which the word "never" is a stand-in. I would want to help her say that she feels really frustrated about the matter and that she is worried about not getting through to Bruce about it.

So here is my revision of the "always-never" rule. Know that:

1. "Always" and "never" are likely to slip out of your mouth even if you work conscientiously to suppress them.
2. Whenever you find yourself saying "always" or "never" you've got a frustrated person on your hands, and that person is you.
3. You are likely to end up feeling even more frustrated because your partner will almost inevitably respond to your "always" or "never" by pointing to an exception.
4. The words "always" and "never" are stand-ins for important feelings and, as such, can serve as clues these feelings.

COMMUNICATION RULE 3: Don't interrupt your partner.

Nancy has barely gotten into what she wanted to say. "You never talk to me anymore," she says. "The only time we …"

And we'll never know how that sentence is going to end because Bruce immediately interrupts: "What do you mean, *never*? We talked the whole time we were walking in the park last weekend. We …"

And we'll never know how Bruce's sentence is going to end because Nancy immediately interrupts back: "You have a funny definition of talking? You were trying to make me feel guilty for inviting my mother for dinner."

Everyone knows about the disadvantages of interrupting:

- It deprives your partner of the chance to have his or her say.
- It makes your partner angry.
- It makes your partner stop listening to you.
- Since you aren't letting your partner finish, you may be jumping to false conclusions about what he or she was going to say.

So it's understandable that communication skills trainers would make the rule: Don't interrupt your partner. But *not* interrupting has disadvantages also. The more you force yourself to sit there quietly while your partner makes what seem to you to be unfair charges:

- The less you'll be able to listen to what he or she says
- The angrier you may be when you finally get your turn (By that time, you may be unable to do anything else but throw a tantrum.)
- The more dispirited you may be when you finally get your turn (By that time, you may not feel like saying anything at all.)

The more you interrupt your partner, the more you may squelch him or her. But the less you interrupt your partner, the more you may squelch yourself.

So here is my revision of the "don't-interrupt-your-partner rule":

1. Interrupt your partner if that's what you want to do, but know the danger: that your partner may become an angry or dispirited person who can't listen.
2. Refrain from interrupting your partner if that's what you want to do, but know the danger: that you may become an angry or dispirited person who can't listen.

And here is the third part to this rule:

3. Become an expert in the art of interrupting without interrupting—that is, in finding ways of expressing your objections that don't completely cut off your partner.

Here are some examples of interrupting without interrupting:

- "I'll want my chance, because you're saying a lot of unfair things. But go on."
- "It's taking all my effort to keep from interrupting you."
- "You may be making some good points, but I'm too upset by your tone to be able to listen."

In each case, the speaker is making enough of an objection—enough of a statement about how he or she feels—so that he or she might now be able to listen. At the same time, the objection is sufficiently non-inflammatory, and sufficiently short, so that the person who has been talking is able to continue without feeling cut off.

COMMUNICATION RULE 4: Paraphrase what your partner just said.

Bruce, in responding, "What do you mean? We talked the whole time we were walking in the park last weekend," is violating another communication rule. He is reacting to what Nancy just said rather than taking it in. When your partner is trying to tell you how he or she feels, communication skills trainers say, paraphrase what he or she says (put it in your own words) and check to see if you have it right. For example, say, "I hear you saying that you feel … Do I have it right?" Or say, "Let's see if I understand what you're saying. You're saying … Am I right?"

> **SKEPTIC:** Do you really believe anyone can say things like that with a straight face? It's so stilted. If you wanted to get me talking like that, you'd have to pay *me* for the session.

> **WILE:** Well sure, it can sound stilted. And that's too bad because communication skills trainers are onto something pretty important here. One of the main reasons fights get started and become irresolvable is that neither partner listens to or acknowledges what the other says. Bruce immediately refutes what Nancy has just said. He says, "What do you mean? We talked the whole time we were walking in the park last weekend."

And here's where the paraphrasing rule can be useful. Paraphrasing—that is, saying, "I hear you saying … Is that right?"—would get Bruce listening to what Nancy just said rather than refuting or ignoring it. He wouldn't be able immediately to go on to give his view. He would have to think about what she said. His whole attention would be directed to trying to understand what she said and to make clear to her that he understood it. And all this seems like a good thing, even though, as the skeptic says, paraphrasing can seem contrived.

And there's a bigger problem. People feel like paraphrasing least just when they need to do it the most.

Here are Nancy and Bruce in the office of a communication skills trainer, who is trying to teach them to paraphrase.

TRAINER: Okay, let's start again. But this time, Bruce, remember to paraphrase. Go ahead, Nancy.

NANCY: Well, as I said, I'm worried that we're about to spend another weekend without talking to each other. You'll invite your buddies over to watch football, and I'll feel deserted and resentful.

BRUCE: I can understand how you feel, but …

TRAINER: No, Bruce. Telling Nancy you understand isn't the same as paraphrasing what she says. How does she know you understand? The only way she can tell for sure is if you put it in your own words.

BRUCE: Okay. (*Turns back to Nancy*) I hear you saying that you're afraid that we won't talk and that I'll leave you out and get all involved with football and the guys, but …

TRAINER: Check it out with her.

BRUCE: Is that right?

NANCY: Yes.

TRAINER: Good.

Bruce's heart is clearly not into paraphrasing. He is showing only token compliance with the task. The reason, we can imagine, is that he is eager to get to the "but"—that is, to the place where he can begin to state his defense. He wants to state his defense, we can also guess, because he feels unfairly accused. In other words, Bruce feels too misunderstood by Nancy to *want* to try to understand her.

What often underlies the communication error of not para-phrasing is that people don't feel like paraphrasing—they don't feel like acknowledging their partners' feelings—when they feel that their partners aren't acknowledging theirs.

The paraphrasing rule is based on an important insight—namely, that people often stop listening to one another without realizing it. They don't fully see that they have temporarily slipped into an adversarial mode. The paraphrase rule is an effort to get partners to listen to each other when they hadn't realized that they weren't.

I suggest keeping the insight but throwing away the rule. Here is my revision of the "paraphrasing rule":

1. Appreciate how important listening to your partner is, how quickly problems arise when you don't, and how easy it is to think you are listening when you're not.
2. Realize that you are not listening because you feel unheard yourself.
3. Know *how* to listen to your partner's feelings (how to acknowledge what he or she says) so that you will be able to listen when you want to.

If you appreciate all this, you will see that your arguments with your partner are often not even about the issues that you and your partner think they are. They are results of the fact that both of you feel unheard.

Realizing that your partner feels unheard—and that's why he or she isn't listening to you—you will find yourself automatically *trying* to listen and trying to prove to your partner that you *are* listening. To prove that you are, you will repeat what your partner just said, but you'll do so in your own informal way rather than in the contrived manner that communication skills trainers teach. You will engage in your own *unstilted* version of paraphrasing. You may say, for example:

- "Am I crazy? Is that really your point? That …"
- Or, "I've been so busy trying to get you to see … that I hadn't noticed that what you're trying to get *me* to see is that …."
- Or, "I know you're trying to tell me …. But I can't listen because it makes me too mad."
- Or, "Okay, you telling me …, but here's why I don't buy it."

- Or, "You've said that eight times now. The repetition is driving me crazy. But, you know, maybe you're repeating it because you don't think I've heard—and, well, actually, maybe I haven't."

COMMUNICATION RULE 5: Don't mind read.

Let's return to Nancy and Bruce's original argument. Bruce responds to Nancy's charge by saying, "What do you mean, *never*? We talked the whole time we were walking in the park last weekend."

Nancy replies, "You have a funny definition of 'talking.' You were trying to make me feel guilty for inviting my mother for dinner."

Nancy has just committed another communication rule error: mind reading. Mind reading is telling people what they are thinking, feeling, or trying to do rather than asking them or waiting until they tell you.

Mind reading can be clearly provocative. Statements such as: "You're trying to punish me;" "You're trying to make me feel guilty;" "You must want to suffer;" "You always have to be in control;" and "Unconsciously you're angry" can bring reasonable conversation to a dead stop. People don't like others making such guesses about their feelings and intentions.

The mind reading statement, "Why are you so angry at me?" can lead into the following familiar argument:

WIFE: (*mind reading*) Why are you so angry at me?

HUSBAND: I'm not angry.

WIFE: Yes, you are.

HUSBAND: (*raising his voice*) No, I'm not.

WIFE: (raising hers) Listen to your voice. You sound angry to me.

HUSBAND: Well, I'm angry *now*. I'm angry because you kept insisting I'm angry.

Such exchanges are frustrating to both partners. It is understandable, therefore, that communication skills trainers would offer the rule: "don't mind read."

There is a problem with this rule, however. Although mind reading can be jumping to conclusions, it can also be drawing conclusions. In this latter meaning, even therapists mind read. They tell their clients, for example, "You seem angry" or "You seem depressed."

Even when mind reading is jumping to conclusions—that is, when it is a clear communication error—it isn't just an error; it is a clue.

When a person says, "You don't like any of my friends," what he or she might really mean is, "I'm worried that you don't like them."

That's what mind reading often is. It's a worry put in the form of an assertion. It's a fear stated as a fact. Thus, "You're bored to death" might mean "I'm worried I've been boring." And the wife's statement, "Why are you so angry at me?" might mean: "I'm worried that you are angry at me. I've been withdrawn lately, and I'd be angry if you had disappeared on me that way."

Such mind reading is an incomplete statement. Rather than tell this wife "don't mind read," I would help her complete the statement.

So here is my revised mind-reading rule:

1. Know the dangers of mind reading, so that when you do it, you won't be surprised by the effect; namely, your partner getting angry or defensive.
2. Realize that mind reading may be an incomplete statement.
3. Recognize that certain types of mind reading are expressions of worries or fears put in the form of assertions.

COMMUNICATION RULE 6: Stick to one topic.

Nancy and Bruce were already having trouble discussing Nancy's mother. Shifting the subject to Bruce's brother and then to Nancy's sister brought it to a grand total of three unmanageable issues to deal with rather than just the one. It's understandable, therefore, that communication skills trainers would offer the rule "Stick to one topic."

But let's look at why people *don't* stick to one topic. They don't because they feel that the topic being discussed places them at a disadvantage.

Nancy feels at a disadvantage in discussing her mother. She thinks that Bruce might be right that her mother visits too often. So, in order to gain more credibility, she shifts the topic to Bruce's brother. Bruce can hardly complain about her mother's visits, she figures, if he takes into account how often his brother visits.

Bruce feels at a disadvantage in discussing his brother's visits. So he shifts to a topic (Nancy's sister) that he feels might enable him to regain the advantage.

Nancy and Bruce aren't changing the subject simply because they have bad communication habits. They are jockeying for position.

So here is my revised "stick-to-one-topic" rule:

1.   Know that shifting topics will complicate the situation, frustrate your partner, and make your partner even less likely to listen to you.
2.   Know why you are doing it; that is, (a) to put yourself in a better position in your argument with your partner, (b) to move away from a point your partner made that you fear may be valid, and (c) to amass further evidence in your effort (futile though it may be) to convince your partner that you are right.
3.   Know that your efforts to convince your partner are futile. You're in an argument, and in an argument, the point is for each of you to refute what the other says.

COMMUNICATION RULE 7: Don't dig up old grievances.

In complaining about the time ten years ago when Nancy's sister came for dinner and stayed for several months, Bruce is digging up an old grievance.

"The grudges that partners have now are difficult enough to deal with," communication skills trainers say. "It only complicates matters to bring up sensitive and unresolved issues from the past."

Communication skills trainers may fail to appreciate, however, that grievances from the past often are about the present. People frequently bring up past events when they have difficulty justifying complaints they have in the present.

Bruce feels that Nancy pays more attention to other people's wishes than she does to his. But it's a subtle feeling, and he has difficulty pointing to anything specific. In fact, Bruce himself can often feel that his complaint is invalid. He has to go back ten years—to Nancy's choosing her sister's needs over his—to find a clear example of what he is experiencing in more subtle form now.

Bruce's bringing up the past is unfortunate. It makes Nancy even less interested in listening to what he has to say. But he may be lucky to have at least this means of representing the feelings that he is having now.

So here is my modified version of the "don't dig up grievances from the past" rule:

1. Know that your bringing up grievances from the past is likely to offend your partner and make him or her even less likely to listen to you.
2. Realize that you may be going to the past because your partner just criticized you and that you are in great need of evidence—even if it requires bringing up something from long ago—to defend yourself.
3. Realize that what you may be going to the past to find is a dramatized version or clearer form of an important concern that you have now.

Bruce's complaint has a grain of truth. Nancy isn't attending to many of his most important needs. And he isn't attending to many of hers.

COMMUNICATION RULE 8: Don't get sidetracked arguing about irrelevant details.

Nancy and Bruce's argument about her sister's visit contains another communication skills error. It doesn't matter whether this sister came to stay with them fifteen years ago or just ten. The main point is simply that it was a long time ago. Nancy and Bruce are getting hot and bothered over nothing.

So, it's understandable that communication skills trainers would offer the rule: "Don't get bogged down arguing over irrelevant details."

Nancy and Bruce's argument looks so ridiculous, in fact—we can easily think that they are acting like children and should just stop—that we may forget to consider why they are so stubbornly holding onto it. They are holding on because, as things exist between them at the moment, any and every detail is:

- A place to make a stand against what each sees as the other's unreasonable, disagreeable, or provocative behavior
- An opportunity to react against what each sees as the other's unyielding, know-it-all, or self-righteous attitude
- A chance to give expression to the general displeasure that each feels toward the other

Nancy and Bruce feel so aggravated that neither has any wish to go along with *anything* the other says. In such a situation, there is no such thing as an "irrelevant" detail.

So here is my revised "don't-get-sidetracked" rule:

1. Whenever you and your partner get bogged down discussing "irrelevant" details, realize that the argument is no longer about issues (if it ever was), but is about your general frustration with each other.
2. And realize that whatever sense of good will (or willingness to give each other the benefit of the doubt) may have existed between you and your partner before has, for the moment at least, disappeared.

COMMUNICATION RULE 9: Don't label or name-call.

Nancy responded to Bruce's complaint about her sister's long visit by saying, "You know, you're a real nutcase. It's crazy to hold a grudge that long."

Saying "You're a real nutcase" destroys whatever possibility might still exist for useful conversation. It is understandable, therefore, that communication skills trainers would offer the rule: "Don't name-call."

Instead of telling people not to name-call, however, I would want to tell them:

1. Know that, when you name-call, you are momentarily feeling so frustrated, hurt, stung, put upon, or un-listened-to yourself that you are willing to resort to almost anything, even to statements that a moment's reflection would tell you will achieve the opposite of what you want. They will just get your partner angrier and even less likely to listen.
2. And know that, at such times, you may not want to take that moment to reflect and may not care whether your partner becomes angrier and less likely to listen.
3. Use the recognition that you are name-calling as a clue that the intensity of your feelings has temporarily exceeded your ability to sort out, think through, and talk about these feelings.

Our ability to sort out and think through our feelings is often imperfect even in calm moments. The result at such times is a kind of quiet name-calling. We don't yell, and we don't seem angry, but what we say about our partners is essentially name-calling. We use words like "egotistical," "narcissistic," "hostile," "irresponsible," "babyish," "dependent," and "controlling."

COMMUNICATION RULE 10: Don't dump out stored-up complaints.

Bruce is so angry at Nancy's calling him a nutcase that he blurts out:

BRUCE: I'll tell you what's crazy. What's crazy is telling me over and over again to be ready to leave in time for a party and then keeping me waiting half an hour [this happened twelve days ago]. It's worrying about a stray dog [this happened three days ago], but ignoring my migraine. It's …

Bruce had been holding these things back because he didn't want to hurt Nancy's feelings or start a fight. He blurts them out now because he doesn't *care* if he hurts her feelings or starts a fight. His main concern is that what he says won't have *enough* impact. This is the opposite of his usual concern, which is that what he says will have too much impact.

We all store up complaints. We do it all the time. And we often do it without knowing it.

We are told to be polite, respectful, and tactful. In fact, being polite, respectful, and tactful is an *eleventh* rule that communication skills trainers often tell us. But being polite, respectful, and tactful requires suppressing complaints. And suppressing complaints means storing them up. And storing them up leads to dumping them out.

So here's my suggestion. Instead of telling Bruce that he shouldn't dump out stored-up complaints, I recommend that he and Nancy use his "dumped out" complaints as clues.

In complaining about Nancy's keeping him waiting, and paying more attention to a stray dog than to him, Bruce is saying, in essence, that he feels neglected.

Ironically, Nancy has been trying to tell Bruce that *she* feels neglected. That's what her complaint, "You never talk to me anymore," is all about. Accordingly, instead of just telling Bruce that he shouldn't dump out stored-up complaints, I would want Nancy and Bruce to use what he does "dump out" to discover that they both feel neglected.

So here is my revision of the "dumping-out rule":

1. Expect that you and your partner will dump out stored-up complaints. The suppression of complaints is too automatic a process to be able to eliminate entirely.
2. Appreciate that such "dumping out" serves a necessary function. If these things are not "dumped out," they might never get out at all. And it's important that they get out (that is, that they be brought to the surface) so that they can be talked about.
3. Use what you and your partner dump out as clues to important hidden feelings.

Two New Rules

In addition to the common communication rules just described, I propose two others: the recovery rule and the prefacing rule.

NEW COMMUNICATION RULE 1: The recovery rule.

As I have said, obeying the ten classic communication rules is impossible. Everyone repeatedly:

- Makes "you statements"
- Says "always" and "never"
- Interrupts
- Fails to paraphrase
- Mind reads
- Changes topics in the middle of an argument
- Brings up resentments from the distant past
- Argues about irrelevant details
- Name-calls
- Stores up complaints

So I recommend that you expect to make such "errors" and that you devote yourself to recovering from them. By "recovering," I mean becoming familiar enough with how you and your partner make these "errors" and with the effect that these "errors" have, so that later, when the dust has settled, you and your partner will be able to sit down together and figure out what happened.

Here is an idealized version of how Nancy and Bruce might sit down to try to figure out what happened.

NANCY: Poor guy. There you were minding your own business without a care—well maybe just a couple of cares—and I get on your case for not talking. (Nancy recognizes that she criticized him; that is, that she began with a "you statement.")

BRUCE: (*appreciating Nancy's admission, makes one of his own*) Well, you were right about my not talking, and how, when I did, it was mostly to complain about your mother.

Nancy and Bruce are in a positive cycle in which each admits things in response to the other doing the same. In their earlier fight they were in a *negative* cycle in which each automatically attacked or defended in response to the other doing the same.

NANCY: (*admitting changing topics*) Well, you were right that we see her too much. But I didn't like your saying it. So I brought up how often we see your brother. Well, that turned out to be a big mistake because then you dragged my sister into the ring.

BRUCE: (*acknowledging digging up an old grievance*) I had to go back fifteen years to do that. You've got to admit my memory is good.

NANCY: (*admitting name-calling*) Oh, I do. And it got me so frustrated I started calling you names—definitely my low point.

BRUCE: (*admitting dumping out stored-up complaints*) And my low point was bringing up all that stuff about that dog and my migraine. It wasn't even a migraine—just a headache.

NANCY: (*using what Bruce dumped out as a clue*) Yes, well, actually that kind of shocked me. There I was trying to tell you that I felt neglected, and it turns out that you've been feeling that way too.

> **SKEPTIC:** Let me tell you right now that I couldn't possibly talk that way. I don't know if I'd even want to.

> **WILE:** Yes, it's hard to imagine people so thoroughly reviewing their fight. I just wanted to give an example of what it would look like if they could. In this exchange, Nancy and Bruce are:

> - Recovering from their communication errors by having a follow-up conversation
> - Using their communication errors as clues to uncover an important issue in the relationship

- Beginning to have the conversation that Nancy had originally wanted to have and, as it turns out, Bruce wants to have also

NEW COMMUNICATION RULE 2: The prefacing rule.

Recovering is what partners can do after a fight. "Prefacing" is what can be done *before* a fight. Nancy had a vague sense that her original statement—"You never talk to me anymore"—wasn't going to go over well. But she gritted her teeth and said it anyway. Things might have gone differently had Nancy, before saying it, told Bruce one of the following:

- I'm angry, so this is probably not going to come out in a very good way, but …
- I've been mad about this for so long, I've got to say it no matter what.
- I know this isn't fair—it's putting all the blame on you—but …
- This may sound critical, but that's not my intention—or maybe it is just a little.

The typical effect of such prefacing remarks is to make what the person then goes on to say easier to hear. The listener is less likely to be angered by his or her partner's complaint if he or she knows that:

- The partner is having difficulty making the complaint
- The partner, himself or herself, is worried that the complaint might be provocative
- The partner feels at least partly unjustified in having the complaint
- The complaint is coming out in an exaggerated way because the partner has been holding it back
- The complaint is coming out in an awkward and provocative way because the partner feels uncomfortable about having it

Shifting from the Content to the Overview Level

Recovering and prefacing have something in common. And to show what this is, I'm going to talk about Johnny Carson.

There are certain comics—Johnny Carson is an example—whose humor is based not only on good jokes but also on recovering from bad ones. The masterful way in which Carson dealt with a difficult situation (telling a joke to a room full of people and having it fall flat) is often more entertaining than a simple good joke would have been. It is possible to suggest, in fact, that Carson would have lost much of his effectiveness were his jokes all good.

Carson is having two relationships with the audience. The first is on the content level. He tells a joke and waits for laughter. The second is on the overview level—what I call stepping up on the platform. He interacts with the audience about his material, noting how and why they might have liked it, jokingly threatening them if they don't laugh, making humorous excuses for a particularly poor one-liner, and so on. It is the overview level that, at least for Johnny Carson, is the critical one.

Applying the example of Johnny Carson to couple relationships, I suggest that the overview level—having a relationship about the relationship and making partners observers of their own interactions—may be a major part of the solution to partner difficulties.

And that's what prefacing and recovering are: ways of shifting from the content to the overview level.

- In prefacing, the person shifts to the overview level *before* the conversation. Nancy describes her feelings, fears, hopes, or reservations about what she is about to say.
- In recovering, the partners shift to the overview level *after* the discussion. They step back from the argument and try to figure out what happened.

Recovering is prefacing that occurs at the end. Prefacing is recovering that occurs at the beginning.

It is possible, although difficult, to shift to the overview level right in the middle of an argument and make what psychologists John

Gottman and Robert Levenson call a repair effort. In the course of their argument, Nancy or Bruce could have said, for example, one of the following:

- I'm too angry to listen to anything you say right now.
- That's a good point, but I'm way too pissed to admit it.
- Or, "I'm angry now so I'm saying a lot of things that I don't even mean."
- I know what I'm saying is making things worse, but I'm so angry that I don't even care.
- We've ruined the evening. Should we try for the whole weekend?

In each case, the speaker is shifting from arguing to talking about the argument. If there is any chance to end the argument while still in it, this is how to do it. So here are my recommendations:

1. Make good use of the communication rules; they can point out ways that you are provoking your partner without knowing it.
2. Make good use of your communication errors; they can reveal unrecognized elements in your feelings.
3. Develop skill in recovering from your communication errors; that is, become adept in shifting to the overview level and having a conversation about these errors (and about your fights).

Part III

SOMETHING IS WRONG
WITH THE WAY WE THINK

Chapter 8
Feelings We Think We Shouldn't Have

So far in this book, I've discussed how to use our relationships to solve problems, fill gaps in our personalities, learn to love ourselves, become skillfully dependent, and become independent. But the question remains: Why don't we do these things already?

And my answer has been: because they all require skillful talking, and something is wrong with the way we talk. Many couples have their most bitter fights when they sit down to talk about their relationships.

> **SKEPTIC:** Oh, is that all you're trying to tell us: that everything would be solved if only we learned to communicate better?

> **WILE:** Well, actually there's a deeper problem. Something is wrong with the way we talk because something is wrong with the way we think. Our thinking continually breaks down. We go along fine, thinking more or less logically, when, *zap*, we start accusing ourselves or our partners, and useful thinking comes to a halt.

For example, one evening while driving over to see his girlfriend Louise, Mel realizes that he isn't looking forward to seeing her. This puzzles him because seeing her has always been the high point of his day. He remembers that his previous girlfriend told him that he was afraid of intimacy. He discounted her criticism as psychobabble (and as retaliation for him breaking up with her)—but he begins to worry now that she might be right.

Zap, Mel has stopped thinking and has started accusing himself. "I'm afraid of intimacy" sounds like a neutral and objective statement that will help him understand his behavior. But it isn't. He just feels beat-up and gloomy—a failure as a human being—which means that he is in no shape to think further about the matter.

If he were able to think further, he would realize that he's not looking forward to seeing Louise for understandable reasons. He's worried that, as Louise often does, she'll want to cook him a big meal. He feels that he doesn't have the right to tell her that he's on a diet and would prefer cottage cheese. He's afraid that doing so would hurt her feelings. He's worried that, as Louise sometimes does, she'll suggest that they visit her parents the next weekend. He feels that he doesn't have the right to say that he'd rather that just the two of them go to the park.

Mel's problem is his belief that intimacy requires completely sacrificing his needs to those of Louise. But defining himself as "afraid of intimacy"—using this global term to describe himself—brings an end to useful thinking about this matter. He just feels hung up and immature. He never gets to learn that it is his exaggerated belief of what intimacy entails that dampens his spirit for it.

"Fear of intimacy" is only one of a number of commonly used ideas or explanations that can bring an end to useful thinking. Others include "dependency," "selfishness," and "jealousy." Early in our lives, as soon as we begin to learn anything, we start hearing:

- It's bad to be selfish; we should share
- It's bad to be jealous; we should love our baby brother or sister
- It's babyish to be dependent; we should be a "big boy" or "big girl" and "do things for ourselves"

Ideas such as these become so ingrained in our thinking that they can be thought of as a new set of commandments. In addition to "thou shalt not kill" and "thou shalt not steal," we also have thou shalt not be:

1. Dependent
2. Self-centered (selfish)
3. Jealous (unless you have a reason)
4. Boastful
5. Withdrawn (or withholding)
6. Afraid of intimacy

I say they're *commandments* because they are fixed and immutable as natural laws. No one would think to question them. These new commandments are the laws that our internal prosecutors accuse us of violating and that we accuse our partners of violating.

Included on the list of new commandments are reactions and vulnerabilities we think we shouldn't have. Thou shalt not be:

7. Depressed
8. Oversensitive
9. Unwilling to take risks

And thou shalt not:

10. Worry about things you can do nothing about
11. Wallow in self-pity
12. Run away from your problems

Also included in what I'm calling the new commandments are discredited ways of relating to others. Thou shalt not be:

13. Controlling (bossy, manipulative)
14. Defensive
15. A nag
16. A wimp

People differ in which commandments affect them the most. Women with a traditional upbringing are usually more afraid of being bossy than they are of being a wimp, whereas men with such an upbringing are usually more afraid of being a wimp than they are of being bossy.

Four "thou shalt nots" are of special interest because they imply attitudes toward life in general. Thou shalt not:

17. Be perfectionistic
18. Have unrealistic or unrealizable expectations
19. Fail to take responsibility for yourself
20. Have a negative attitude (be grouchy, pessimistic, a poor sport)

Some thou shalt nots contradict other thou shalt nots. Victorian women lived by the commandment: Thou shalt not enjoy sex. Post-Victorian women live by the opposite commandment:

21. Thou shalt not be sexually cold

A modified form of the Victorian commandment persists, however:

22. Thou shalt not be promiscuous

Men have a parallel set of contradictory commandments

23. Thou shalt not be a dirty old man
24. Thou shalt always be eager and willing to have sex

Each generation adds its own special thou shalt nots. Here are four from ours. Thou shalt not:

25. Fail to fulfill your potential
26. Be a workaholic
27. Be codependent
28. Suppress your anger (because it will just build up)

This last coexists (often confusingly) with the incompatible longtime commandment:

29. Thou shalt not express anger (because it will just cause problems)
30. In fact, thou shalt not be angry at all

Of course, it's okay to be angry under certain specific conditions—for example, if you can point to a clear provocation such as your partner coming home two hours late. Similarly:

It's okay to feel depressed if you can point to a clear reason, such as being jilted. But it's not okay if you can't. And even then, it's only okay if the depression doesn't last "too long." It's okay to be jealous if your partner gives you cause, such as flirting with other people. But it's not okay if he or she doesn't. And it's not okay to be jealous of your own child. A husband is supposed to be charmed by his newborn infant and not feel jealous of his wife's intimacy with it.

The effect of all this is to make life a minefield. For example, Phil gets along fine until he transgresses the seventh commandment (thou shalt not be depressed). It's the middle of breakfast and, suddenly, he feels a little depressed. He would have been all right if he had something to point to that would justify feeling this way. But he doesn't. Everything is going well. It's Saturday, the sun is shining, and he and Ellen have been getting along fine. In fact, she is particularly cheerful this morning.

What makes it even worse is that this is the kind of Saturday that is supposed to make all his hard work worthwhile. He and Ellen are going on a picnic. He isn't looking forward to it, however. In fact, he finds himself wishing it were Monday and he was going to work. And now he is *really* worried. He has just trampled on commandment 26 (thou shalt not be a workaholic).

Phil doesn't know that it's Ellen's cheerfulness that's depressing him. He has no way to know this because he thinks cheerfulness is a good thing. He thinks *he* should be cheerful. And the fact that he isn't sets off another mine: commandment 20 (thou shalt not be grouchy).

Phil hasn't even finished his eggs, and he's already violated three commandments. Everyone's subjective life is such a minefield. And the mines are the feelings that people think they shouldn't be having.

Phil is so quick to blame himself that he's unable to see that Ellen's cheerful mood is forced and hollow, which is why he is turned off by it. Since it was Ellen's idea to go on a picnic (she isn't sure that Phil really wants to go), she feels responsible for making it fun.

And, as often happens with such a forced attempt to be cheerful, it rings false. Not just Phil but anyone sitting at the table might have been put off by it.

The effect of the new commandments is to prevent Phil from thinking and talking usefully about the situation. In fact, he stops thinking entirely. He believes that he should simply stop being the way he is, and that's all there is to it.

Even if Phil had told Ellen what he was feeling, the situation wouldn't necessarily get better. Ellen might simply have agreed with him that he *was* a grumpy and depressed workaholic. After all, she too believes in the new commandments.

The partners are thus unable to discover the important needed information that:

1. Phil's reactions make sense. It's understandable that he would be put off by Ellen's failed attempts at cheerfulness.
2. Ellen's reactions also make sense. She is faking enthusiasm because she is oppressed by a feeling of responsibility for the success of the picnic.

If Ellen and Phil are ever to have conversations in which they make such discoveries, they will need to develop a new way of thinking. After describing the principles underlying our old way of thinking (Chapter 9), I will describe this new way (Chapter 10).

Chapter 9
Hidden Accusations

The new commandments interrupt thinking by interposing accusatory judgments. Fran goes to the refrigerator and is about to finish the last of the ice cream when she suddenly remembers, "How selfish! I was saving this for Dave. I almost ate it."

Labeling herself as "selfish," and thus in violation of commandment 2, ends Fran's thinking about the matter. She thinks she shouldn't be selfish, and there's nothing more to think about. If she hadn't stumbled into a commandment, Fran might have realized that there *was* more to think about. If she were able to continue her thinking, she might have thought, "Since it's so unlike me to forget about David's needs, I must be craving something really badly. And, now that I think about it, I am. I've been feeling pretty empty lately because our relationship feels empty."

Suddenly, Fran's eating the ice cream makes sense. Her wish to eat the last of the ice cream isn't just a violation of a commandment. It's a clue. My purpose in this chapter is to show how the new commandments interrupt our thinking and prevent us from using our feelings as clues. There are four types of explanation that we commonly use to understand our behavior that are based on the new commandment and that prevent us from using our feelings as clues. I will describe these four in a parable.

Four Types of Explanation

Judy and Tom are a married couple in their mid-twenties. In her distress over an argument with Tom the evening before, Judy asks the advice of four people, each of whom uses one of the four types of explanation.

Character Flaws

Judy visits her upstairs neighbor Lucy and pours out her sad story:

JUDY: I'm so upset. You know me; I like to go out, and Tom likes to stay at home and watch TV. But last night, he actually suggested going out to dinner. There was dancing, and he didn't ask me to dance. And when I asked him, he said he didn't have the right shoes. So I told him he didn't need ballet slippers just to bump around the floor a few times. But still he said no, which really burned me. When we got home, I called him names I didn't even know I knew. And I'm still furious.

LUCY: He wouldn't dance with you? What a jerk! Doing something to please someone else probably never occurs to him. He reminds me of my first husband: totally self-centered.

How did Lucy arrive at this conclusion so quickly and with such little evidence? She used the character-flaws explanation. She scanned what Judy told her in search of character flaws. If Tom refuses to put himself out a little, that means he's self-centered.

The character-flaws explanation is closely connected to the new commandments. In fact, the new commandments are in essence a menu of possible character defects from which a person using the character-flaws explanation can choose. Here Lucy is invoking commandment 2 (thou shalt not be self-centered).

The character-flaws explanation can be applied at all times and to all people. Were Tom to tell Lucy the same story, she might have told him:

LUCY: You do what Judy says she wants (you take her to dinner) and immediately she finds something *else* to complain about. She's a control freak.

No matter what people do, their character can be impugned. Not getting married can be viewed as fear of commitment. Getting married can be seen as fear of being alone. Going to college can be viewed as irresponsibility and laziness—an unwillingness to get a real job. Not going to college and going to work can be seen as irresponsibility and laziness—a lack of ambition.

One effect of the character-flaw explanation is that it forecloses useful thinking. Lucy says in essence: The problem is Tom's self-centeredness and Judy's need to control. That's all there is to it. And there's only one thing to do about it: they should stop behaving that way.

Perhaps Judy's mistake is that she's seeking advice from a nonprofessional. Perhaps she should be talking, instead, to a therapist. Although that might be a good idea, the results might not be that different since some therapists share Lucy's style of thinking. They scan their clients' behavior for character defects in a manner that is parodied in the following joke:

> If patients are early to their therapy appointments, they're anxious. If they are late, they're hostile. And if they are on time, they're compulsive.

You Must Have Wanted It That Way

But let's continue the parable. Since her talk with Lucy doesn't make her feel much better, Judy tells the same story to her office mate Ken during a coffee break later that morning.

KEN: I'll tell you, Judy, something's fishy. Why would Tom take you to a place where there's dancing and then refuse to dance with you? He must have *wanted* to frustrate you.

Ken came to as quick a conclusion as Lucy did, but to a *different* one. That's because he has a different stock explanation. As he sees it, whatever happens is what people unconsciously *want* to happen. If Judy is upset by Tom's behavior, Tom must have *wanted* to upset her.

A person who uses the you-must-have wanted-it-that-way explanation sees people as obtaining secret gratification from their problems. "People think they don't want the bad things that happen to them," such a person says in effect, "but they really do. People always get what they want. There are no victims in this world, only perpetrators."

Judy must also have gotten what she wanted, Ken thinks. She may have set up the whole thing. Tom's refusal to dance may be just the excuse she needed to do what she wanted to do in the first place— throw a tantrum, give Tom a piece of her mind, and show him who's boss. (Ken doesn't tell Judy about this part of his idea, however. He has to work with her after all.)

Returning from her coffee break, Judy continues to mope around the office. Ken is disappointed that what he told Judy didn't cheer her up. He concludes: Judy must want to be miserable. Depression is the ultimate self-indulgence, he thinks, and she's having a wonderful time wallowing in self-pity.

Anything can be seen as serving a secret purpose. When a paralyzed woman fails to rise from her wheelchair after the laying on of hands, the faith healer may say that some people don't want to be cured. They need their sickness to get attention. When a wife doesn't immediately leave her physically abusive husband, her friend may think that she must want to be beaten-up. Maybe she likes knowing that she can get a rise out of him whenever she wants to. Or maybe she enjoys the fact that she can be the sane one while her husband loses it.

While Lucy accuses people of having character flaws, Ken accuses them of having secret ways of getting what they really want. But the secret motives that Ken sees people as having are typically character flaws and violations of the new commandments. He sees people as controlling others (commandment 13), for example, or as manipulatively getting others to take care of them (commandment 1), or as wallowing in self-pity (commandment 11).

The you-must-have-wanted-it-that-way explanation has a particularly chilling effect on thinking: it disqualifies the person as an observer of his or her own motivations. The person who adopts this way of thinking believes that people aren't going to want to admit their unconscious motives. That's why these motives are unconscious in the first place: because people don't want to admit them. Judy's never going to admit that she set up the argument so that she could show Tom who's boss. She's never going to admit that she prefers to wallow in self-pity rather than to be cheered up. You can't talk to people about their secret motives.

Here again we might recommend that Judy talk to a therapist rather than to a nonprofessional like Ken. But, again, that's not a surefire guarantee that the result will be different since some therapists agree with Ken's style of thinking. They employ some of the terms used by Ken: "wallowing in self-pity," "doing it for attention," "manipulation," "you're doing it to yourself," and "you don't want to be helped." But they go even further and talk about "self-destructive drives," "secondary gain," "masochistic gratification," and "vindictive enjoyment in defeating people who try to help you."

In *Heartburn*, an autobiographical novel about her husband's divorcing her, Nora Ephron describes how her friend, Vera, told her that she, Nora, set things up so that they would happen the way they did. Here is what Ephron wrote in objection to her friend's way of thinking:

> I love Vera, truly I do, but *doesn't anything happen to you that you don't intend?* "You picked him because you knew it wouldn't work out." "You picked him because his neuroses meshed perfectly with yours." "You picked him because you knew he'd deprive you the way your mother or your father did." That's what they're always telling you ... "You picked the one person on earth you could have problems with." "You picked the one person on earth you shouldn't be involved with." ... Robert Browning's shrink probably said it to him, "So, Robert, it's very interesting, no? Of all the women in London, you pick this hopeless invalid who has a crush on her father." Let's face it: everyone is the one person on earth you shouldn't get involved with.

Not only will therapists tell you that "you picked him because you knew it wouldn't work out," Ephron says, they will also tell you that "your problem is fear of intimacy; that you're connecting to your mother, or holding on to your father."

Therapists who say that you're connecting to your mother or holding on to your father—that is, that your problem is unresolved issues from the past—are using the back-to-childhood explanation.

Back to Childhood

Let's continue the parable. Judy feels even worse after talking with Ken than she did after talking with Lucy. So she calls her old school friend, Rose, and tells her the story. Rose uses the back-to-childhood explanation.

ROSE: Well, I'm not the least bit surprised. Tom's an only child. He doesn't know what it's like to extend himself for another person, which is something *you're* sensitive to, because of your father; he was always promising you things and not coming through.

According to the back-to-childhood explanation, people have unfinished business from childhood that they carry into the present. Just bringing it to their attention may be all that's necessary to free them from it. On the other hand, these patterns may be deeply engrained and difficult to change.

In explaining the present in terms of the past, Rose is trying to be sympathetic. And for a moment at least this helps. It protects Judy against self-criticism and enables her to forgive herself. It's not her fault, after all, that her father didn't come through for her. But she sees herself as hung up, as damaged goods. And she can't imagine how she and Tom are going to be able to change such long-term, deeply engrained character defects as "self-centeredness" and "sensitivity to neglect."

The problem with back-to-childhood explanations, ironically, is that they are so convincing. They drive out all other explanations. It's so clear that our problems *do* go back to childhood—and that childhood factors need to be taken into account—that it's easy to see such explanations as the complete answer. Once Judy and Tom trace their problem to Tom being a spoiled only child and Judy's having been neglected by her father, that may be all they see: a spoiled little boy and an insecure little girl. It may become difficult for them to consider the possibility that Tom might have an important and understandable reason for not wanting to dance and that Judy might have a similar understandable reason for getting upset because he didn't.

Unrealistic Expectations

The more Judy hears, the worse she feels. She worries that what her friends are saying might be correct: Maybe Tom is self-centered, as Lucy says, and can never give me what I really want. And if, as Ken says, Tom is trying to frustrate me, he's certainly doing a good job. And Rose may be right that he has been ruined by his parents. And maybe I've been ruined by mine. Maybe were just two screwed up people who deserve each other.

Judy runs into her friend Marlene on the bus home and spills out her story.

MARLENE: (*a bit smugly*) Your problem is that you think a marriage is dancing, romancing, and flowers. That's a honeymoon. A marriage is compromise, aggravation, and diapers. You can't expect one person to satisfy all your needs, even if he is your husband. Dancing? Be glad you've got someone who comes home at night.

Marlene uses the unrealistic-expectations (stick-to-reality) explanation for understanding what she sees. While Lucy looks to see what character defects are being revealed, and Ken looks to see what secret wishes are being fulfilled, and Rose looks to see what early relationships are being repeated, Marlene looks to see what unrealistic expectations are being expressed.

The unrealistic-expectations explanation is based on commandment 18 (thou shalt not have unrealizable expectations). According to this explanation, all problems stem from perfectionism.

Show me someone who is forever being disappointed, and I'll show you someone with unrealistic goals. Show me someone who is always depressed, and I'll show you someone who expects too much. Show me someone who carries a grudge, and I'll show you someone who is unwilling to compromise.

Although there is some truth to these statements, the implicit suggestion is that you should just stop having these unrealistic expectations, which itself is an unrealistic expectation. A person's expectations don't just come out of the stuff of fairy tales, but they often represent wishes and goals in which he or she has considerable stake.

According to the unrealistic-expectations way of thinking, 99 percent of divorces are caused by unrealistic beliefs and, in particular, the beliefs that people who love each other should:

- Be able to maintain the honeymoon feeling throughout marriage
- Be able to satisfy all of the other person's needs
- Want to spend all their time together
- Know what the other wants without having to be told
- Be able to avoid getting really angry at each other

These beliefs can be burdensome. If you believe that the honeymoon feeling should last throughout your marriage, you may worry that something is seriously wrong when you find that it doesn't. You may be relieved to hear, accordingly, that this is an "unrealistic expectation" that you'll need to give up—that is, until you realize that:

- Giving up these wishes and expectations may be hard to do.
- These wishes and feelings may be clues to important lifelong yearnings that it is important to bring out into the open. The psychologist John Gottman says that behind each instance of couple gridlock (entrenched positions) are hidden dreams.

As Judy gets off the bus, she feels discouraged. She doesn't see how she's going to get rid of her "unrealistic expectation" for greater intimacy and more romance.

Like the previous explanations, the unrealistic-expectations explanation can limit any further thinking. You're just supposed to toss these expectations out the window and be done with them.

Judy comes away from these four people feeling badly. They have told her that she is overly sensitive to rejection, is still hung up on her father, has unrealistic expectations, and is married to a self-centered man who enjoys frustrating her. She'd feel even *worse* were she to hear what Ken and Lucy were thinking but not saying, which is that she's a control freak, that she is having a wonderful time wallowing in self-pity, and that she set the whole thing up in the first place.

> **SKEPTIC:** Sure, Judy's upset by what these people said, and I feel sorry for her. But not *everyone* who is accused of such things would feel as bad as she does. In fact, she could just as easily feel inspired to stop being so sensitive, to give up her unrealistic expectations, or any of these other things.

> **WILE:** Yes, but her enthusiasm is likely to disappear when she finds out that it's not so easy to stop being sensitive and give up her unrealistic expectations. It's like parishioners reacting to a hellfire-and-damnation sermon. Some leave the sermon feeling sinful and hopeless, whereas others leave inspired never to sin again. But, of course, they're *going* to sin again; their inspiration is only temporary.

Who Are These People and Why Are They Saying These Things?

My point in this chapter is that we all have Lucys, Kens, Roses, and Marlenes within our minds. And their effect may be to prevent us from using our feelings as clues.

What is needed is a whole new way of thinking that allows us to use our feelings as clues.

That is what I will talk about in the next chapter.

But let's return to the parable. Judy started the day feeling down-in-the-mouth. She ended the day feeling down-on-the-floor. Everyone she talked to made her feel worse. Walking home from the bus stop, she imagined what the evening would be like. Tom, in his usual way of not dealing with situations, would act as if nothing had happened. He would give her a peck and ask how her work went. After a dinner where the only talk would be a few words about dinner, he would probably spend all night watching television. She, in her usual way, would answer his question about work only briefly, assuming that he wasn't really interested. She'd ask how his work went and expect to hear "Oh, pretty good" and nothing more. And she'd probably spend all night reading in bed and feeling lonely.

But Tom was waiting at the door. "I've been doing a lot of thinking about what happened last night," he said. "And I could hardly wait for you to come home to talk about it." Judy couldn't believe what she was hearing. Tom had just said more in the first ten seconds than he usually said throughout a whole evening. And he was confronting a problem. And he seemed lively and engaged.

"What's gotten into him?" Judy thought. "Who is this strange man?"

Chapter 10
Eliminating Accusations

What has gotten into Tom is that he has spent an hour with people who helped him use his feelings as clues.

The four types of explanation described in the previous chapter are built into everyone's thinking—and, for the most part, rightly so. But they can get in the way of productive thinking. To keep this from happening, I recommend supplementing them with the following explanations.

Seven Additional Explanations

While Judy was upstairs talking to Lucy, Tom was on his way to work. It was his day to drive the carpool. There were seven people in his van, each of whom had his or her own way of thinking.

Hidden Appropriateness

Tom tells them the story of what happened the night before and adds:

TOM: Everything would have been all right if only I had danced with Judy. Why didn't I just do it?

Tom is worried that his refusal to dance was inappropriate to the situation. Cloe is the first of Tom's passengers to speak up. She uses the hidden-appropriateness explanation. She believes that things that appear inappropriate often turn out to make a lot of sense once you get to the bottom of them.

CLOE: Well, let's look at it. Suppose you had danced. How would it have gone?

TOM: Not well. I'm a klutz, and Judy doesn't like my stepping on her toes.

CLOE: (*thinking that she has found an understandable explanation already*) Oh, could that be why you didn't dance—to avoid displeasing Judy by stepping on her toes?

TOM: (*thinking he's being let off too easily*) Maybe. But I still should have made the effort. Judy's right. I'm selfish.

Understandable Feelings

Joe, a second passenger, uses the understandable-feelings explanation. He believes that underlying our seemingly childish or irrational behavior are unexpressed feelings that, if brought out into the open, would elicit compassion for oneself and empathy in others. When he hears Tom say he's selfish, Joe immediately thinks that there's got to be a feeling in there somewhere that if brought out would give Tom and us a new, more favorable view of him.

JOE: What made you decide to take her out to that restaurant?

TOM: I know she likes elegant restaurants, although any place that has a headwaiter makes me uncomfortable.

JOE: (*thinking that he has found a hidden feeling already*) Okay, so what ended up as your "selfish" refusal to dance started out as an unselfish wish to do something for her.

TOM: I got in over my head. Going to that restaurant was already extending myself. Dancing was *way* beyond what I had in mind.

Point Not Gotten Across

Camille, a third passenger, uses the point-not-gotten-across explanation. She believes that people get upset when there is something important that they're unable to say.

CAMILLE: Is that what you wish you had said to Judy—that you're upset that your effort to extend yourself resulted in her feeling that you *won't* extend yourself?

The hidden-appropriateness, unrecognized-feelings, and point-not-gotten-across explanations can be applied at all times and to all people. Let's imagine what would have happened if Judy rather than Tom were in the car.

JUDY: I acted like a child. I really blew it.

CLOE: (*looking for a hidden appropriateness in Judy's behavior*) Well, let's figure it out. What's been going on between you and Tom lately?

JUDY: Same as usual. Everyone thinks he's great, and in some ways he is, but he doesn't come through. Sure, he helps with the housework, but I'm the one who always ends up with the really dirty jobs like cleaning the toilets. I thought we'd be raising the kids together, but *I'm* always in charge of telling him what needs to be done, and when.

If Lucy were there, she'd say, "Judy, you're too demanding." Ken would chide her, "Girl, you're only happy if you've got something to complain about." Rose would be certain that she was just angry at her father. Marlene would say, "Judy, you're expecting too much." But Cloe is there, and she says:

CLOE: (*finding a hidden appropriateness in Judy's behavior*) No wonder you're upset. What happened last night perfectly represents what most upsets you about Tom, which is that he goes through the motions but then doesn't follow through. He took you where there was dancing and then didn't dance.

JUDY: But it was childish of me to get so upset.

JOE: (*finding an understandable feeling*) But anyone—adult or child—would get upset when confronted with such a clear example of what most bothers them about their partner.

CAMILLE: (*pinning down what Judy might have needed to say*) Maybe that's what you needed to tell him: "This is our whole marriage. I feel totally alone."

It's obvious that Judy would have had a better day if she had talked to the people in Tom's van rather than her own bunch.

Universal Issues

But to return to Tom on his way to work, Stan, who uses the universal-issues explanation, now speaks up. As Stan sees it, partners with problems simply experience more intense forms of difficulties every couple has.

STAN: It sounds as if you ran into the common problem in which one partner (Judy) holds back a complaint to avoid a fight, but that just leads to a buildup of anger and a worse fight later on.

Stan is the opposite of Lucy, who, as you might remember, uses the character-flaws explanation. Whereas Lucy combs through normal behavior looking for an underlying abnormality, Stan combs through abnormal behavior looking for an underlying universality. He believes it is easier to deal with a problem if you don't think there's something wrong with you for having it.

A Clue to an Underlying Reality

Carl, a fifth passenger, uses the hidden-clue explanation. He agrees with Cloe, who uses the hidden-appropriateness explanation, that a person's seemingly inappropriate behavior has an underlying appropriateness. But he goes further. He believes that this seemingly inappropriate behavior may be useful. It may reveal an important hidden issue in the relationship.

CARL: Look at it this way. The fight gave you a chance to bring up something you hadn't been able to discuss before.

TOM: Like what?

CARL: Like your worry about letting Judy down. It might be a relief finally to talk about that.

TOM: Yes, but the fat would be in the fire, *my* fat. She might say some things I don't want to hear.

CARL: True, that could happen, but ...

TOM: Right, *but*. It could be a relief to get some of that stuff into the open.

Tom feels like turning the van around and going directly home so he can talk to Judy. Unfortunately, there are these people who expect him to drive them to work. Anyway, Tom almost immediately has second thoughts. He starts doubting that he could have a conversation with Judy that would actually work out.

The Canary in the Coal Mine

It's crowded in the van. But Tom doesn't mind. He's just glad they're all there. Everyone who speaks makes him feel better.

- Cloe showed that underlying Tom's seemingly inappropriate behavior was a hidden appropriateness.
- Joe showed that underlying Tom's "bad" reactions were understandable feelings.
- Camille showed that Judy's "bad" reactions were a result of her inability to express what she really needed to say.
- Stan showed that he and Judy were experiencing a common couple problem.
- Carl showed that their fight brought into the open an important hidden issue.

Amy, the sixth passenger, uses the miners'-canary explanation. She believes that the difficulties people experience in childhood make them sensitive observers of certain subtle undercurrents in the present—much as canaries are sensitive to oxygen loss, which is why miners brought them down into the mines with them, as an early warning system.

Amy's explanation is an alternative to Rose's back-to-childhood explanation. Amy would agree with Rose that a person's past may produce a special sensitivity. He or she may react in intense ways to things other people hardly notice. Amy insists, however, that there's some truth in the person's response. He or she is reacting in an intense way to things that are actually happening.

In fact, the sensitivity produced by a person's childhood may make him or her a good observer of certain areas of reality. For example, the rejection that a wife suffered as a child may make her a sensitive observer of the subtle ways she and her husband slight one another now. This wife and husband may wish that she didn't have her childhood-based special sensitivity to rejection. It's a nuisance how she gets upset at even minor slights by her husband. Her sensitivity has one important benefit, however. She and her husband will never wake up one day, as some people do, and find themselves in a detached, withdrawn relationship without knowing how they got there. She's their protection against that. She's an expert at detecting the subtle and often unnoticed slights and rejections that regularly occur between people.

TOM: It all goes back to Judy's father. He constantly let her down. I'm tired of having to pay for what happened with her father

AMY: Yes, because of her father, she may have become an expert in observing the subtle ways in which people let her down

TOM: That's why I try to be there for her. I don't want to be like her father. So I took her to that restaurant, even though it made me itchy.

AMY: Yes, you weren't sharing her enthusiasm, so in that way, she may have felt you weren't really there.

Solutions Become Problems

Jacob, the seventh and last passenger, uses the solutions-turn-into-problems explanation. He believes that much of the problem is how people handle problems.

JACOB: There you are doing something special for Judy. You take
her out—something she really wants. And because you're out
of your element, your heart isn't totally in it, and the whole
thing turns sour. It doesn't seem fair.

Jacob's explanation is in some ways the opposite of Ken's you-must-have-wanted-it-that-way explanation. While Ken sees people as devilishly successful in getting what they want, Jacob views them as tragically unsuccessful in that way. Their efforts to solve their problems make them even worse. (This idea that solutions become problems was developed by Paul Watzlawick, John Weakland, and Richard Fisch in their book, *Change.*)

TOM: Yes, it doesn't seem fair. But what am I supposed to do?

ALL THE PASSENGERS: Talk to Judy in the ways that we've been talking
to you here.

The Conversation

Tom, of course, has never talked to Judy in the ways his carpool-mates suggested. That's because his thinking is dominated by the same four classical explanations that Judy's is.

- Lucy, who attributes problems to character defects, says
  it's just a matter of admitting your defects and correcting
  them.
- Ken, who attributes problems to hidden motives, says
  that people don't want to admit the real truth, even to
  themselves. They're not going to admit, for example, that
  they really want to keep their problems.
- Rose, who attributes problems to childhood, says that it

is just a matter of realizing that your partner is not your
parents.

- Marlene, who attributes problems to unrealistic
  expectations, says that it's just a matter of facing reality.

These four explanations fail to recognize the hidden way in which
the behavior in question makes sense—and in terms of the present
and not just the past. The seven explanations make up for this lack
by pointing to:

1. A hidden appropriateness in the person's seemingly inappro-
    priate behavior
2. An ordinary feeling that is being expressed in indirect and
    offensive forms because the person feels uncomfortable with
    it
3. An understandable point that the person is having difficulty
    getting across
4. A common couple issue that the person is experiencing in a
    particularly intense form
5. A hidden reality for which his or her behavior is a clue
6. A present reality to which the person has a childhood-based
    special sensitivity
7. An ordinary and understandable problem that has gotten worse
    because of the person's efforts to solve it

Let's imagine the kind of conversation that Tom might have with
Judy were he to use the explanations that his carpool mates taught
him rather than the classic explanations that he and Judy ordinarily
use.

Tom tries to call Judy at work and tell her what he has just
learned, but she's at lunch with Ken and getting a very different
kind of advice.

As Judy straggles in after her distressing day, Tom says:

TOM: I've been doing a lot of thinking about what happened last
night, and I could hardly wait for you to come home to talk
about it.

JUDY: (*interested*) I'm listening.

TOM: I'm upset with how I behaved last night. I wanted you to have a romantic evening, and I wouldn't even dance with you.

Tom is applying what he learned from his carpool mates. He is recognizing a *hidden appropriateness* in Judy's anger (Cloe's principle explanation). He is discovering the *understandable feeling* (disappointment) that was underlying Judy's rage (Joe's explanation). And he is showing Judy that her message has *gotten across* to him (Camille's explanation).

Judy likes the sound of this, but she hasn't fully expressed her resentment.

JUDY: Well, why didn't you?

The goodwill with which Tom's carpool buddies infused him enables him to deal with Judy's snippy remark without becoming defensive.

TOM: (*smiling*) I wish I had, but your toes might be a little sore today.

Judy is now able to recognize the "hidden appropriateness" in Tom's behavior.

JUDY: Oh, is *that* why you didn't dance—because of what I said that time about your, er, lack of rhythm?

TOM: I took it to heart.

JUDY: As I did your not dancing with me last night. But how can I expect you to dance with me if I'm going to criticize the way you do it?

Judy and Tom are in a positive cycle in which each automatically admits things in response to the other doing the same, just as earlier they were in a negative cycle in which each automatically blamed the other in response to the other doing the same. In this positive cycle, each is able to listen to what the other has to say. In fact, as often happens in a positive cycle, each begins to make the other's points.

TOM: I shouldn't be so sensitive.

JUDY: I shouldn't be so critical.

TOM: Well, I do let you down.

JUDY: Only because I have magical expectations no one could meet.

TOM: I'm not sure why it should have to take such magic for me to learn not to step on your feet.

Judy and Tom are discovering a "hidden reality" in the relationship: his sense of failure in meeting her expectations and her concern that these expectations may be unrealistic. They are tapping the fight for the information it reveals about the relationship.

Conversations like this one are not just a means for solving Judy and Tom's problem. They are a solution in themselves. Having a husband who talks with her this way (who listens, admits things, and appreciates how she feels) is more important to Judy than being taken dancing. Tom is coming through for her. He is providing what she is most wanting—emotional engagement—of which dancing is only a surface expression.

People are at an advantage in dealing with their problems to the extent that they think the way that the passengers in Tom's car do.

In working out a relationship with your partner, much depends on which theories you have, which theories your friends have, and, perhaps, who's in your carpool.

Part IV

SOLUTIONS THAT CREATE WORSE PROBLEMS

Chapter 11
Makeshift Solutions

The best way to solve the problems that come up in a relationship is to talk about them in the manner that I just described for Judy and Tom. If you can't do that (and it is *hard* to do) you may be left without an effective way to deal with these problems. In such a case, you do the best you can. You engage in makeshift solutions that often make matters worse.

That's what I want to talk about in this section: makeshift solutions. There are three types—action-solutions, slogan-solutions, and fantasy-solutions—all of which are demonstrated in the following example.

Katie and Burt have been married twenty-five years and have three grown children. Katie is unable to think or talk about certain problems in their relationship. Here is what she needs to be able to say to Burt:

KATIE: Haven't you noticed how things have gotten a little stale, lately? I miss the fun we used to have.

Since Katie can't bring up this concern (she's not used to talking this way and she worries it would upset Burt too much), she deals with it in another way. She engages in a fantasy. She thinks longingly back on the days when the relationship *was* fulfilling. She and Burt used to party, dance, and stay up all night talking and making love.

This fantasy does, at first, solve the problem. For a moment, Katie is back in the old days, passionate and full of life. But her memory of how she and Burt's marriage used to be makes her all the more aware of how different it is now. She worries that her lack of romantic feeling means they have a bad marriage. In an attempt to talk herself out of this worry, Katie tells herself that it's unrealistic to expect the honeymoon feeling to last.

Katie is engaging in a slogan-solution. She is using a familiar saying to try to convince herself that there's nothing to worry about. Then she engages in an action-solution. She tries to get Burt to do something that might snap them back into their early romantic feeling.

KATIE: Let's go rowing on the lake. What do you say?

Katie is having a positive fantasy. She thinks rowing under a full moon will revive their romance. But Burt is having a negative fantasy. He thinks rowing will show how unromantic they really have become.

He says, "Let's talk about it later," hoping she'll forget about it.

Katie doesn't bring it up again, but she doesn't forget about it, either.

Here, in miniature, is the heart of their problem. Burt's indirectness (he says "let's talk about it later") and Katie's withdrawal (she doesn't press the matter) are typical of the way in which they (and almost everyone else) interact. Being indirect and withdrawn solves one problem—Katie and Burt no longer have the distressing fights they used to have—but it creates another: a lack of spark in their marriage.

Remembering the spirited and playful conversations that she and Burt had at the beginning of the relationship, Katie tries to think of questions that might get them energized. And she thinks she's found one. She asks Burt:

KATIE: If you could be any animal on the planet, which one would
       you choose?

Burt can't figure out what's gotten into Katie. He compliantly answers her question. He says "I'd be a goat because I could eat and at the same time mow the lawn, which I'd better go out and do now." And he goes outside.

Katie, still dwelling on the rut they're in, remembers reading a magazine article that recommended spicing up your marriage by doing dramatic, sexy, unpredictable things. The next day, when Burt comes home from work, she greets him at the door with nothing on but a smile.

Now Burt feels really on the spot. He read the article too, and he knows he's supposed to find her nakedness enticing and want to have sex with her right there in the hallway. But the hallway floor doesn't look appealing and neither does Katie, standing there self-conscious and shivering. (The magazine didn't talk about hard and dusty floors or about awkwardness and goose bumps.) Fortunately for Burt, a neighbor rings the bell, and Katie runs to the bedroom to put on her clothes.

Slipping into her skirt and feeling foolish, Katie has an even more upsetting thought: "I did everything the article said, and Burt wasn't turned on at all. Maybe he just doesn't find me attractive anymore."

But quickly she reassures herself: "Who am I kidding? Why should seeing me naked get him all excited? He's seen me naked every day for twenty-five years."

Then she wonders: "Why am I getting so upset in the first place? I should be happy with what I've got. We've got a better marriage than anyone I know."

This attempt to talk herself out of her worry reassures her for a moment. But it's soon replaced by the opposite thought: "But I don't want to make my parents' mistake and remain forty years in a dead relationship."

Katie is back where she started—worried about the situation and thinking that something needs to be done but not knowing what to do. "Maybe I'm thinking about this all wrong, Katie decides. Instead of trying to get Burt to pay more attention to me, maybe I should try to be more caring toward him. If he felt that I really cared about him, maybe he'd reciprocate."

So Katie begins doing special things for Burt. She buys his favorite foods. When he's working on the bills, she brings him coffee. She gardens with him. She goes through *TV Guide* and notes the times of the football games so that she can tell him about them and watch them with him.

And then, when she notices how little he is responding, she reacts against the whole enterprise. She is sick of forcing herself to watch football and she has always hated gardening. She grasps at another slogan-solution:

KATIE: I can't expect my marriage to satisfy all my needs. I have to look elsewhere.

This slogan-solution sets the scene for a series of action-solutions. Katie thinks of ways to broaden her life. She signs up for a class in Japanese printmaking. She calls a few old friends and makes dates for lunch with them. And she begins to talk more with her neighbors.

And out of that a new fantasy-solution emerges. One of the neighbors is a divorced man who has had a crush on Katie for a long time. Unlike Burt, he doesn't take her for granted. In fact, he is super-attentive.

Katie finds herself having romantic daydreams about him.

And now Katie has a new problem. She can't stop thinking about this man and she feels terribly guilty about it. She engages in a slogan-solution to try to talk herself out of her feelings.

KATIE: Men always look better before you start living with them. I've got to be careful not to throw away all I have with Burt just for a fling.

It's hard for her to remember, however, just what she does have with Burt and even harder to believe that things wouldn't be better with her neighbor. So she shifts from a talk-yourself-*out*-of-a-wish type of slogan-solution into a talk-yourself-*into*-a-wish slogan.

KATIE: Well, kid, you only live once.

She puts on the sexiest dress in her closet and pays her neighbor a surprise visit on a day when no one else is around. However, he turns out not to be around either. Disappointed, but also a little relieved, she changes her clothes and goes to a movie.

And when she returns, she finds Burt cleaning the garage, something that Katie had wanted him to do for six months. And he has brought her some flowers. Katie's earlier plan was working after all. Burt finally was responding to all the gardening, football-watching, coffee-bringing, and special meals.

And all these things that Burt was doing made a difference. They gave Katie more of a feeling that they were in it together. She felt a little more hopeful about their marriage, at least for a while. She stopped thinking so much about her neighbor.

Katie had engaged in the following fantasy-solutions:

1. Recalling the excitement of the early part of her relationship with Burt
2. Engaging in romantic daydreams about her neighbor

She had also engaged in the following slogan-solutions, telling herself:

1. It's unrealistic to expect the honeymoon feeling to last forever
2. I can't expect that seeing me naked will turn him on when he's seen me naked every day for twenty-five years
3. I should be happy that the relationship is as good as it is
4. I mustn't make my parents' mistake of remaining in an unhappy marriage
5. Instead of expecting things from Burt, I should do things for him
6. I can't expect my marriage to satisfy all my needs
7. I've got to remember that men don't look as good when you begin to live with them
8. You only live once

And she had engaged in the following action-solutions:

1. Asking Burt to go rowing on the lake
2. Asking what animal he would like to be
3. Meeting Burt at the door without any clothes on
4. Doing special things for him
5. Taking classes, calling friends, meeting her neighbors
6. Trying to have an affair

One of the action-solutions did work, at least partly. Doing thoughtful things for Burt did eventually lead to his doing thoughtful things for her. And she began to feel a little better about the relationship. However, her way of getting Burt to act more caring was not one that she could use very often. There was just so much football and gardening that she could stand.

So that's what Katie, Burt, and the rest of us do when the accusing explanations block our thinking and talking. We engage in action-solutions, slogan-solutions, and fantasy-solutions. I'll discuss action-solutions in this chapter, slogan-solutions in the following chapter, and fantasy-solutions in Part VII.

Trying to Avoid Falling Out of Love

Let's use two related situations—feeling less sexually attracted to your partner and fearing that you are falling out of love—to suggest the range of action-solutions that people use.

Claude suddenly feels sexually turned off by his, wife Beth. If he were able to think and to talk about this feeling, he might realize that it is appropriate to the situation. It is a reaction to an argument he had with her the day before. However, he can't think or talk about feeling sexually turned off by Beth, because he just thinks he shouldn't feel this way. He's convinced something is wrong with him.

So what does Claude do? He engages in an action-solution. He deals with his inability to think or talk about feeling sexually turned off by engaging in an action that he hopes might solve the problem. He asks Beth to put on her short black dress with the low neckline.

Beth is upset by the fact that *she* suddenly feels turned off by Claude. If she were able to think and talk about these feelings, she might be able to trace them to the argument they had the day before and to Claude's strange behavior tonight. He keeps insisting that she wear this stupid dress and that they go out to this fancy restaurant. Were Beth able to think and to talk about these feelings, she'd see that they were, in a way, appropriate to the situation. But Beth is unable to do so. She, too, believes that she just shouldn't be having them.

So what does Beth do? She engages in an action-solution. She asks Claude if he loves her. She hopes that hearing him say it will bring back her positive feelings for him and counteract her doubt as to whether he loves her and whether she loves him.

Dean Delis, a psychologist in San Diego, lists a number of common action-solutions that people use when they find themselves falling out of love. In an effort to make their partners more appealing, they try to:

- Get their partners to act and to dress in ways that might attract, intrigue, or turn them on
- Get their partners to eliminate mannerisms and habits that turn them off
- Turn their partners into more interesting and intelligent people, urging their partners to take night courses and to read more books and newspapers

These people are worried about the fact that they are losing interest in their partners. They don't want to be losing interest. They feel guilty about it. They dread the prospect of having to deal again with the singles scene. They wonder if they have unrealizable expectations and think that they should be happy with the relationships they've got. They wonder whether they're incapable of long-term relationships. And they have no effective way of talking or thinking about any of these feelings. So they engage in these action-solutions.

And their partners are even more upset. Noticing that their lovers are falling out of love with them but feeling too threatened to talk or think about it, they engage in action-solutions in an effort to rekindle their partners' love:

- They engage in what Delis calls "hypercourtship behavior." They try to impress their partners with their intelligence, wit, attractiveness, sexiness, charm, and achievements. Or they do the opposite. They try to be good listeners and engage their partners by letting these partners impress them.

- They make themselves more available. They go along with everything their partners want and try to show how warm and loving they are. Or they do the opposite. They make themselves less available and try to show how independent they are. They try to intrigue their partners by playing hard to get and by making their partners jealous.
- They seek reassurance. They ask, "Do you love me?" Or they do the opposite. They play it cool. They try not to make complaints or demands or to ask for reassurance. And they try not to act hurt or jealous.

SKEPTIC: This list makes me nervous. I've done most of these things myself.

WILE: I'm not surprised. Just about everyone does. And they can be at least *partly* successful, although often they are extremely *un*successful:

- Attempts to be impressive often come across as boorishness and self-centeredness.
- Attempts to please your partner by going along with everything he or she wants can make you boring to be with.
- Attempts to play hard to get often fool nobody and just prove how totally available and easy to get you are.
- Reading a few books rarely turns anybody into a fascinating conversationalist.

An Action-Solution That Worked

Everyone uses action-solutions. The words of advice that people give each other and that they give themselves are essentially action-solutions. Women who wish to spice up their marriages or who are worried about losing their husbands are instructed by self-help books to be more mysterious and unpredictable. The wife isn't advised to talk with her husband about her worries. Instead, she is told to *do* something.

I use action-solutions myself often, and I've gotten some mileage out of them. Relationship problems are difficult to deal with, and any means that gets you an edge is fair game. The problem is that action-solutions often don't work and may even be counterproductive.

But here is an extended example of one that *did* work.

Gloria tries to talk herself out of her complaint that her husband George doesn't help with the housework. She's worried about being a nag (commandment 15) and about being pushy (commandment 13). And despite all that is said these days about husbands doing 50 percent of the housework, she thinks the idea that a man might actually make a major contribution in that area is an unrealistic expectation (commandment 18).

Accordingly, instead of making a general complaint about George's not helping with the housework, Gloria talks herself out of the complaint. In its place, she makes a simple request. She asks him to take out the trash. Taking out the trash is a classic male chore and therefore something that she thinks George won't object too much to doing, although it is only a very small part of the help that she really wants.

Gloria's request is an action-solution. It's a way of not making a complaint while, at the same time, producing a change that might resolve the complaint. She hopes that his taking out the trash will decrease her resentment about having to do most of the work.

And Gloria's action-solution works, at least partly. George responds positively to her request: he takes out the trash immediately. And he does it cheerfully. And on the way to doing it, he gives her a sexy hug. And he does a particularly good job of taking out the trash. He even puts new plastic liners in the wastepaper baskets. And he adds a little something extra: he rinses out the trash can. And then, instead of continuing to watch TV, he balances their checkbook.

Gloria had wanted some sign that she wasn't the only one doing things. And that's what she got. It was a solid sign, since George did such a good job of it. And the cheerful way he did it reassured her that he didn't feel nagged. The spontaneous hug he gave her made her feel that they were in it together. And his turning off the TV and balancing the checkbook reminded her that George had his own ways of contributing to the household. And this was a real contribution, since she hates balancing the checkbook.

So, without their even having to talk about it, the problem was solved. Or was it? To Gloria's surprise, she continued to have nagging feelings about it. While she no longer felt all alone in the housework, she wasn't sure that, in a few days, the feeling wouldn't return. George had taken out the trash, but he hadn't thought to do it himself; it was still she who had to do all the initiating. After all was said and done, she was still in charge of all the operations.

But she was feeling good at the moment and dismissed these doubts as quibbles.

Tokens

In trying to get George to take out the garbage, Gloria is asking for a token of what she really wants, which is his full participation in the housework. She hopes that this token will snap her into a less lonely and less resentful frame of mind.

Getting our partners to engage in token acts is a common type of action-solution. Life is in some sense a search for tokens that will snap us into better frames of mind. Everyone has wishes and feelings that can't be talked about or even fully thought about. And everyone makes do with token fulfillment

Jennifer doesn't have a good way to talk to her husband, Alan, about feeling taken for granted. They have never learned how to think about and discuss such things. She simply feels that she shouldn't have such complaints. So instead of thinking or talking, she just suddenly finds herself wishing that Alan would bring her flowers. As people often do, she expresses this wish as an accusation: "Why don't you ever bring me flowers anymore?"

Jennifer hopes that if Alan were to engage in this token act, that is, if he were to bring her flowers, this might revive some part of the early excitement of the relationship and make her feel less taken for granted.

And it does. Two days later, Alan dutifully brings home a dozen roses. And Jennifer melts. She feels loved. She thinks it's the most beautiful bouquet that anyone has ever received. And she feels this way even though the flowers are from the supermarket and Alan isn't doing it out of love but simply to try to prevent her from complaining about him in the future.

> **SKEPTIC:** Well yeah, women are forever complaining that their husbands aren't demonstrative enough; at least, my wife is. They place all this importance on tokens of affection.

> **WILE:** But men do, too; it's just not as obvious. Alan thinks it's silly for Jennifer to place such importance on flowers, although he is willing to provide them to keep the peace. But he doesn't think it's silly for him to place a great deal of importance on Jennifer having his dinner ready when he gets home. Alan thinks that he wants his dinner simply because he's hungry. He doesn't realize that the more important reason is that it makes him feel loved. It gives him the feeling that Jennifer really cares about him and wants to do things for him.

Having his dinner made is as much a token to Alan as getting flowers is to Jennifer. If Jennifer is sentimental about flowers, then Alan is sentimental about dinner. And Alan is as easily pleased as Jennifer is. Jennifer isn't much of a cook. But just as she feels that Alan's flowers are the most beautiful in the world, Alan thinks that Jennifer's dinners could be served in the best restaurants in town.

And having his dinner ready isn't the only token that Alan seeks. He's touched when Jennifer agrees to watch Monday Night football with him. He feels really loved. He thinks that they have a terrific relationship.

Sex is another important token for Alan. He believes that he is always wanting sex with Jennifer because he is just a very sexual person. He doesn't think it has anything to do with how he feels about her. And that's what Jennifer thinks too. And that's what turns her off. Alan *is* always eager for sex. But what he is really eager for is reassurance that Jennifer cares for him and will accept him. Sex is as much a token for Alan as flowers are for Jennifer.

Snapping into a Better Frame of Mind

We all have a set of potential tokens that can snap us into a better frame of mind.

- Some people melt when they are given flowers. Others feel nothing at all. Or they feel unloved because they wonder what the giver might be trying to atone for. Or they notice that one of the flowers looks wilted and wonder whether these are week-old flowers sold at a reduced price.
- Some people melt when they are given a compliment. It makes their day. Others, given the same compliment by the same person, feel nothing at all. Or they wonder what the person wants from them.
- Some people melt when somebody wants to have sex with them. They feel desirable and that raises their spirits. Others feel degraded because is makes them feel like sex objects.
- Some women melt when their husbands take out the trash. They suddenly feel close to them. For other women it may be just a reminder of all the things their husbands *aren't* doing.

If people are to use their partners' token acts to snap themselves into better frames of mind, they must get their partners to engage in these acts. Some people require very little on the part of the other. They need only a token of a token. For such people it might be enough that their partners:

- Bring them an aging dandelion from the lawn
- Notices their new haircut, and it's not even necessary that the partner say that he or she likes it
- Is willing to sit in the same room reading during just the

first quarter of the football game
- Halfheartedly empties one wastepaper basket after three reminders

Other people require more wholehearted efforts from their partners to snap themselves into better frames of mind. Two weeks after George took out the trash and then came back and balanced the checkbook, Gloria again became resentful about being the only one doing housework. This time when she asked George to take out the trash, he was engrossed in what he was reading and put it off.

"I went a little crazy," Gloria told her friend the next day. I told him, 'Get off your ass and take it out right *now*.' He told me that *he'd* decide when to take it out, and to stop trying to control him. He's right. I'm a control freak."

What Gloria and George fail to see is that:

- Underlying Gloria's seemingly childish outburst is an understandable adult feeling—resentment about having to do all the housework. She wishes that *she* had the luxury of being able to read and watch TV more often. Maybe she could if George would share the chores.
- Gloria is uncompromising in her demand that George take the trash out right away because she has already compromised so much. She is asking for only a fraction of what she really wants. The fact that he hesitates to do even this is understandably upsetting to her.
- Gloria needs complete control of George's trash-emptying behavior because she feels she has such little control of so much else in the relationship.

A large part of what passes between partners consists of action-solutions. People try to get one another to engage in token acts that will enable them to snap into better frames of mind. Taking out the garbage can be such a token. So can giving flowers. Tokens are the currency of relationships.

Anthropologists say that a lot can be told about a people by the nature of their garbage. I suggest that a lot can be told by the way they take out the garbage.

Chapter 12
Self-propaganda

Slogan-solutions, like the other two types of makeshift solutions, are efforts to solve problems despite the fact that we can't think or talk about them. But unlike action-solutions and fantasy-solutions, slogan-solutions give the *impression* of thinking. They are *self-propaganda*, however, rather than thinking. They are efforts to deal with thoughts and feelings that we think we shouldn't be having:

1. By talking ourselves into them (that is, by trying to convince ourselves that it's okay to have them)
2. Or by talking ourselves out of them (that is, by trying to convince ourselves more fully that we shouldn't be having them)

In the following example, a woman uses an action-solution and, when that doesn't work, a slogan-solution: she tries to talk herself out of her worry.

This woman feels bad about her loss of sexual interest in her husband. She is so worried that it means that she has a bad marriage that she's unable to talk or even think clearly about it. She engages in an action-solution. She tries to get her husband to behave in ways that might make him more attractive to her. She asks him to dress more stylishly.

He buys some new clothes, but when this doesn't help, she engages in a slogan-solution. She tells herself that "passion mellows over time" and that she shouldn't take her reduced romantic feeling so seriously.

This woman is using an *idea* to try to solve a problem. But she isn't really thinking—that is, she isn't conducting an unbiased inquiry into her loss of romantic feeling. Instead, she's trying to convince herself of something. She's trying to prove that her loss of sexual interest is nothing to worry about. She's engaging in self-propaganda.

In the following example, a woman attempts an action-solution and then uses both types of slogan-solution: talking herself out of her complaint and talking herself into it. Like Gloria, she is upset that her husband doesn't help more around the house.

1. She engages in an action-solution. She convinces him to make the token contribution of clearing the table each night after dinner. She hopes that if he agrees it will reduce her feeling that it's all up to her. He does clear the table, but whenever she watches him do it, she's reminded of how she does everything else, and her resentment just intensifies.

2. So she engages in a slogan-solution. In her effort to talk herself *out* of her complaint, she appeals to the idea that housework has traditionally been woman's work. But these aren't traditional times so that doesn't work either. She *remains* resentful.

3. So she shifts to a slogan-solution of the *opposite* type. In an effort to talk herself *into* her complaint, that is, to justify her right to have it, she appeals to the contemporary idea that husbands should share the housework. She tells him: "Marriage is a fifty-fifty proposition. I've just vacuumed my 50 percent of the carpet. Here's the vacuum cleaner. Now you can do yours."

Much of our mental life is devoted to trying to talk ourselves into or out of our feelings.

Thinking as an Exercise in Self-propaganda

Where do the slogans come from that people use in slogan-solutions? They come from the general culture, that is, from folk wisdom, kitchen philosophy, street talk, pop psychology, locker room wisdom, and so on. The following shows how ideas can be pulled in from these various sources.

Walt is uncomfortable with his attraction toward, Angie, his best friend's wife. He sees it as an act of disloyalty to his wife, Nora, and to his friend. In an effort to talk himself *out* of his attraction, he tells himself "the grass is always greener on the other side of the fence." This old saying helps him feel that his attraction toward Angie is only an illusion.

But a few minutes later, Walt finds himself again preoccupied with thoughts about Angie, which he deals with this time by trying to talk himself *into* his feelings. He seizes upon a common cultural belief and tells himself "Men are basically polygamous. Feeling attracted to Angie doesn't mean that I'm a bad person. It just means I'm a man."

The reassuring effect of this self-propaganda is short-lived, since the fact that all men want to cheat on their wives just makes him feel that all men are bad, including him. So he makes another attempt to talk himself *out* of these feelings. Turning to an idea from pop psychology, he tells himself, "I want a meaningful, committed relationship and not just an affair." But this thought doesn't get him very far either, because he's not sure that his relationship with his wife *is* that meaningful. And he figures that if he is going to have a committed relationship, he could just as well have one with Angie.

He appeals next to locker-room wisdom, and he starts putting the blame on his fantasy woman. He sees her as playing with him. "She doesn't have the good qualities that my wife has. She looks sexy, but she's probably cold in bed." But watching the sultry way Angie moves, he has a hard time believing it.

For a moment, he gives up trying to talk himself out of his sexual feelings and, instead, gets angry at his wife. "If she were sexier, I wouldn't be longing after women like Angie."

Walt probably believes he is thinking. But "thinking" is an attempt to figure out what's going on. And what he's doing, instead, is applying slogan after slogan in an effort to find something that might ease his mind.

Culturally Sanctioned Complaints

What do people do when they have feelings, wishes, or complaints that they think they shouldn't have and don't know how to talk about?

Max feels neglected by his wife, Liz. He doesn't know *why* he feels neglected. In fact he doesn't know he *does* feel neglected. None of the men in his family ever thought or talked about such things. Feeling neglected is an experience Max never learned how to recognize.

So Max is in a lot of trouble when he is suddenly faced with this feeling that he can't put words to. He takes advantage of Liz coming home a few minutes late to justify a complaint.

MAX: (*accusingly*) Why are you always so late?

Max is unable to say "I've been feeling neglected." But he is able to say, "Why are you always so late?" It's a complaint that people in our culture (and in Max's family) feel justified in making. People are supposed to be on time. And if they are not, others are allowed to complain about it. Liz's lateness provides Max with a culturally sanctioned way of saying that he feels neglected.

Max's complaint may be culturally sanctioned, but it doesn't make much sense. Liz isn't always late. In fact, she's almost never late. If there is anyone who's late, it's usually Max himself. Liz can't understand why Max is so angry at her. And she doesn't like it.

LIZ: I am *not* always late. And if you'd think to ask me, I could
    tell you why I was late tonight. I was standing in line at the
    market getting us a salmon steak for dinner.

Max doesn't have an answer for this. If complaining about Liz's lateness is a stab at discovering and saying that he feels neglected, then it is monumentally unsuccessful. How can Max justify feeling neglected when Liz has gone out of her way to get his favorite meal?

Now, ideally, there *is* a way that Max could rescue the situation—by acknowledging that Liz is right.

MAX: (*sighing*) It's true that you're hardly ever late. And I feel like a
    fool. Here I was feeling neglected while you're standing in a
    boring line after a day of work, just to please me.

SKEPTIC: (*to Wile*) It's hard to imagine Max saying anything like that.

WILE: Yes, and that's too bad, because if he had said it, Liz might be able to respond:

LIZ: Well actually, I have been neglecting you. In fact, we've been neglecting each other, what with our crazy schedules. The salmon was an attempt to turn things around—to do something a little special for you.

Max and Liz would be using his complaint about her lateness as a lead-in to a conversation about what has been going on in the relationship.

Traditional Husband and Wife Complaints

Liz and Max are unable to have this conversation, however. In fact, they hardly talk at all. Instead, Max continues to make complaints. When they sit down to dinner, he tells Liz the salmon is too dry. His hidden message is that Liz's overcooking the salmon indicates her neglect of him.

His message is too well hidden, however. Not even Max knows that this is what he is saying. Complaining that your wife has over-cooked the fish that she has gone out of her way to get for you would strike many people as ungrateful.

After dinner, when Max goes upstairs to change his clothes, he criticizes Liz for putting his socks in his underwear drawer. This complaint is another ineffectual way of saying that he feels neglected.

Again, Max's complaint doesn't make much sense. Max realizes that he's lucky that Liz put his socks away at all. It's supposed to be his job to do the laundry.

These complaints are slogan-solutions. They are appeals to cultural catchphrases to justify feelings or complaints. They enable Max to convey to Liz a feeling that he is having difficulty discovering, justifying, and expressing: that he feels neglected.

These particular complaints are traditional husband complaints. They are slogans that husbands—even many of those who think of themselves as nontraditional—call upon when they are having difficulty justifying certain wishes and feelings. They are criticisms that husbands feel they can stand behind, are justified in making, and have an unquestionable, almost God-given right to have. Most husbands have difficulty saying, "I feel neglected" or "You don't seem to love me anymore." But they *are* able to complain about their wives being late, their meals being overcooked, and their socks being put in the wrong drawer.

Wives, of course, have their own set of traditional wife complaints that they feel they can stand behind.

TRADITIONAL WIFE COMPLAINTS	TRADITIONAL HUSBAND COMPLAINTS
You're always late for dinner.	Dinner's never ready on time.
I wish you'd dress more stylishly	I wish you'd dress more sexily.
You're too strict with the kids.	You spoil the kids.
You never spend any time with the kids.	You're too involved with the kids.
You love your work more than you do me.	You just want a meal ticket.
You're insensitive.	You're oversensitive.
You don't listen to me.	You're always nagging me.
You never want to talk.	You always have to talk everything into the ground.
You don't appreciate what it's like to be with the kids all day.	You don't appreciate what it's like to work all day.
You don't help enough around the house.	You criticize the way I do things when I try to help around the house.
The only time you kiss me is during sex.	You never want to have sex.
You don't bring me flowers anymore.	You don't fix yourself up anymore.
You leave the house a mess.	You keep the house a mess.
You never support me when your mother criticizes me.	You always argue with my mother.
I wish you'd be nicer to my parents.	Why do we have to see your parents so often?
You're like another child I have to take care of.	When I come home tired from work, I expect a little consideration.
You want a mother, not a wife.	You're just like my mother.

Husbands have no parallel for the following important complaints that many wives are able to make:

- You don't love me anymore.
- You're not affectionate enough.

There is also a set of traditional partner complaints. These are complaints that both husbands and wives feel relatively free to make:

- You never want to go out anymore.
- It's always about you.
- You always have to have the last word.
- You always have to have things your way.
- Nothing ever satisfies you.

Traditional husband and wife complaints are based on stereotypic male and female roles. When in doubt many people revert to them. These complaints are time-honored and provide a more solid place from which to make a stand. People employ them even though they may not entirely believe them.

Max feels uncomfortable complaining about the salmon and his socks. He doesn't like the image he presents of himself as an old-style dictatorial husband. But he has no other way to talk about feeling neglected. And, as many people do when they have feelings they don't know how to talk about, he gravitates towards the classics.

Borrowing the Other Sex's Complaints and the Other Sex's Answers to These Complaints

In the stereotype, the husband comes home and goes on the Internet. The wife, who wants a little contact, complains that he's not talking to her. The husband replies that he's tired and needs a little peace and quiet. This conflict can be difficult to resolve.

And it is just as difficult if it's the *husband* who feels neglected and the wife who wants a little peace and quiet. The husband may come home raring to go and the wife may need time to herself after a day dealing with preschoolers. Or, it is the wife who comes home tired from work. Many husbands are unable to say that they feel neglected and uncared for. Since traditional husband complaints do not provide ways of doing so, husbands may appeal at such times to traditional wife complaints.

After dinner, Max washes the dishes and then goes into the living room to watch a crime show. He expects Liz to join him. But she stays in the dining room catching up on work from the office. Max had been feeling neglected all evening. Now he *really* feels neglected.

If it were Liz who was feeling neglected, she might be able to say something about it. As I said, because of their social training, women have an easier time talking about such matters, although it is difficult even for them. But Max is totally unable to do so. So he casts around for complaints that he *does* feel comfortable with.

MAX: (*calling from the living room*) What are the kids doing? Are you keeping an eye on them?

Max can't talk about Liz neglecting him, but he can talk about her neglecting the kids. Liz doesn't know what Max is going on about. And neither does he. The kids are safely in their room, playing and giggling. So Max quickly skips to another complaint:

MAX: You know, your problem is that you don't know how to relax.

This complaint is a traditional partner complaint. It is gender-neutral and used equally well by husbands *and* wives. And it is more to the point than his previous comment. Sensing that he is now on the right track, Max takes it a step further.

MAX: You're a typical type A workaholic.

This is a traditional wife complaint. It is one, however, that husbands can now employ also without feeling too uncomfortable. Max continues:

MAX: You're married to your work.

This is *another* traditional wife complaint. It's one that men generally feel too ashamed to make, at least in its usual form: you're married to your work rather than to me. Omitting the "rather than to me" enables Max to say it without feeling like a wimp.

Liz responds to Max's traditional wife complaints by making a traditional husband complaint:

LIZ: Why do you have to be such a nag? I wish you'd support my work instead of giving me such a hard time. I'm doing it for us, you know.

Liz caps it off with particularly powerful traditional wife complaint:

LIZ: Admit it—you want a mother, not a wife. You're like another child I have to take care of.

Why do Max and Liz pick the particular accusations they do? They pick them because they are culturally sanctioned. Everyone immediately sees them as irrefutable. No one even thinks of replying, "What's so bad about being a nag?" or "What's wrong with wanting a mother rather than a wife?" or "What's the crime in being a workaholic?"

And everyone immediately thinks that people so accused are guilty, even the people themselves. How does a woman answer the charge that she's a "neglectful mother"? How does a man answer the charge that he "wants a mother, not a wife"? Although people accused of these sins might try to defend themselves, they secretly worry that the charges might be true.

Max scans his past relationships looking for evidence that he might really be looking for a mother, and of course he finds some. When people scan their pasts looking for such things, their worries distort what they see. Max had generally thought of himself as having good, healthy relationships with women. But now all he remembers are the times that they fed him or comforted him when he was down.

Similarly, Liz anxiously tries to figure out whether she is a neglectful mother, and she has a hard time convincing herself that she isn't. Of course she has a hard time. Parents can easily worry that they are not doing enough for their kids.

The problem with such traditional complaints is that they are too powerful. They wipe out the other person. They put that person on the defensive and make it impossible for him or her to think coherently.

At the same time they are too powerful, they are not powerful enough. They don't say what you really want to say. Max doesn't get to say that he feels neglected. And Liz doesn't get to say that she feels hurt by Max's accusations.

But slogan-solutions are also opportunities. Practically everything that Max said was a clue to the fact that he felt neglected:

- Why are you always late?
- You overcooked the salmon.
- You put my socks in my underwear drawer.
- You're neglecting your children.
- You don't know how to relax.
- You're a workaholic.
- You're married to your work.

And practically everything that Liz said was a clue to the fact that she felt criticized and unsupported:

- Stop nagging.
- I'm working late for the good of the family.
- You want a mother, not a wife.
- You're like another child I have to take care of.

Ideally partners will be able to use their slogan-solutions not just as solutions but also as clues.

In this chapter and the previous one, I have tried to show the extent to which action-solutions and slogan-solutions dominate our thinking and behavior:

- We engage in action-solutions and slogan-solutions
  to solve what appear to us to be unsolvable problems.
  (A wife who doesn't know how else to deal with her

resentment about having to do all the housework engages in an action-solution: she asks her husband to take out the garbage. And then she engages in a slogan-solution: she tries to talk herself out of her resentment. She tells herself, "Housework is woman's work.")

- We seek tokens from our partners to snap us into better frames of mind. (The wife hopes that her husband's taking out the garbage will help her feel less resentful.)

- We appeal to cultural slogans to talk ourselves into or out of our feelings, wishes, and complaints. (The wife appeals to the cultural slogan "marriage is a fifty-fifty proposition" to convince herself that she has the right to complain about her husband's not helping more with the housework.)

- We engage in such action-solutions, slogan-using (self-propaganda), and token-seeking because we are unable to accept our feelings and thus to think and talk about them. The wife doesn't realize that feelings are their own justification; that is, she doesn't see that her feelings of resentment are important—they are deserving of her and her husband's attention— simply by virtue of the fact that she has them.

- We are unable to think and talk about our feelings because we are possessed by accusing inner voices. (The wife thinks that her feelings are unjustified because she believes that they are the result of her "character defects;" that is, her "need to control," "predisposition to nag," and "tendency always to make a big issue out of everything.")

This is how we operate. And we are at a great advantage if we acknowledge and appreciate this fact. We are at a great advantage because it can be useful to realize that:

- Our partners are continually struggling to make sense of their feelings, which is why they say some of the weird things that they do.

- We are continually struggling to make sense of our feelings, which is why we say some of the weird things that we do.
- Our partners are trying to get us to engage in token acts, which is why they get into some of the arguments with us that they do.
- We are trying to get our partners to engage in token acts, which is why we get into some of the arguments with them that we do.

This information will allow us:

- To *not* take these tokens and slogans so seriously (They're just slogans and tokens after all.)
- To *take* these tokens and slogans seriously (You can use your own or your partner's token-seeking and slogan-using as clues to important, often hidden, issues in the relationship.)

Part V

FIGHTING

Chapter 13
To Fight or To Withdraw

When people think of couple problems, they usually think of fighting. "We had a bad week," partners might say. "We fought the whole time." Or, "We had a good week. We didn't fight at all."

If fighting isn't the couple's main problem, then withdrawal often is. "We lead basically separate lives," the partners might say. Or they may say, "We hardly ever have anything to say to one another lately." Or, "There's no spark in the relationship. It's boring."

Fighting and withdrawal may seem like different problems. But they are intimately related, and each can lead to the other. Partners withdraw in order not to fight. They suppress their anger. But at some point this anger breaks through, resulting in a worse fight than if the anger had been expressed in the first place. Upset and frightened by this fight, the partners may rededicate themselves to suppression. Again they withdraw.

Thus, withdrawal leads to fighting and fighting leads to withdrawal just as dieting leads to binging and binging leads to dieting. Fight-withdrawal cycles are occupational hazards of being a couple:

- Even couples who appear consistently withdrawn have fights. But their fights, limited as they are to looks and innuendoes, are easy to miss.
- Even couples who appear continuously in battle withdraw. But their periods of withdrawal, overshadowed as they are by the dramatic nature of their fights, are easy to miss.

Fight-withdrawal cycles are unavoidable. Couples differ only in which of the elements (the fighting or the withdrawing) predominates and the extent of the damage. For some these cycles are merely bumps in the road; for others they are lethal blows to the relationship.

I said that fighting is a major problem. But it can also be a major solution. Fighting can clear the air. A husband and wife who begin an evening feeling withdrawn and grumpy can feel connected and cheerful following a fight. "We needed that," they might say.

> **SKEPTIC:** You'd never hear that in my house. When my wife and I fight, at least one of us ends up feeling worse.

> **WILE:** Well yeah—if fighting is to clear the air, both partners need to feel that they have thrown some heavy verbal punches, and both need to tolerate receiving some too. And that usually doesn't happen. What happens is that one or even both partners come away feeling beaten-up.

The give-get ratio is delicately balanced. If one partner feels he or she hasn't gotten his or her point across or feels particularly stung by something the other says, then the result can be further embroilment rather than a clearing of the air.

"You should be like me," June tells her partner, Megan. "I get mad and then it's over. You nurse your anger for days."

The reason June gets over her anger is that she gets her licks in. And the reason Megan hangs onto her anger is that she doesn't get hers in and, instead, feels verbally trounced by June.

So here's the problem of fight-withdrawal cycles: people can fight, which too often leads to one or both partners feeling verbally beaten-up, or they can avoid fights, which, as I will now show, leads to boredom, loss of love, *and* to fights.

Boredom

Long-term relationships are boring. At least that is what everyone assumes. The classic picture is of a middle-aged couple watching television together, yawning, and saying little.

In order to keep your relationship alive, the women's magazines say, you must work at it. Spice it up. Break out of your routine. Become unpredictable. Greet your husband at the door wrapped in Saran.

I'm not against breaking out of routine or standing plastic-wrapped in a doorway. But I do think this misses the point. The question is not whether partners have routines, but whether these routines are *satisfying*. Boredom is the result not of routines but of *unpleasant* routines. It's the result of unexpressed feelings, held-back complaints, and suppressed anger.

Carol and Fred have been married twenty years. They are bored by their life of watching TV and going out once a week. The problem is not this routine in itself, although this is what they believe, but what happens while they're carrying it out.

It's Saturday night and Carol suggests they see a movie. Although she would like to see the new romantic blockbuster, she mentions an action film, which she thinks Fred might prefer. Although Fred really wants to go bowling, he agrees to the movie. He has said "no" to several of her recent suggestions for movies and thinks he owes her a "yes."

To start with, then, neither is doing what he or she really wants to do. Fred doesn't want to go to a movie, and Carol wants to see a different one. Each feels a little resentful. Neither says anything about it, however. Each is trying to be considerate of the other— an example of the unspoken compromises and self-sacrifices that everyone makes.

So off to the movies they go. On the way there, Carol is upset by the way Fred cuts in front of another driver. But she keeps this criticism to herself, knowing that Fred hates her backseat driving. (In fact, she hates it in herself. She doesn't want to be like her mother, who is an award winner in this category). Although Carol says nothing about it, Fred senses her criticism. He, too, says nothing about it.

Later waiting on line to get into the movie, they stand apart, not talking. Whatever enthusiasm or good will they might have had at the beginning of the evening is gone. They notice a young couple arm-in-arm, laughing, talking, and involved. They think to themselves, "We used to be like that. What's become of us? We've become a tired and bored middle-aged couple in a rut. Look what twenty years have done to us."

What has become of Carol and Fred is not twenty years, but twenty years of evenings like this one. Boring evenings, which lead to a boring relationship, are the consequence of sitting on your feelings.

Let's try to imagine the conversation that might rescue Carol and Fred.

CAROL: (*touching Fred's arm*) Look at that couple over there
       laughing, talking, holding hands. What's happened to us?
       That's how we used to be—before things got so predictable.

It is a relief for Carol to say this. For a moment at least, she is confiding what's on her mind rather than feeling all alone in it. Of course, there are hazards in making this statement, which is why Carol hesitates to do it. Fred could easily think that she holds him responsible for the problem, which he does:

FRED: (*defensively*) Have you noticed how young they are? They've
      probably just met. You can't expect that to last.

Fred is trying to talk Carol out of her concern, which leaves her feeling even more alone. Seeing the disappointment in her eyes, Fred continues:

FRED: (*softly*) But I know what you mean.

It is an intimate moment, even if they are expressing the worry that they are not intimate. Their worlds temporarily interlock.

SKEPTIC: Yeah, but what are they going to say next? "Maybe we
         should get a divorce"? I don't see how this conversation
         can go anywhere.

WILE: Well, if it is to go somewhere, Carol and Fred need an
      important piece of information. They need to know
      that their boredom isn't just something that happens
      over time, but is being re-created in the moment.

Here is what Carol might say were she to have this important piece of information:

CAROL: You know, maybe the problem is that we're just too nice to each other. For one thing, I didn't even want to see this movie. I suggested it only because I thought *you* wanted to see it. So I started being bored even before we got here.

It would be a relief to Carol to say this. She would be taking a major step toward un-boring herself. Fred might then be able to say:

FRED: Well, I've bored myself, too, by not telling you that I really wanted to go bowling.

Having said this, Fred, too, would feel better.

CAROL: I can't believe this. We've come all the way across town to stand in a line to see a movie neither of us has any interest in.

FRED: It's pretty funny when you stop to think about it.

CAROL: The next time I drag you to a movie, remind me to take you to one I like. At least one of us will be happy.

FRED: What are we doing in this line? Let's go get some ice cream.

And as Carol and Fred walk down the street laughing, the young couple who were holding hands say to themselves, "Wouldn't it be wonderful if we were still that much in love when we're their age?"

Falling out of Love

Relationships get boring—and people fall out of love—when they are unable to say what they need to say. Joseph and Karen are a couple in their thirties. Joseph is a dentist. Karen left her job as a surgical nurse to take care of their three small children. Joseph comes home tired from work. Karen meets him at the door and barrages him with problems from the day. She says that the kids were wild and uncontrollable and he will have to speak to them, that the refrigerator is on the fritz and he will have to fix it, and that the bank misprinted his business checks and he will have to straighten it out.

Joseph *feels* like telling her, "Can't you even wait until I take off my coat? I don't want to hear about anything until I've had a chance to sit down and relax a little. And, by the way, can't you take care of *anything* by yourself?"

I said that Joseph *feels* like saying this. But before he gets a chance even to begin, his internal prosecutor tells him, "Wait a minute, fella. If you want to start a fight and ruin the evening, go right ahead. Be my guest. But if you want to have any kind of decent evening at all, cool it. You don't mean half of it, anyway. You're just mad. Getting angry isn't going to help. Look at it from Karen's point of view. She's clearly had a hard day. Show a little consideration."

> **SKEPTIC:** Joseph's internal prosecutor is my kind of guy. I hope Joseph listens to him.

> **WILE:** He does. He says he'll speak to the kids after dinner, look at the refrigerator when the kids go to bed, and take care of the bank in the morning. Then he does what he wanted to do in the first place: he gets a lukewarm beer and sits down with the paper.

Joseph's internal prosecutor is pleased. "Now, isn't that better? You avoid a fight, you avoid hurting Karen's feelings, and look, you even get what you wanted in the first place: a chance to sit down and read the paper in peace."

Unfortunately, Joseph doesn't quite get what he wants, even though he and his internal prosecutor think he does. He wants to sit down with the paper, and he gets that, but he wants to do so feeling content with his wife, and he doesn't get that. Instead, he feels distant from her.

No one realizes that anything is wrong. Joseph is sitting there as always reading the paper. The kids wander through checking him out for signs that he's been told about their behavior, but they don't see any difference. Karen comes out to water the plants, and she doesn't see any difference. Joseph himself, sitting there, doesn't think there's any difference either. There are clues that something is wrong, but they are easy to overlook:

CLUE 1: Joseph isn't enjoying the paper as much as usual, a clear sign that he hasn't recovered from feeling barraged at the door. But he dismisses this sign. He just thinks the columnists are dull today.

CLUE 2: Joseph doesn't feel like doing what he usually does: put the paper down when he's finished and wander into the kitchen to chat with Karen. But he figures that it's because he's tired. And Karen figures that it's because Joseph has found a particularly interesting article.

CLUE 3: Joseph doesn't have much to say during dinner, which surprises him because a couple of things happened today that he had been looking forward to telling Karen. But he figures that he's just tired of thinking about work.

By this time, Karen begins to sense that something's up.

KAREN: You're quiet tonight. Is something wrong?

Since by this time Joseph has forgotten what's wrong (that he felt barraged at the door and was unable to say anything about it), he can't tell her. All he can say is:

JOSEPH: No, I'm just tired.

Karen is mostly convinced by this. People do get tired. She knows she feels tired herself. She prepares herself for an evening with a tired and withdrawn man.

After dinner and after talking to the kids as he said he would, Joseph goes out and tinkers with the car. Karen, feeling shut out, thinks of joining him in the garage, maybe just hanging out for a while. But she can't think of what she'd say. Instead, she calls a friend. Joseph comes in and, overhearing the call, feels left out himself. Karen seems so much more spirited and lively talking to this friend than she is with him. After helping her put the kids to bed and after looking at the refrigerator as he said he would, Joseph sits down with her to watch TV. Again, they find themselves with little to say.

The withdrawal isn't a clearly angry one. If it were, they would at least know what was happening to them. And Karen and Joseph aren't completely silent, since they talk about practical matters such as babysitting arrangements and weekend plans. In fact, it's easy to miss that they are withdrawn at all. Their evening doesn't seem that much different from the ones that many couples have.

When you think about it, withdrawn partners are just more successful at doing what everyone else is trying to do. Nearly everyone thinks it's a good thing to overlook petty annoyances (don't sweat the small stuff) and to avoid unnecessary conflict (pick your battles). But whereas most people can hold out for just so long before rebelling against the whole effort and becoming angry or sarcastic, withdrawn couples can remain polite and respectful indefinitely. They are particularly good at what we were all taught to do.

Partners who can't stop fighting might long for such a relationship in which they are spared the bitter, irresolvable arguments and the demoralizing, unrelenting bickering that plague so many couples.

By suppressing his anger, Joseph has avoided a demoralizing fight. But the cost is an evening of flatness and disengagement.

The effect of many unstated complaints over many evenings is a steadily increasing withdrawal between partners and a steadily increasing loss of energy, interest, love, and intimacy.

Expressing Versus Suppressing Anger: A Debate

Here's the problem: expressing anger can lead to a loss of love. But suppressing anger can do the same. It's an issue that requires a full-fledged debate. Here are the debaters:

- To argue for the importance of expressing anger, we will reintroduce Camille. Remember her? She was the passenger in Tom's car who used the point-not-gotten-across explanation. Camille is the natural person to represent this side in the debate, since she believes that problems arise when partners are unable to express what they need to say.

- To argue for the importance of suppressing anger, we will call upon the skeptic, the reader who's been arguing with me throughout the book. The skeptic is the natural person to take this side in the debate, since he believes that problems take care of themselves if you simply refrain from talking about them.

I'm on Camille's side, since she represents a point of view with which I agree, but the skeptic does have some important points to make.

CAMILLE: It's important to express your anger. If you don't, you're going to pay for it eventually. It will fester and come back to haunt you

SKEPTIC: But it doesn't always fester. And it doesn't always come back to haunt you either. I was mad at my wife last week because she made us late for a movie, but I held my tongue, and we went on to have a great evening.

CAMILLE: Well sure. Suppression sometimes works, at least for the short term, which is why it's so tempting to try. But remember, we're talking about how boredom develops and how love is lost. And, the irony is, love is lost by what we do to try to keep it. We suppress our negative feelings. How are we going to develop positive feelings if we don't have a way to express our negative ones?

SKEPTIC: Well, that *sounds* good, but what really happens when we express our negative feelings is that our partners get angry, and we get into fights.

CAMILLE: That *is* a problem.

SKEPTIC: And what about people who don't want to express their negative feelings? They're *proud* that they can turn the other check and stay polite, respectful, and gracious no matter what. What about them? Are you saying that they have to express their anger even if they don't want to?

CAMILLE: Well, no …

SKEPTIC: You're talking like someone stuck in the sixties. Before then, people were told "you shouldn't express your anger." Then they went away to an encounter group weekend and were told "you've *got* to express your anger." They came home and immediately alienated everybody. It didn't take them long to realize they'd better cool it if they wanted to keep their friends and their jobs.

CAMILLE: I'm not saying that people *have* to express their anger. I'm just saying that they're at an advantage if they know that suppressing it can lead to boredom and loss of love. People may nevertheless decide to build their relationship on politeness and self-restraint. They may devote themselves to avoiding expressing any anger at all. But at least they won't be surprised when the cost is a weakening of their passions.

Conclusion

The skeptic is right about the danger of expressing anger. Camille is right about the danger of suppressing it.

We can express our anger and get into a fight that spoils the evening. Or we can withhold our anger and become withdrawn, which spoils the evening. It seems like the choice is only which way to a miserable time.

What's needed is a new way of thinking about anger and fighting. That's what I'm going to talk about in the next chapter.

Chapter 14
The Facts of Fighting

If avoiding fights isn't the answer, let's have fights but do a better job of it. Let's become skillful fighters. In this chapter, I will try to describe how to do this. The ideal is to be able to:

1. Express your anger
2. Without permanently damaging your relationship, and
3. Instead, *benefit* from it.

When people discuss skillful fighting, they usually talk about limiting and controlling the fight. Partners are told to express anger in a way that doesn't get their partners too upset. They are told to obey the following *rules of fair fighting*, which parallel the rules of good communication described in Chapter 7 (the idea of "fair fighting" was developed by George Bach in his book, *The Intimate Enemy*):

- Don't hit below the belt.
- Don't name-call.
- Don't dredge up things from the past.
- Don't store up complaints and then dump them on your partner.
- Express feelings rather than make accusations.
- Make only constructive criticisms.
- Acknowledge what your partner has just said rather than immediately arguing with it.
- In general, cool it.

These seem like good principles, and I follow them whenever

possible. Unfortunately, the rules of fair fighting are hardest to follow just when you need them most.

People aren't interested in fair fighting when they're angry. They are interested in winning, that is, in landing verbal punches and ducking those of their partners. In the middle of a fight, the rules of fair fighting seem ridiculous, assuming you can remember them at all.

Feeling stung by their partners' accusations, people have an overpowering need to sting back. Feeling frustrated by their partners' refusal to acknowledge any of their points, they seek ever more powerful—which means ever more inflammatory—means to make these points. Feeling increasingly less understood, they feel increasingly less like providing the one thing their partners need: acknowledgment of their points so that *they* can feel understood. So, here's my idea:

If getting people to obey the rules of fair fighting—limiting themselves to non-inflammatory forms of fighting—doesn't work, let's not require it. In fact, let's not require that they necessarily say or do anything different at all. Let's just have them think differently.

In fact, let's have them think differently in eighteen ways.

The Eighteen Facts of Fighting

People may think they know everything about fighting, but they don't. Here are eighteen things that they don't know or that they forget when they most need to remember them.

I will use the case of Karen and Joseph as a frame of reference. As you remember, these were the partners who spent the evening in mutual withdrawal. Each wished to be greeted by a loving and attentive partner who would make up for a difficult day. It didn't work out that way, however. Karen greeted Joseph not with the Bloody Mary and smile he would have liked, but with a request that he speak to the kids, fix the refrigerator, and straighten things out with the bank. Joseph *suppressed* his resentment, and the result was an evening of mutual withdrawal. Let's now imagine now what would happen if he were to *express* his resentment.

JOSEPH: Can't you even wait till I take off my coat, for heaven's sake? I don't want to hear about anything until I've had a chance to sit down and relax a few minutes. You never think of anyone but yourself.

KAREN: Well, you don't have to jump down my throat.

JOSEPH: And you don't have to ambush me at the door with an endless list of things to do.

KAREN: Endless? It was three things.

JOSEPH: Three things too many. It wouldn't occur to you that I've been working hard all day.

KAREN: Oh, you think I spent the whole day polishing my nails, huh?

JOSEPH: What I think—if you really want to know—is that you could have handled these problems. I don't see why I have to do everything around here.

KAREN: Excuse me! You hardly do anything around here. You're like a third child I have to take care of.

JOSEPH: I'd do a lot more if you didn't nag me all the time.

KAREN: Well, if it bothers you so much, why do you stick around?

JOSEPH: I wonder that myself sometimes. Times like this, in fact.

KAREN: I must say, that's just like you. A little squabble, and you start talking divorce.

JOSEPH: I'm not talking divorce. You're the one talking divorce with your "Why do you stick around?"

KAREN: And *you're* the one who said maybe you'd think about it.

JOSEPH: This isn't getting us anywhere. (*Turns to leave.*)

KAREN: That's just like you, too—one little fight and you head for the hills. Obviously, you don't have the guts to stay and talk it out.

JOSEPH: Talk it out to a crazy woman? There's no way to reason with you.

KAREN: How would you ever know? You're never around long enough to find out.

JOSEPH: What a good idea! (*Slams the door behind him.*)

This is an example of a quickly escalating fight. It is a negative cycle in which each partner stings in response to feeling stung. Five exchanges, and the subject of divorce comes up. Five more, and Joseph can't stand it and has to leave.

With this interchange in mind, let's go over the facts of fighting. People in a fight need to know that:

1. If their fight is irresolvable, it is because neither is able to get across the important points he or she needs to make.
2. Their fight may be a consequence of efforts to keep the peace.
3. What people are saying may be more accusing than they realize.
4. Accusing turns the other person into someone who can't listen.
5. Fighting and discussing don't mix, and it may be necessary to have the fight first. A fight is not a time to expect to work out issues, even though this may be the only time that partners ever bring them up.
6. People employ powerful, irrefutable, culturally sanctioned complaints to try to get across points they are having difficulty getting across.
7. Fights lead to predictable spin-off fights that may be as distressing as the original fight.
8. The initial statements of held-back complaints are likely to be exaggerated.
9. The initial accusations may simply be first draft approximations.
10. A fight may be the only entry point to a needed conversation.
11. Fighting can escalate so quickly that partners may fail to realize

that the issue is based on a simple misunderstanding. Or they may be so angry by the time they *do* realize it that they no longer care.

12. Making a complaint may be an alternative to withdrawing.

13. Anger drives out feelings; people who are angry don't realize that they aren't talking about any of their feelings and that they have lost all awareness of most of them.

14. Your partner is more likely to listen to you if you report your anger (that is, say that you are angry) than if you express your anger (that is, say angry things). Your partner is even *more* likely to listen to you if you report the hurt or disappointment that underlies your anger.

15. Complaints, however inflammatory, are often remnants of forgotten fantasy expectations.

16. Complaints are often remnants of simple and ordinary wishes.

17. One way to get your partner to listen to you is to discover the ways in which you agree with what your partner has just said and to then go on from there to make your own point.

18. Talking about your partner's contribution to the fight is likely to rekindle the fight.

Let's take these one at a time.

> **SKEPTIC:** I'm not sure I'm entirely up to taking eighteen facts one at a time.

> **WILE:** Well, if you like, skip them for the time being and turn to the last two pages of this chapter where I describe how knowing these facts puts you in a better position. You can come back to them later.

> **FIGHT FACT 1:** Fights are intrinsically frustrating because neither partner is able to get across any of his or her points.

That's what a fight is: an exchange in which two people become increasingly frustrated because neither is able to have his or her say.

Whenever I see a fight (or find myself in one), I immediately assume that *this* is what's happening. People are unable to make their points because:

- They aren't stating them clearly
- They don't know what their points are (and thus have no chance at all of getting them across)
- Their partners aren't listening

And, of course, their partners aren't listening. A fight is going on, and the point in a fight is to refute what the other says rather than to listen to it. In a fight, neither participant has any interest in hearing what the other has to say until the other hears what he or she has to say.

- Joseph needs Karen to appreciate that he felt ambushed at the door before he will have any interest in appreciating that she felt jumped on. But that won't happen because Karen needs Joseph to appreciate that she felt jumped on before she will have any interest in appreciating that he felt ambushed.
- And Joseph needs Karen to appreciate how he could feel that everything is up to him before he will have any interest in acknowledging that actually she does most of the work at home. But that won't happen because Karen needs Joseph to acknowledge that she does most of the work before she will have any interest in appreciating how he could feel that it's all up to him.

If a fight is created by each partner feeling un-listened-to, then the way out of it is for one of the partners to begin to listen. As soon as Partner A acknowledges a little of what Partner B has been trying to say, Partner B might immediately feel like acknowledging a little of what Partner A has been trying to say.

Were Karen to say "Well, I can see how you could have felt ambushed by all the things I asked you to do," Joseph might say, "Well, I overreacted. I had a bad day and I took it out on you."

I don't mean that people should be able to make such acknowledging statements during the fight. That's too much to ask. It's certainly more than I want to ask of myself. But knowing that your fight is irresolvable because neither you nor your partner is getting across any points can enable you to feel less bewildered by the fight and make it easier to pick up the pieces afterward—that is, to sit down with your partner and figure out what happened.

The following is the inner dialogue of a person who is able to make use of this first fact of fighting: "Since Karen and I were fighting, that means that neither of us felt heard. So let me figure out what she needed me to hear and, also, what I needed her to hear."

FIGHT FACT 2: Fights are often consequences of efforts to keep the peace.

The readiness with which partners accuse one another makes it easy for them to forget that the cause of their fights may be their efforts to avoid fighting. They have suppressed their resentment, which sets the stage for sudden mutual outpourings of resentment (fights).

Partners who recognize that fights may be consequences of their efforts to keep the peace may be protected against the nightmare view that their fights simply are signs that they are incompatible or basically hate one another.

FIGHT FACT 3: The accusations that partners make in a fight are typically more provocative than they realize.

In a fight, people tend to underestimate, or even be oblivious to, the provocativeness of what they say while fully experiencing the provocativeness of what their partners say. Joseph thinks it's irrational and oversensitive of Karen to get so upset over his saying "This isn't getting us anywhere." He thinks he's just saying what's obviously true. Karen thinks it's irrational and oversensitive of Joseph to get so upset over her saying "*That's* just like you. One little fight and you head for the hills." She thinks she's just saying what's true. Neither realizes how provocative his or her remarks are.

If people believe that they are simply stating facts, expressing feelings, and responding to their partners' accusations, and don't realize that they are doing so in an accusing way, they will be puzzled by their partners' angry and defensive responses. They may conclude that there is no way to reason with their partners and that talking doesn't help.

The following explanations can be used to protect against this danger:

- If my partner starts accusing or getting defensive for no apparent reason, it's possible that I have just accused him or her without knowing it.
- If my partner is surprised by how accusing or defensive I get, it's possible that he or she may have just accused me without knowing it.

Let's look at the inner dialogue of a person (let's say Karen) who uses this explanation. Karen thinks to herself later, "Joseph made that totally jerky statement about my being a 'crazy woman'—so maybe I accused him without even knowing it. And well, actually, I did. I told him he had 'no guts.' That's pretty provocative. 'Crazy woman' is mild compared to what he could have said."

In realizing that Joseph was responding to what she now recognizes as her own provocative remark, Karen is discovering an appropriateness in what she first believed to be Joseph's totally inappropriate comment.

> **FIGHT FACT 4:** Accusing turns the other person into someone who can't listen.

We all sort of know this. We sense that the more we argue and accuse, the less our partners listen. However, in the heat of the moment, it is easy to lose awareness of this fact and to feel that we can force our partners to listen if only we find the right arguments.

> **FIGHT FACT 5:** Fighting and discussing don't mix, and it is generally necessary to have the fight first. A fight is not a time to expect to work out issues, even though this may be the only time that partners ever bring up these issues.

We often try to express anger (have a fight) and discuss issues (have a conversation) at the same time. We forget that the two are incompatible. The point of a conversation is to listen to what the other person says. The point of a fight is to ignore or dismiss what the other person says and force that person to listen to you.

I'm not saying that partners shouldn't express anger and argue with each other, just that it is difficult to have a conversation and a fight at the same time and that, for most people, it is necessary to have the fight first. That's because people who have strong feelings about a matter can't listen or think until they've had a chance to express some of these feelings. Later on, if the fight provided each partner a chance to have his or her say, it may be possible to have a conversation.

The belief that you are having a discussion when you are really having an argument is what has given talking a bad name. Partners come away from such an interaction all the more convinced that talking just makes matters worse.

> **FIGHT FACT 6:** In a fight, people employ powerful and, at times, devastating and irrefutable culturally sanctioned complaints or slogans in an attempt to make points they are having difficulty getting across and justify feelings and wishes that they are having difficulty justifying.

In an attempt to get their points across, people appeal to anything that they think might break through the other person's defenses, as I described in the chapter on slogan-solutions:

- Joseph called Karen a "nag," a powerful insult in our culture, particularly when directed to a woman.
- Karen accused Joseph of "having no guts," another powerful insult in our culture, particularly when directed to a man.

People use slogan-solutions not only to break through their partners' defenses but also to override their own personal doubts about what they are saying. In an effort to justify feelings they are having difficulty justifying, people latch onto whatever complaints they can feel at least a little justified in making. Karen and Joseph did not feel entitled to tell each other they were disappointed that the other didn't cheer them up after their difficult days. So they had to resort to slogans.

- Joseph felt, at least at the moment, justified in making certain standard, culturally sanctioned husband complaints: "It wouldn't occur to you that I've been working hard all day."
- Similarly, Karen felt at least partly and momentarily justified in making certain familiar, culturally sanctioned wife complaints: "You're like a third child I have to take care of."

Such culturally sanctioned complaints are the closest that Karen and Joseph came to talking about the wish that each had that the other make up for his or her difficult day.

If partners are aware that they both use powerful, irrefutable culturally sanctioned complaints, they will understand why they are so affronted by what their partners say and why their partners are so affronted by what they say. And knowing this may enable them to feel less affronted.

> **FIGHT FACT 7:** Fights lead to predictable spin-off fights that may be as distressing as the original fight.

Partners will be at an advantage if they establish a joint awareness of the pattern of their fights, and, in particular, the common spin-off fights they can get into. The more they know about their fights, the better prepared they will be to handle them and the better able they will be to talk about them afterward.

The following pattern occurs with such regularity with so many couples that it can be considered a standard sequence in a couple fight:

> **STAGE ONE:** *A slashing argument.* For some couples a "slashing argument" is a three-day yelling match; for others it is

an exchange of looks. For Karen and Joseph it is two minutes of angry exchange in which both partners feel so stung by what the other says that they lash out with anything that might penetrate the seemingly impenetrable defense of the other.

STAGE TWO: *An argument over whether to continue the argument.* Joseph says that it's stupid to continue arguing and that they should each go off alone and cool off. Karen says that they shouldn't run away from their problems but should try to talk them out. A new argument, even more intense then the original one, occurs over this issue.

STAGE THREE: *Sulking.* At some point they do stop. Each goes off and sulks.

STAGE FOUR: *Peacemaking attempt by Partner A.* Karen, who cools down quicker and who is made more nervous by the fight, makes a peace overture. Joseph isn't ready, and he rebuffs the overture. This enrages Karen, who becomes particularly incensed at the fact that she's always the first to try to make peace.

STAGE FIVE: *Peacemaking attempt by Partner B.* Joseph cools down later and makes a peace overture. But Karen, angered by the rejection of her own attempt, is no longer interested. She rebuffs his attempt.

STAGE SIX: *Cooling-down period.* Nothing more is said that evening, and they go to bed without a word. Karen sleeps poorly, upset about the fight. Joseph is also upset, but he is able to sleep, which infuriates Karen.

STAGE SEVEN: *End of fight.* They wake up the next morning and go on as if nothing has happened. They don't want to talk about the fight in fear of restarting it.

This is the general pattern that Karen, Joseph, and a great number of us continually repeat.

We're in a better position if we are able jointly to construct such a natural history of our fights. The realization that these are common scenarios for a great many other couples can make them easier to deal with. We won't have to feel that there is something wrong with us if we are among such a large crowd.

As the example shows, much of the problem comes from attempts to solve the problem. Karen's efforts to seek reconciliation before Joseph was ready, or before *she* was ready, led to intensified fighting. Recognizing this irony—that attempts to solve the problem may increase the problem—can help partners deal with the intensified fighting that follows.

> **FIGHT FACT 8:** The initial statements of held-back complaints are likely to be exaggerated.

If people take their partners' initial wild accusations and angry ultimatums at face value (as how their partners really feel about them deep down) they may have no alternative but to feel threatened and to respond angrily and defensively. If they realize, however, that their partners' accusations and ultimatums are exaggerated and that their partners are likely to take a more moderate stance in a little while, they will feel less threatened by them, will take them less personally, and may choose simply to wait for the explosion to pass.

Here is what Karen might say to herself if she realized that Joseph's statement, "You never think of anyone but yourself," was exaggerated: "Maybe Joseph is coming out with this stuff in such an angry way because he's been holding it back. Maybe he doesn't really hate me as much as he seems to right now and, if I wait a few minutes, he'll be calmer and not so harsh."

Karen may still go on to say exactly what she was going to say ("Well, you don't have to jump down my throat"), but she'll feel less upset and less provoked. And any shift in the direction of feeling less upset and less provoked can make a big difference.

> **FIGHT FACT 9:** The initial accusations may be only first drafts.

Not only are these initial statements exaggerated, they may not even be about the right issues. Although partners may know they are angry, they may not know exactly what they are angry about.

People who realize that their partners' initial accusations may be first drafts will be able to avoid mistaking these accusations as the final word on the matter. They may thus be able to avoid getting into arguments over statements that the accusing person might completely disavow a few minutes later. Here is what Karen might say to herself if she knew this fact of fighting: "I don't like it that Joseph is accusing me of being self-centered. But before I get too upset, I'll wait to see if he really means it."

Joseph may need the chance to lay out all the different feelings and complaints he has in order to discover what his real concerns are. He may need to say, "You never think of anybody but yourself" in order to realize that what he's really upset about is that he and Karen seem to have drifted apart: that they haven't been talking lately.

What Joseph originally experienced as Karen's not having enough sympathy for his rough day ("You never think of anybody but yourself"), he would now see as a mutual problem: they had drifted apart.

It would be a shame if Joseph and Karen were to become bogged down arguing about whether or not Karen thinks only about herself when Joseph's real concern is that the two of them haven't been talking.

> **FIGHT FACT 10:** An argument may be the only entry point to a needed conversation.

Everyone knows that people say many things in fights that they don't mean. And everyone knows that fights may be the only times that people are able to say certain things that they *do* mean. People don't sufficiently appreciate, however, how this latter fact can be turned to advantage. Joseph's complaint that Karen thinks only about herself could lead later on to a conversation in which they discover that:

- Joseph misses talking with Karen.
- Karen misses it too.

- It's easy for them to get caught up in the rush of everyday activities and forget to talk.
- They are already feeling much better now that they are talking, even though what they're talking about is how they haven't been talking.

Joseph's angry statement that Karen never thinks of anybody but herself could be used as an entry point to this important conversation.

> **FIGHT FACT 11:** It is easy when angry to overlook the possibility that the argument may be based on a simple misunderstanding.

Two teenagers—a boy and a girl—were eating a pizza. There was one piece left. The boy asked "Are you going to eat that?" The girl got enraged, stalked out, and didn't talk to him for two weeks.

What happened? The girl took the boy's question as disapproval of her for eating so much and for being so fat. And that's too bad, because the boy wasn't thinking about her being fat at all; he was thinking about *his* being hungry. He asked if she wanted the last piece of pizza because if she didn't, *he* did.

Joseph was upset at Karen for failing to turn on the coffeemaker one morning when she got up before he did. He was the only coffee drinker in the house, and he saw this as demonstrating a lack of interest in his needs. He got so angry about it, and Karen got so angry in return, that they never discovered that the problem arose from a simple misunderstanding. Karen hadn't started the coffee because she didn't know when Joseph would get up and had thought that he would want his coffee fresh. What Joseph took as a disregard of his needs (Karen's not turning on his coffee) was actually an expression of concern for them (wanting his coffee to be fresh).

I don't mean that people should hold off getting angry until they check out every avenue of possible misunderstanding. But there is an advantage in simply considering the possibility that the whole thing is based on crossed signals. This would make it easier to sit down together after the fight and to figure out what happened.

And I don't even mean that Joseph was necessarily mistaken in his general point. It is possible that many of his important needs are *not* being appreciated. His complaint about the coffeemaker may be one of the few times that he is able to raise this issue, even though it turns out not to be an example of what he is trying to demonstrate. The ideal would be for Karen and Joseph to be able to use his anger as an entry point into a conversation about his feeling that his needs aren't being appreciated.

> **FIGHT FACT 12:** Making a complaint may be an alternative to withdrawing.

Joseph knew that if he failed to complain about feeling ambushed at the door, he would probably remain emotionally detached for the rest of the evening. Thus, as ironic as it may seem, Joseph's complaint was a potential contribution to the relationship. It may have been an effort not to withdraw. Karen would have felt very different about Joseph's outburst if she had known that his complaint was an attempt to keep in touch.

> **FIGHT FACT 13:** People who are angry don't realize that they aren't talking about any of their feelings and that they have lost awareness of most of them.

People who are angry are so filled with feelings that it's easy to miss the fact that they aren't talking about any of them. Joseph isn't saying that he feels overwhelmed and neglected, and Karen isn't saying that she feels hurt and abandoned. The omission of feelings isn't surprising, however. In a fight, all the important feelings are left out, and that's what causes the fight.

People start spouting accusations when the press of events overwhelms their ability to handle and express the feelings generated by these events.

When Joseph said, "Can't you even wait until I take off my coat, for heaven's sake … you never think of anyone but yourself," Karen was unable to tell him (or even fully to register within herself) that she felt:

- Shocked by how angry he seemed to be with her
- Angry at what seemed to her in some ways an unfair charge
- Guilty about what she felt in other ways might be a fair charge
- Bad about letting him down
- Hurt and unloved

Instead of saying any of these things, she said, "Well, you don't have to jump down my throat."

People fight because they can't talk. If Karen had been able to express the feelings just described, she wouldn't have had to snap back in the accusing and ineffectual way she did. Fighting is what people are left to do when they lose track of their feelings. If Karen and Joseph were to realize this important fact about fighting, they would be in a favorable position to try to figure out what their feelings are and, perhaps, to tell the other about them.

> **FIGHT FACT 14:** People are more likely to get their partners to listen to them if they report their anger (talk about the fact that they are angry) rather than simply unload it (say angry things). Their partners are even more likely to listen to them if they report the hurt or disappointment that may underlie their anger.

I said that Karen and Joseph weren't talking about any of their feelings. They do appear to be talking about at least one kind of feeling, however: anger. But they aren't. Instead, they are saying angry things. There's a difference. Talking about their anger—saying "I'm angry"—would provide at least the possibility of having a conversation. The other person might then ask what he or she is angry about and the two might be able to discuss the matter. Saying angry things—such as "You're a nag" and "You don't have any guts"—is inflammatory and ends all possibility of discussion.

For example, your partner is much more likely to listen to you if you say, "When you showed up late, I got angry," than if you say, "You're an irresponsible jerk for being so late." The former is reporting your anger and the later is expressing it. And your partner is even more likely to listen to you if you add, "And I felt hurt about it."

FIGHT FACT 15: The complaints that partners make in a fight are often remnants of forgotten hopes and dreams.

If partners feel uncomfortable with their fantasy wishes (because they see them as childish), they will be unable to talk about them and may lose partial awareness of them. Karen didn't know about Joseph's fantasy wish that she rescue him from his difficult day. All she heard were comments such as:

- "There aren't enough potatoes."
- "You really should throw that old blouse away."
- "You left the light on in the bedroom."

Karen was offended by these complaints—she had no way of knowing that they were the result of the disappointment of Joseph's unexpressed fantasy wish—and she and Joseph got into a fight.

If Karen and Joseph were to recognize his disconnected complaints as remnants of fantasy wishes, the two of them might be able to use these complaints to bring out these wishes. Joseph could say: "I just figured out why I've been crabbing at you all evening. I had this hope that you would do all kinds of wonderful things to make up for my difficult day. I know that's ridiculous because I didn't even tell you that I had a miserable day and, besides, you had a hard day of your own."

FIGHT FACT 16: The blurted-out complaints that partners make in a fight are often remnants (distorted expressions) of simple and ordinary wishes.

People often feel uncomfortable, not simply about their fantasy expectations, but also about their ordinary wishes. Karen and Joseph had rather extravagant hopes of what the other might do for them. When it came down to it, however, all each really needed was a kind word. Since neither was able to talk about his or her disappointment at the frustration of these ordinary wishes, each was forced to express this disappointment in indirect and, as it turned out, offensive ways. Karen said, "You're like a third child I have to take care of." And Joseph complained, "You don't think of anyone but yourself."

Since Karen and Joseph were unaware that they hadn't told the other what they wanted (a little warmth to make up for the difficulties of the day), they were forced to conclude that the other was just unwilling to provide it.

If you don't know that the problem is your own inability to ask, then you may be stuck concluding that the problem is your partner's unwillingness to give.

> **FIGHT FACT 17:** One way to get your partner to listen to you is to discover the ways in which you agree with what your partner just said and then go on from there to make your point.

What is easy to miss, since Karen and Joseph seem to be stating their positions so forcefully, is how poorly they are doing it. When Joseph accuses Karen of ambushing her with an endless list of things to do, she insists that it *wasn't* endless, but just three things. Arguing with him—calling him on his exaggeration—gets him angrier. It isn't a good way to get him to listen to her. But suppose Karen had acknowledged Joe's point:

> **KAREN:** Yeah, you're right, I did ambush you. And I'm sorry I did, because I had a really awful day, and I so wanted things to go well between us tonight.

Agreeing with what Joseph just said is a good way to get him to listen to her. He is less likely to want to continue the fight after hearing this. The problem is that when under attack you don't have the least wish to agree with *anything* the other person says.

> **FIGHT FACT 18:** In your effort to talk afterward about a fight, commenting on your partner's contribution to the fight, rather than sticking exclusively to your own, will just rekindle it.

It is reminiscent of the old principle: "It's okay for me to criticize my family, but I won't tolerate your doing so." In this case the principle is: "It's okay for me to admit I'm wrong, but for you to do it is just asking for trouble."

If you talk about only your own contributions to the fight—that is, if you focus on the ways in which you were provocative—your partner isn't going to be offended by what you say. In fact, he or she might come to your rescue. Here is Joe talking about only his contribution to the fight:

JOSEPH: I did jump down your throat, and you're right, that was pretty dumb.

Joseph's willingness to admit his contribution to the fight makes Karen feel like admitting hers.

KAREN: True enough, but that's only because I ambushed you.

Karen and Joseph are in a positive cycle in which each automatically looks at things from the other's point of view in response to the other doing the same.

JOSEPH: You'd been with the kids all day. I should help more when I get home.

KAREN: You'd been working hard too. You deserve some time to relax.

As long as Karen and Joseph talk this way—that is, as long as they discuss only their own personal responsibility for the fight—they can't possibly spin off into another fight. Each partner's admitting things leads the other to feel like doing the same.

But the spell could be broken at any point. After saying, "You know, you're right. I did jump down your throat," Joseph could add:

JOSEPH: But you had a part in it, too. After all, you did ambush me.

Here, Joseph is talking about Karen's contribution to the fight. If

Joseph had refrained from saying this, Karen might have made this same comment about herself. Coming from Joseph, however, she can't tolerate it:

KAREN: What do you mean, "ambush"? I was just asking for a little help. And the only reason I even had to ask is that it would never occur to you to offer it on your own.

And immediately Karen and Joseph would be back in the fight, which they would have avoided if they had stuck exclusively to their own contributions to the fight.

> **SKEPTIC:** I don't want to always have to stick to my contribution to a fight. And it's too hard to do even if I did want to.

> **WILE:** And you don't have to. This fact of fighting and the others facts on the list are things to know, not things you have to do.

Here is my recommendation: Talk about your partner's contribution to the fight if you want to, but be aware that you are doing it, so that you won't be surprised by the effect—namely, your partner getting defensive or angry. The greater danger isn't getting back into fights. It's getting back into fights without knowing why.

Conclusion

Preventing fights is difficult. There's always going to be something that will set you off or that will set your partner off. So rather than devote yourself entirely to preventing fights, I recommend that you develop skill in recovering from them. By recovering, I mean sitting down with your partner afterward and talking about the fight.

> **SKEPTIC:** I don't think that's such a good idea. Most people I know get into their worst fights when they sit down to talk about them. That's what certainly happens with my wife and me. When our fights are over we're just glad

they're over. We don't want to tempt fate by bringing
them up again.

WILE: Well, that's what this list of eighteen facts of fighting
is for. It's an attempt to provide enough information
about what fights are about so that you'll have a better
chance to work things out if you do sit down later to try
to talk about them.

How can these eighteen facts of fighting help you? You still may have
a lot of fights and you still may say a lot of angry things, but:

- Since you'll know that you're saying a lot of angry
  things, you won't be surprised by your partner's angry or
  defensive response.
- You'll know that you and your partner are caught in a
  stinging back-and-forth exchange that might need to run
  its course.
- You'll know that a lot of provocative things are being said
  that need not completely be taken at face value; they are
  exaggerations and first drafts.
- You'll know that the fight is temporarily irresolvable
  because neither partner is able to have his or her say.
- And you'll know how, later on when you're not so angry,
  you'll be able to resolve it—by helping your partner have
  his or her say.
- You'll know that you're in a kind of classic battle that
  nearly all couples get into, and so the fact that you're in
  it doesn't necessarily mean that something is wrong with
  you, your partner, or the relationship.
- You'll know that all the important feelings that could
  soften the interaction and help make sense of things are
  being left out.
- You'll know that this isn't a time to expect to work out any
  issues.
- Nevertheless, you'll know that there may be important
  issues somewhere in there among the accusations.
- And you'll know that it will be possible, following the

fight, to sit down with your partner to figure out what
happened and to discuss the issues that emerged during
the fight.

- And you'll know, when you do sit down, what will lead to
  a restarting of the fight and what won't.
- And because of all this knowledge, your fights will seem
  very different to you.

Part VI

TWO RELATED PATTERNS
THAT DRIVE US CRAZY

Chapter 15
Pursuing and Distancing

As I said, fighting and withdrawing are the major problems in a relationship. But two other problems are almost as important:

- Pursuing and distancing
- Bypassing and nonbypassing

Fighting and withdrawing, pursuing and distancing, and bypassing and nonbypassing occur with such frequency that they deserve to be considered the occupational hazards of being a couple. Hardly anyone escapes them. Couples differ primarily in the degree of wreckage the problems create. These three patterns are so common, and they exert such a powerful effect on our relationships, that I would amend the marital vows to read:

> Do you, Joseph (Karen), take this woman (man) to be your lawful wedded wife (husband), for better or for worse, in sickness and in health, and through the inevitable periods of fight-withdrawal, pursuit-distance, and bypassing-nonbypassing?

"Pursuit and distance" is a term coined by Thomas Fogarty, a well-known family therapist in New York. Here it is in a nutshell:

> In pursuit and distance, one partner, the "pursuer," seeks increased involvement, intimacy, engagement, talking, affection, sex, or time together, while the other, the "distancer," seeks increased separation and privacy.

The pattern is self-reinforcing and self-escalating. The more the pursuing partner pursues, the more trapped the distancing partner feels and the more he or she needs to get away. The more the distancing partner needs to get away, the more deserted the pursuing partner feels and the more he or she needs to pursue.

Pursuer-distancer conflicts are as difficult to resolve as are fight-withdrawal cycles. In fact, pursuit-distance difficulties are often what partners in a fight-withdrawal cycle fight about. In such a fight:

- The pursuer accuses the distancer of being withdrawn, withholding, unavailable, unloving, uncommitted, afraid of closeness and needing to control.
- The distancer accuses the pursuer of clinging, nagging, demanding, and needing to control.

I expect that you will recognize yourself in some aspects of the following extended example, since almost every couple gets caught up in some version of pursuit and distance. Paula and Jay are a married couple in their early twenties. Paula is a waitress and Jay, who makes his living teaching tennis, has cut back to half-time so that he can go back to school. Jay can't understand why Paula acts the way she does. He thinks:

> **JAY:** I'm going to school for us, so that I can get a job that pays well enough so we can start a family. But instead of helping, she's become my biggest problem. She's jealous of the time I spend studying. Even when she's working, she finds excuses to call me a million times a day. She always has to be the center of my attention, but even when she is, she seems sulky and resentful. I deliberately plan picnics and things. And it's unbelievable that it's just those times that she picks a fight. And whenever we have even the slightest little problem, she always has to talk it into the ground. Things would probably take care of themselves if she didn't talk about them so much.

Paula sees Jay as the problem. She thinks:

> **PAULA:** Jay says he has to do schoolwork, but that's just an
> excuse. He ignored me even before he went back to
> school. It's just worse now. I think he just doesn't want
> to be with me. Sure, once in a blue moon we'll go out
> together, but mostly what free time he does have, he
> plays basketball or goes out for a beer with friends.
> He's hardly said two words to me in a week. Whenever
> I try to talk about our problems, he heads for the door.
> And we haven't had sex in a month. It's the old story.
> I'll support him through school, and then he'll find
> someone new to ignore all the time.

Paula is the pursuer. She feels abandoned by Jay's withdrawal and
reacts by pressuring him. Jay is the distancer. He reacts to Paula's
pressure by withdrawing.

The problem, in part, is their differing character styles:

- Throughout her life, Paula has dealt with problems
  by engaging (that is, by talking to people and seeking
  reassurance).
- Throughout his life, Jay has dealt with problems by
  disengaging (that is, by keeping things to himself and
  going on long, solitary walks to think things over).

At the source of Paula and Jay's problems is this incompatibility in
character style.

> **SKEPTIC:** I think you're missing the point. Their
> incompatibility is what brought them together.
> They probably wanted their marriage to fail, at least
> unconsciously. Why else would they marry someone
> who is so clearly inappropriate?

> **WILE:** That's the you-must-have-wanted-it-that-way style of
> reasoning. You're saying that Paula and Jay got married
> because of their problems. An alternative view, and the

> one that I believe, is that Paula and Jay got married
> in spite of these problems. What they liked about one
> another outweighed what they didn't like.

Of course, what people don't like about their partners is often the other side of what they *do* like. In fact, a relationship is, in some sense, the attempt to work out the negative side effects of what attracts you to your partner in the first place:

- Jay was fascinated by someone who could express her feelings and reach out to others the way Paula could. One relationship task—what Paula and Jay may need to accomplish to make the relationship work—is to find a way for Jay to deal with the aspects of these characteristics that he doesn't like. A person may reach out and be expressive in both appealing and unappealing ways, and his or her partner will understandably like the former and dislike the latter.
- Paula, for her part, was fascinated by Jay because he could remain self-possessed and self-reliant. Another relationship task—what Paula and Jay may need to accomplish to make the relationship work—is to find a way for Paula to deal with the expressions of Jay's self-possession and self-reliance that she doesn't like.

Whereas Paula and Jay see the other as unwilling to make the commitment to try to solve their problems, I see them as continually trying to solve their problems. And that's the problem: the ways these partners attempt to deal with their problem reinforce the problem.

The primary way Paula and Jay try to deal with the problem is to downplay it. Each evening, Jay sneaks into the bedroom to do his schoolwork hoping Paula won't notice. He worries that she will resent his having to spend so much time on his studies and away from her. Paula does notice, of course. What she notices is Jay sneaking away, as if she were the enemy.

The irony is that if Paula felt secure about Jay's affection for her, she wouldn't mind his studying—or, at least, she wouldn't mind it so much. She would be more content to do things on her own: catch up on her reading, talk to friends on the phone, or surf the Net. But the creepy way Jay slips into the bedroom, as if she were a danger to avoid, makes Paula feel insecure and unloved, and none of these options even occurs to her. She mopes around the apartment waiting for him to finish.

- Jay's effort to keep his studying from becoming a problem has turned it into a problem.
- Jay's attempt not to abandon Paula leaves her feeling abandoned.

All the ingredients are on the stove, and now they begin to thicken. Feeling that Jay already sees her as a burden, Paula pretends she doesn't mind his slipping into the bedroom. And she tries to hide the fact that she's just killing time waiting for him to come out and talk to her.

Jay senses what she's doing, of course, and feels pressured. He resents her hanging around, ready to pounce as soon as he emerges. He has begun to feel that she is a needy, neurotic woman who is always ready to accuse him of abandoning her. (In seeing Paula as having these character flaws, of course, Jay is using the character-flaws habit of thought.) By the time he emerges from the bedroom at the end of the evening, he no longer wants to be with her. He calls a friend to meet him for a beer.

Incidents like this poison the relationship. Jay feels he is continually letting Paula down and that he is a failure as a husband. Being away from her starts to feel like a relief, although he feels too guilty to admit this, even to himself. When he gets home from school, he hopes that she will be out so that he won't have to be with her. Even sex becomes a pressure. Previously, Jay could hardly keep his hands off Paula. Now he hardly ever wants to touch her.

This whole unfortunate interaction exaggerates the dependence of Paula and independence of Jay. It changes Paula from a person who could potentially have made good use of her time alone into a person whose main preoccupation is whether Jay loves her. And it changes Jay from a potentially involved person who needs Paula into a detached person who doesn't even want to be near her. If it were earlier in their life together, before this pursuer-distancer interaction developed, Jay would likely have said something to Paula that would reassure her of his need for her:

JAY: I don't feel like studying tonight. Something upsetting
     happened at school today. But I've got to put in at least
     a couple of hours. After that, how about we go out for a
     beer—that'll be my reward—because I want to tell you what
     happened.

Paula is suffering from not hearing such things. And Jay is suffering from not feeling like saying them. He is deprived and doesn't know it. Paula, who could have been his major resource in dealing with problems, has become his major problem.

Paula's Private Problem-solving Effort

Paula tries to deal with Jay's unavailability, and with the worry that she's "too dependent" by trying to prove her independence. She goes to a movie with a friend and signs up for a pottery class.

The movie, however, is about unrequited love and just reminds Paula of her own situation. The pottery class seems filled with lonely people making a big mess with clay, and it depresses her. As often happens with such attempts to prove one's independence, Paula comes home feeling even more needy.

And there's a further disappointment. Paula secretly hoped that Jay would worry she was becoming too independent and would miss her. He doesn't ask her any questions about her time away and, if anything, he seems relieved by it. Frustrated by the failure of her plan, Paula throws aside all pretenses and insists that Jay should appreciate her more:

PAULA: You didn't even notice that I was gone all evening. You never
     pay any attention to me or to what I might like. I can't even
     remember the last time you bought me flowers. It was so long
     ago, they hadn't evolved yet. You had to bring me ferns.

Paula's attempt to be independent and undemanding thus ends in this dependent and demanding complaint. And Jay is too upset to see the humor in her crack about the ferns.

Jay's Private Problem-solving Effort

Later, Jay engages in his own attempt to make things better. Feeling pressured by Paula's complaint and in an effort to give her what he thinks she wants, he arranges a picnic. He does the shopping, gets the deviled eggs she loves, brings her flowers *and* ferns, and takes her to the park they went to on their first date.

Jay's plan fizzles. Since it's clear to Paula that he's just going through the motions and he'd really rather be studying, she doesn't get much satisfaction from the big day. Furthermore, she's not in the mood for a picnic. But she tries to act pleased in order to reward him for the effort and to avoid disappointing him. It is evident, however, that her heart isn't in it any more than Jay's is.

Paula's reaction to the picnic is frustrating to Jay. Since he's already overextending himself to please her, he has little patience with her lukewarm response. And when she comments that he forgot to bring mustard, it's more than Jay can stand.

JAY: Look at all the trouble I went to—all this food, all the effort, and the only thing I hear is "Where's the mustard?"

PAULA: A-hah. So you went to a lot of trouble. You really didn't want to do this in the first place, did you? Well, that's fine with me. Next time, don't bother.

JAY: I shouldn't have bothered *this* time. If we were at home, both of us would have been happy. I could have studied, and you could have had all the mustard you wanted.

Jay's attempt to be loving thus ends in this unloving argument. They go into a ten-minute mental divorce:

- Paula's ten-minute mental divorce: I shouldn't have married him. I should have listened to my mother about all the other fish in the sea. He's a sardine. He doesn't care about me. The whole marriage is a charade. He's married to his books. He only thinks of himself. And I can't stand myself the way I get so clingy. He brings out the worst in me.

- Jay's ten-minute mental divorce: What a mistake to marry a Virgo. She's just too neurotic. No matter what I do she's always going to complain. And I don't need complaints. I need support. I should never have broken up with Vickie. But then, I wasn't able to satisfy her, either. Maybe I'm too selfish to be married to anyone.

The rest of the day is spent in a mutual sulk, and neither Paula nor Jay sleep very well that night. But at breakfast the next morning, Jay acts as if nothing has happened. He chats in his usual way about interesting things in the newspaper. Paula, grateful that the crisis has passed, also acts as if nothing has happened.

Is the Problem Merely a Matter of Faulty Communication?

A communication skills trainer might point to the fact that at no time did Paula and Jay ever really talk. The day of the picnic began with a long period in which both partners tried to act pleasant to each other in an effort to make the outing work. That was followed by:

- A short argument about mustard
- A ten-minute mental divorce
- An afternoon sulk
- A sleepless night
- A sudden return to "normal."

What Paula and Jay need, this communication skills trainer might suggest, is to sit down and discuss what had happened.

TRAINER: Let's imagine how things would have gone if the two of you had talked about things the morning after the picnic.

Who would have begun?

PAULA: It would have had to be me. I'm the one who always has to start everything. And I would have said what I said at the time (*turning to Jay*): Why did you suggest a picnic when you really didn't want to go?

JAY: I did want to go—until you complained about the mustard.

PAULA: That's the problem. Something always upsets you. You're like a fussy child. Like the time in Mexico when …

JAY: You never forget anything. For heaven's sake, we went to Mexico four years ago.

PAULA: Our first trip and you don't even remember? It was less than three years ago, and …

JAY: We went to Mexico after my brother's wedding.

PAULA: No way! It was three years ago. It was after I got my new job.

JAY: You're wrong. You're dead wrong.

PAULA: Of course, I am. I always am.

In just two minutes, Paula and Jay have broken nearly every communication rule in the book.

TRAINER: I think we need some ground rules.

The following is a condensation. The trainer didn't give all these rules at once. He gave them a few at a time over the course of several sessions.

1. Don't ask "why" questions. Asking "Why did you suggest a picnic when you really didn't want to go?" is blaming. And blaming doesn't help.
2. Paraphrase what the other has said so that he or she knows that you have heard. Instead of saying, "I did want to go," say, "I hear you saying that you felt that I didn't want to go."
3. Try to stick to one topic. Things went downhill when you shifted from the picnic to talking about Mexico.

4. Don't bog down in irrelevant issues. It doesn't matter whether you went to Mexico three years ago or four.

5. Don't dredge up events from the past. The issue is what is happening now, not what might or might not have happened three or four years ago.

6. Don't name-call or label. Calling Jay a "fussy child" doesn't add anything and just makes him mad.

7. Don't make "you" statements. Statements such as "You always get upset about everything" are accusations. Instead, say how you feel.

8. Don't say "always" or "never." Such exaggerations just provoke the other person.

9. Don't interrupt. Give the other person a chance to finish.

It's hard to imagine that Paula and Jay, as angry as they are, will be able to apply any of these rules. Here is their attempt:

PAULA: (*attempts to express feelings rather than state accusations, with a sidelong glance at the trainer looking for a sign from him whether or not she is doing it right*) I feel bad about some of the things I said at the picnic yesterday. I was upset because I felt that you really didn't want to be with me.

JAY: (*takes a deep breath and conscientiously tries to paraphrase what Paula just said*) I hear you saying that you feel bad about what you said and that you felt I didn't want to be with you. I appreciate your saying this. I feel bad about some of the stuff that I said, also. But it's not that I didn't want to be with you. I was just disappointed because we were doing something I thought you'd like.

PAULA: (*obviously with much effort and with another quick, sidelong glance at the trainer, tries to paraphrase what Jay just said*) I hear you saying that you were disappointed that I didn't enjoy the picnic. I don't know why I didn't. For some reason the idea of a picnic never hit me right.

TRAINER: (*speaking with emphasis because he now believes he has discovered the critical communication error*) Jay, you were mind reading. Instead of asking Paula whether she wanted to go on a picnic, you just assumed that she did. That's where the trouble began. You can never assume that you know what the other person wants. The next time you plan something, Jay, you should ask Paula what she wants. In fact, as a practice exercise, why don't the two of you plan something now.

JAY: (*privately vowing to himself never again to second-guess Paula's wishes*) Okay. (*To Paula.*) What would you like to do Saturday?

PAULA: (*seems uncertain*) I don't know. (*Long pause.*) Maybe it would be nice to go to the beach.

JAY: (*quickly*) Okay, we'll go to the beach.

The result is that Paula and Jay engage in another problem-solving effort. And it's the picnic all over again. Before Paula and Jay even arrive at the beach, Paula senses that Jay really wants to be home studying, and she becomes disheartened. Jay, noticing her lack of enthusiasm, becomes frustrated. And when Paula doesn't immediately go into the water, it's the mustard incident all over again.

JAY: (*trying to imagine what the communication trainer would want him to say, but then giving up entirely and blurting out*) We drive across three counties so you can go to the beach, and you don't even go into the goddamn water?

Since going to the beach was her idea, Paula doesn't feel entitled, as she had on the picnic, to complain about his not really wanting to be there in the first place. She is forced to resort to more primitive arguments:

PAULA: (*completely forgetting everything the trainer has taught her*) I don't see a sign anywhere ordering me into the goddamn water. I came here to relax. Maybe I'll go in the water later, and maybe I won't.

If talking is to help, Paula and Jay need to have certain information about their relationship:

- They need to know that they have a severe case of a problem that, to one extent or another, every couple has—a pursuer-distancer problem.
- They need to know that what makes the problem so difficult for couples is that almost every attempt to solve it deepens it.
- They need to know that Jay periodically plans "duty" outings, just as Paula occasionally tries to become "independent."
- They need to know why neither effort ever works out. Jay's effort not to deprive Paula causes him to deprive her, and Paula's effort not to pressure him causes her to pressure him.
- They need to know that Jay also has relationship needs, but that these needs are crowded out by his worry about not satisfying Paula's needs.

Even were they to have this information, there's a danger that they wouldn't be able to use it:

- Paula might be too alarmed at the thought of being a "dependent, nagging woman" to do anything other than to try to be "independent"—and fail.
- Jay might feel too guilty about depriving Paula to do anything other than to try not to deprive her, to make it up to her—and fail. This would lead inevitably to other periods in which he gives up entirely, goes off on his own, and tries not to think about it.

SKEPTIC: You make it all sound pretty hopeless, Dan. Is that what you really believe—that the problem is just too difficult to expect Paula and Jay ever to work out?

WILE: Well, actually, there are a few principles that might help them. I'll discuss them in the next chapter.

Chapter 16
Mastering the Facts of Pursuit and Distance

People have trouble dealing with their pursuer-distancer conflicts because they can't stand the idea that they have them. Pursuers hate it that they pursue, and distancers hate it that they withdraw. Pursuers and distancers see themselves as defective people with defective partners in defective relationships:

- Pursuers are upset by the pictures of themselves as "dependent," "demanding," and "nagging." They often have long, painful histories of criticism from others (and from themselves) about such tendencies. In addition, they frequently associate this characteristic with a parent whom, at least in this respect, they don't want to be like.
- Distancers often have similar experiences and sensitivities about being seen as "withdrawn," "uninvolved," and "afraid of intimacy."

Pursuit and distance provide a field day for the character-flaws form of reasoning, and that is why it is such a big problem. People in such an interaction have an almost irresistible urge to attribute their own or their partners' behavior to character defects.

Paula and Jay don't realize it, but what they are doing (accusing themselves or one another of being "dependent," "demanding," or "afraid of intimacy") is name-calling, which brings an end to useful thinking about the matter. They believe there is nothing further to think or talk about; you're just supposed to stop being demanding or afraid of intimacy or whatever it is you're being accused of.

A Non-accusing View of Pursuit and Distance

If Paula and Jay are to work out their pursuer-distancer conflict, they need a non-accusing way of thinking about it. They need to know that:

1. They have a severe case of a problem that, to one extent or another, every couple has. Realizing this will help Paula and Jay feel less that something is uniquely wrong with them.
2. The persistence of this problem isn't just the result of their failure to try to change. Paula can't simply stop pursuing, and Jay can't simply stop withdrawing.
3. What makes the problem so difficult is that almost every attempt to solve it deepens it. Paula spends most of her time trying not to pursue (and that is part of the problem), and Jay makes ineffectual and counterproductive efforts not to withdraw.
4. They are trapped—they are caught in a difficult dilemma—and they are not the selfish, unreasonable, uncooperative, uncompromising, insensitive, mean-spirited, unfeeling, controlling, or self-destructive people they seem to themselves or to each other.
5. Paula has reason to pursue (she is being abandoned) and Jay has reason to withdraw (he is being pressured).
6. Both of them have important points to make that they are having difficulty getting across. Paula is right that they need to be able to talk about their problems, and Jay is right that their attempts to do so generally lead to fights that neither of them wants.
7. The only way to avoid pursuit and distance is to be completely non-accusing, which is impossible. When the pursuer reaches out, he or she often does so in an accusing way, which causes the distancer to withdraw.
8. Pursuit and distance exaggerate the differences between

partners. Originally, Jay had at least some desire to do the things that Paula wanted to do—talk, spend time together, be affectionate, and have sex. But the more he feels criticized by Paula for not doing these things, the less he finds himself wanting to do them.

9. The pursuer isn't the only person being deprived. The distancer is being deprived too; he or she just doesn't know it. While Paula is deprived of having a husband who would want to spend time with her, Jay is deprived of having a wife he'd want to spend time with.

10. Each partner's attempts to deal with his or her problem increases the problem of the other. Paula deals with feeling abandoned by pressuring, while Jay deals with feeling pressured by abandoning.

11. Pursuit and distance may depend, in part, on situational factors such as simply who is busier.

For those of you who want more details on these eleven points, here they are (for those who don't, skip to the end of the chapter, where I give an example of how partners who have mastered these eleven facts might talk

> **FACT 1:** Partners in a pursuer-distancer conflict are suffering from an intense form of a universal couple problem.

Paula and Jay think that people with good relationships don't have the kind of problems they have. They feel that something is uniquely and dreadfully wrong with their relationship. They would feel better about it if they realized that pursuit and distance are occupational hazards of a relationship. Every couple has the problem at least to some extent, and they just happen to have an extreme version of it. People who view pursuit and distance as a universal couple issue rather than as simply a sign of character defects will be better able to deal with it.

> **FACT 2:** The pursuer can't stop pursuing, and the distancer can't stop withdrawing.

The main advice generally given to partners in a pursuer-distancer conflict is to stop doing what they are doing. Pursuers are advised to:

- Respect their partners' needs for privacy
- Spend more time doing things on their own
- Be a little more standoffish
- Accept a more separated and detached style of relating
- Not always have to talk about everything
- Stop pressuring, nagging, demanding, and controlling
- Play a little hard to get

In other words, stop pursuing. If the pursuer stops pursuing, this reasoning goes, than the distancer won't feel so pressured and have to withdraw.

The problem with this advice is that the pursuer can't stop pursuing. Although Paula can force herself to stop asking Jay for more affection, she can't force herself to stop wanting it. And Jay, knowing that she continues to want it, even though she has stopped asking for it, continues to feel the pressure.

This fact explains why playing hard to get so rarely works. Your partner knows that you are playing, and that, actually, you are still easy to get. Playing hard to get is most likely to work (your partner may actually come around) when you are no longer playing—that is, when you have lost interest and no longer care whether he or she comes around. But by then, of course, it's too late because you really don't care.

Just as pursuers can't stop pursuing, distancers can't stop withdrawing. Distancers don't have any other way to deal with the pressure and criticism.

People who see their partners and themselves as caught in a difficult situation rather than as just stubbornly refusing to change are likely to feel more sympathy about their situation.

> **FACT 3:** The pursuer is spending most of his or her time trying not to pursue, and the distancer is making effortful but hardly noticeable attempts not to withdraw.

Another reason why advising the pursuer to stop pursuing doesn't help is that the pursuer is already trying to stop, and that's what's causing much of the problem.

Paula hates the picture of herself as a dependent person who hangs around waiting for Jay to give her some attention. And she hates the position it puts her in. So she makes her own efforts to go out and do things on her own. But that doesn't help, because her attempts to prove her independence—for example, by taking a pottery class and going to a movie with a friend—typically backfire and result in her feeling even more dependent.

And there's another thing that Paula hates. She hates her picture of herself as the type of person who is always complaining about not being given enough attention. So she makes an effort not to complain. But that doesn't help either, because her efforts to suppress her complaints typically lead to an intense outpouring of complaints later and confirm Jay's view that the complaints have been there all along.

And there's still another thing that Paula hates. She hates the picture of herself as the type of person who is always trying to change her partner. So she makes an effort to accept Jay the way he is. But that doesn't work, because her attempts not to change him typically lead to ever more intense demands for change later on.

At the same time that Paula (the pursuer) is trying not to pursue, Jay (the distancer) is trying not to withdraw. Jay hates the picture of himself as a withdrawn, withholding, and rejecting person. So he makes an effort to act more interested and engaged. It's an uphill battle, however, and he quickly gets discouraged. The need for self-protection soon reasserts itself. When Jay does make energetic and concerted efforts to give Paula what he thinks she wants—for example, his taking her on a picnic—these efforts typically backfire, because his lack of enthusiasm shines through.

Pursuers and distancers are generally seen as wholeheartedly behind what they are doing. What now becomes apparent is that, instead, both are devoted to suppressing the very behavior for which they are being condemned:

- Paula, who is worried about being too pushy, is

> spending most of her time trying not to pursue, though sporadically bursting forth with impulsive and intense episodes of pursuit.
>
> - Jay, who is concerned about being too detached, is continuously, though unsuccessfully, trying to suppress his tendency to withdraw.

Were Paula and Jay to know how hard they were trying to change, they'd have greater sympathy for themselves and for each other.

> FACT 4: People in a pursuer-distancer conflict don't appreciate how both of them are stuck.

Pursuers and distancers often feel that it would be easy for their partners to change. Pursuers don't see why it would be so difficult for their partners to be a little more forthcoming and affectionate. Distancers don't see why it would be so difficult for their partners to be a little less dependent and demanding.

People in a pursuer-distancer conflict fail to realize that their partners are as stuck as they are and that they themselves are even more stuck than they think they are.

Paula and Jay are each faced with unworkable alternatives. Paula can pursue or try not to pursue. Jay can withdraw or try not to withdraw. As we can see, neither alternative works out well for either partner.

Paula and Jay will be at an advantage if they realize that both are caught in difficult dilemmas and they are not simply the selfish, unreasonable, uncompromising, insensitive, mean-spirited, controlling, unfeeling, or self-destructive people they think they are. The recognition that they are stuck in something together may enable them to increase their sense of sympathy for their shared situation.

Partners are in a good position, or at least in a better position, when they jointly appreciate how bad their position is.

Since Paula and Jay don't realize that they are stuck (they think they could change if they really wanted to) they conclude that:

- They must unconsciously want the relationship to fail

- Perhaps they purposefully chose a partner who would
  mistreat them the way they were mistreated in childhood

These accusing and self-accusing speculations, since they suggest that
Paula and Jay secretly want and unconsciously plan the unpleasant
things that happen to them, are expressions of the you-must-have-
wanted-it-that-way style of thinking.

Paula and Jay come to these conclusions because they have no
other way to understand why Paula doesn't simply stop pursuing
and Jay doesn't simply stop withdrawing. They are thus in need of
important information. They need to realize that:

- They can't simply stop pursuing and withdrawing. They
  are stuck (Fact 2).
- They are trying to stop, which is causing much of the
  problem (Facts 3 and 4).
- It is understandable that the pursuer is pursuing and the
  distancer is withdrawing (Fact 5).

FACT 5: The pursuer has reason to pursue, and the distancer
has reason to withdraw.

Since Paula reacts to withdrawal with demandingness, and since Jay
reacts to demandingness with withdrawal:

- Paula actually is being abandoned. She has reason to
  pursue.
- And Jay actually is being pressured. He has reason to
  withdraw.

Given the situation with which Paula is dealing, it makes sense that
she would pursue. What else can a person do who is shut out by
the person with whom it is most important to be able to talk and
abandoned by the individual whom he or she most counts on to be
there?

Given the impossible situation in which Jay finds himself, it makes
sense that he might want to withdraw. He is in an untenable position of working hard to give something (affection) that can only

be given spontaneously (that is, by not working at it) and trying to generate affection toward a person who, since she is angry at him, is not expressing much affection toward *him*.

FACT **6:** Both partners have important points to make that they are having difficulty getting across.

There is an important grain of truth in both partners' positions. A good example of this is the typical argument pursuers and distancers have about talking:

- The pursuer presses for more talking. Paula resents the way Jay leaves the room in the middle of their fights. She sees him as never staying around to talk anything through.
- The distancer thinks that the pursuer talks everything into the ground. Jay says, "Talking only makes things worse. Most problems will take care of themselves if only you don't talk about them so much."

Actually, both partners are partly right. Paula is right that there are problems that need to be talked about. And Jay is right that they presently have no way to do so; all their attempts to talk turn into fights that neither of them wants.

Here, as in many other ways, partners in a pursuer-distancer conflict take opposite sides on an issue on which they basically agree. In calmer moments (when they are not fighting) Jay might agree that there are problems that need to be talked about (even though it's not his natural tendency to talk), and Paula might agree that their talks rarely work out.

FACT **7:** The only way to avoid pursuer-distancer conflicts is to be completely non-accusing, which is impossible.

It is almost impossible for pursuers and distancers not to feel accused. The pursuer feels in continuous danger of criticism or self-criticism for pressuring and nagging. The distancer feels in continuous danger of criticism or self-criticism for withdrawing and withholding.

Pursuit and distance are caused by accusations that the partners may not realize they are making. Pursuers become pursuers because they are more likely than their partners to react to tensions, disruptions, disappointments, or disconnections by reaching out and engaging. That's what Paula does. She deals with a feeling of disconnection from Jay by trying to engage him:

PAULA: You seem quiet tonight.

This looks at first like a reasonable thing to say. First of all, it's true; Jay has been more than usually quiet. Second, it's the kind of observation that partners make all the time to each other without thinking. Third, it seems useful for someone to point out what's going on in the relationship.

But there is a hidden criticism in this statement. "You seem quiet" implies "you shouldn't be quiet." Jay, sensing the criticism, defends himself by criticizing back:

JAY: I'm just tired. Anyway, I don't see why we have to spend every night talking.

Paula and Jay, who may have been having identical desires for intimacy just a moment before, are now polarized. That's what accusing can do. Whatever wish Jay might have had for closer contact has been superseded by the more pressing need to defend himself. Paula is stuck defending why it's important to talk, and Jay is stuck defending why it's important not to have to talk.

It doesn't take much to get a pursuer-distancer interaction going. And once it starts, it can escalate quickly. Since Paula feels she hasn't gotten her point across, she intensifies her charge:

PAULA: Well, it's not just tonight that you haven't talked to me. It's been every night this week, four nights in a row.

And then Jay really feels criticized.

JAY: So, what's the big deal? I've been tired all week. And besides, I have so been talking. Maybe you're just not hearing me.

Now Paula really feels she hasn't gotten her point across. And, as people do at such times, she exaggerates:

PAULA: You call saying "Pass the salt" and "Where's the mail?" talking? Cause that's been just about the extent of it.

To avoid this demoralizing exchange, Paula would have had to begin with something non-accusing such as:

PAULA: I don't know, Jay—maybe it's because our schedules are so crazy right now—but we haven't had much time together, and I really miss it.

Paula is unlikely to say this. She thinks the problem is Jay and not their schedules. But if she were to say this—if she were to talk about the distance between them in this non-accusing way—Jay wouldn't feel the need to defend himself. He'd be able to admit his contribution to the problem:

JAY: Yes, I've been really worried about school this week, and I've been so busy I never even got a chance to tell you about it.

Jay would be able and even eager to talk if he didn't feel criticized. If he and Paula were to have this exchange, they would realize that each missed feeling close. And since they would be saying what was on their minds, they would be reestablishing the sense of closeness.

But, as I said, Paula isn't going to bring up the issue in this way. She is angry at Jay, and the anger is going to show through. Anger is a practically unavoidable part of pursuit and distance. The pursuer inevitably expresses anger toward the distancer for not coming through, and the distancer typically responds with anger of his or her own.

Partners are in a better position to work out their pursuer-distancer conflicts if they realize that:

- Between the two, one is always more likely than the other to deal with uncertainty or tension by engaging.
- This engaging almost always develops an accusing quality

that leads the other to defend, disengage, and withdraw.

It's easier to deal with this pattern of engaging and defending/withdrawing if you see it as inescapable rather than as a sign that there is something basically and uniquely wrong with you, your partner, or the relationship.

> **FACT 8:** Pursuers are in danger of losing whatever wish they might have had for separation, and distancers may lose whatever wish they might have had for intimacy.

A major point in the story of Paula and Jay is how their relationship deprived them of certain wishes and abilities that they had early in the relationship:

- Originally, Jay had at least some desire to talk to, spend time with, be affectionate with, and have sex with Paula. But the more Jay felt criticized for not wanting to do these things enough, the less he found himself wanting to do them. He became "withdrawn" and "afraid of intimacy."
- Originally, Paula liked to do some things on her own. But the more rejected she felt by Jay, the less she found herself wanting to do things on her own. She became more "dependent" and "demanding."

It is important to see the loss of such wishes and abilities as a consequence of what happens in the relationship and not just the result of the partners' personalities.

> **FACT 9:** The distancer is as deprived as the pursuer.

It is easy to see that Paula is deprived. She misses the warmth, affection, tenderness, caring, confiding, and companionship that people seek in relationships and that she originally entered the relationship with Jay to obtain. At times she feels trapped in a loveless marriage.

When Jay comes home in the evening, he greets their dog more enthusiastically than he does her. Anyone would sympathize with Paula for taking second place to a poodle.

What Paula, Jay, and nearly everyone fail to see, however, is that Jay is as deprived as is Paula. Whereas Paula is deprived of having a husband who looks forward to seeing her in the evening, Jay is deprived of being a husband who looks forward to seeing his wife in the evening.

- It's a lot more fun to look forward to seeing your wife than it is to come home to someone you would rather avoid.
- And it's a lot more satisfying to be in a relationship in which you feel warmth, affection, tenderness, caring, companionship, and sexual interest than it is to be in one in which you look forward to a beer with the guys.

Jay is trapped in the same loveless relationship as Paula is. His hopes for the marriage have been similarly dashed. He just doesn't know it. Jay is so focused on what Paula says she is missing and on defending himself against her criticisms that he fails to notice what *he* is missing.

> **FACT 10:** Partners are unable at times to keep from rubbing each other the wrong way.

Even if Paula and Jay did realize that their reactions were justifiable, they might still blame themselves for staying in a relationship that has such glaring problems. They need to realize that all relationships have glaring problems. Areas of vulnerability always exist somewhere in a relationship and, with time, these areas inevitably come into increasing prominence.

The issues and problems that partners can handle well become taken for granted. The ones they can't—the sticking points in the relationship—move into the foreground. Soon it is only these sticking points that the partners are aware of.

Paula and Jay are resources to each other in many ways. When Paula feels threatened, upset, or discouraged, she can usually count on Jay to come to her assistance. When she has problems with friends, family, or work, she can usually rely on Jay's sympathy, concern, and help. And Jay can count on Paula for the same things.

There are always circumstances, however, in which partners are unable to be resources for each other. This happens when each person's way of responding to his or her buttons being pushed pushes the buttons of the other.

- Paula's buttons are pushed when she feels abandoned; she deals with feeling abandoned by pressuring.
- Jay's buttons are pushed when he feels pressured; he deals with feeling pressured by abandoning.

There are times and places in every relationship in which partners can't help rubbing one another the wrong way. If partners realize that there are always such weak points somewhere in the relationship, they may be able to commiserate with one another about them rather than conclude that something is specially and fatally wrong with themselves or the relationship.

People need to know that pursuit and distance cause partners to appear even more incompatible than they actually are. Partners caught in a pursuer-distancer conflict can easily feel that they have completely different wishes, interests, and concerns—so much so, in fact, that they are convinced they are from different planets. This is how Paula and Jay felt in the weeks before their wedding.

- As their wedding day approached, Jay felt increasingly less desire to see Paula. When he did visit, he had little to say, spent most of the time watching TV, and found some reason to leave early.
- Paula, in contrast, felt increasingly more desire to see Jay.

The irony—and it would have helped a great deal if Paula and Jay had known this—is that they were dealing with a shared concern. Both had fears about getting married. While Jay dealt with his by withdrawing and spending more time by himself, Paula dealt with hers by pursuing Jay. She sought to reassure herself about his love for her, her love for him, their general compatibility, and the wisdom of their decision to marry by trying to have continuous contact; long intimate talks; and lots of flowers, gifts, and sex.

The problem was self-escalating. The more Jay withdrew, the more Paula needed reassuring contact. The more she sought contact, the more he needed to withdraw.

The problem was so serious they almost called off the wedding. They were on the verge of doing so, when they went to see a therapist who showed them that they were both feeling the same thing (nervousness about getting married) but were expressing it in different ways.

Paula and Jay's realization that they were worried about the same thing made them feel less at odds with each other, and they began to think that maybe they came from the same planet after all (although maybe from different continents).

Pursuers have a hard time understanding how their distancer partners can possibly act and feel the way they do. They can't see why it should be so difficult for their partners to talk a little more and to be a little more attentive, engaged, and affectionate. Pursuers find it so easy to do these things that they can't see how it could possibly be hard for anyone else.

Similarly, distancers have a hard time understanding how their pursuer partners can possibly need so much affection and why they can't tolerate more independence in their lives. And they can't understand how hugging and talking can mean so much to their partners, since such things mean so little to them (or at least so they think).

The first step in understanding how your pursuer or distancer partner can possibly act and feel the way he or she does is to appreciate that it's going to be hard to understand it.

One way to get a sense of how your partner feels is to recall periods (either in your previous relationships or earlier in your present relationship) in which you were in your partner's position.

When they first met, Jay, who was totally infatuated with Paula, wanted to spend all his time with her. Paula, who was not as infatuated with Jay, felt a little smothered by him. During this period, Jay was the pursuer, and Paula was the distancer. By recalling this early stage in their relationship, Paula can get a feeling for Jay's experience now, and Jay can get a feeling for Paula's.

In some relationships—although not in Paula and Jay's—the pursuer in one aspect of the relationship is the distancer in another. That's the case with Lisa and Bill. Although Lisa is the pursuer, and Bill is the distancer in most areas of the relationship, they switch roles when it comes to sex. Bill regularly approaches Lisa for sex, and she regularly puts him off. Lisa and Bill can use their experiences in their sexual relationship to appreciate what the other feels in the other parts of their relationship.

> **FACT 11:** Pursuit and distance may depend, in part, on situational factors such as who is busier.

Two years have passed. Jay has graduated from school, and Paula has just given birth to a son. Suddenly, Paula is the busier one; she has to devote almost all her time and energy to the baby. Jay tries to help, but since Paula is breastfeeding, she is the main caretaker. Jay feels left out and neglected. Now he is the pursuer and Paula the distancer.

A few years later, with their son in daycare, Paula is ready to spend more time with Jay. By now, however, Jay has become deeply involved in his work, partly because Paula had been so deeply involved with their son. So when Paula reaches out, he is no longer available. Again, the situations changes; Paula is once more the pursuer and Jay the distancer.

Pursuit and distance are to some degree the result of such situational factors and are not just a consequence of the partners' personalities.

But Can Knowing These Things Really Help?

SKEPTIC: I don't see how these ideas you're talking about are really going to help. They seem so intellectual.

WILE: They can help because it's the old ideas—the thinking that Paula, Jay, and the rest of us ordinarily use—that cause the problem. The solution is intellectual because the problem is intellectual. There wouldn't even be a pursuer-distancer problem if people didn't already have the accusing ways of thinking in place and ready to fire.

Paula and Jay's problem isn't that Jay sneaks into the bedroom to study and that Paula hangs around waiting for him. The problem is that they think that something is wrong with them for having this problem. They don't realize that nearly everyone has at least a mild version of it. They think that they should try harder to change, and they don't realize that it's their attempts to change that cause much of the problem.

Imagine what it would be like if Paula and Jay were to know the eleven facts I just described. Instead of seeing themselves as:

- Defective people in a defective relationship,
- Who are unwilling to change, and
- Who may even want their relationship to fail,

they would now see themselves as:

- Trying to change,
- Which, ironically is causing much of the problem, and as
- Struggling with a universal couple problem,
- In which it is impossible for them and their partner not to feel accused (and not to be accusing), and as
- Caught in a trap in which each partner's efforts to make things better tend to make them worse.

In the old way of thinking, there is no way for them to talk usefully with each other about the problem. They feel there is nothing to talk about. They think that they should simply stop being so selfish, unreasonable, and self-destructive.

In the new way of thinking, there is a way for them to talk usefully with one another about the problem, although it's still not easy to do so.

Let's return to when Jay went back to school. But let's say now that Paul and Jay have this new way of thinking. As before, Jay comes home with his arms full of books. Paula's heart sinks since she wants to talk to him, but she knows that he won't want to do anything until he finishes studying. Right away Paula is in a difficult spot. All that she can think to do are things that in the past embroiled her in pursuit and distance. She can:

1. Throw caution to the winds and try to talk to Jay anyway (But this would be pursuing.)
2. Wait until he finishes studying and try to talk to him then (But this would be trying not to pursue, which is part of the pursuit-and-distance pattern.)
3. Decide not to rely on Jay and force herself to do something on her own, for example, see a movie (But this would be trying to prove her independence, which also is part of the pursuit-and-distance pattern.)

When I say that Paula has mastered the facts of pursuit and distance, I don't mean that she wouldn't do any of these three things. In fact, she might do all of them. But—and here's the important point—she'd do them in a new way: she'd know what she was doing (or at least be able to figure it out later) and be able to talk about it with Jay.

PAULA: (*after coming home from the movie*) Well, I did it again! It all started when I insisted on talking to you even though I knew that your mind was on your studies. I don't know why I did it … Well, I guess I do. There were so many things I wanted to tell you. I guess my excitement got the better of me.

Paula is no longer pursuing. Instead, she is talking *about* her pursuing. And that makes a difference. Since Jay doesn't feel pursued, he feels less need to withdraw. Instead of pressing Jay to change his behavior, Paula is drawing him into her experience. She is talking in a self-revealing way that makes Jay feel like doing the same.

JAY: Yes, and I pretended to listen. I don't know why *I* keep doing *that*. You're too smart to be fooled by it.

In making this statement, Jay is no longer withdrawing. Instead, he is talking *about* his withdrawing. And although he is saying things that you'd think might upset Paula, she's *not* that upset. That's because Jay is finally engaged with her, even if it's to discuss how he's been *dis*engaged.

PAULA: Yes, and to prove I don't need you, I went to the movies. I bet you weren't fooled by that little ploy for very long.

Paula and Jay are each admitting things in response to the other doing the same. They are engaged in a collaborative exchange, rather than their usual pursuer-distancer exchange.

JAY: I hope it wasn't that new science fiction film. I'd like to see that with you.

PAULA: You would?

Paula is surprised. Jay hasn't recently expressed interest in doing things with her. Jay is surprised, also. He isn't used to wanting to do things with her. The friendliness of the exchange has produced this shift in his feelings.

Were Paula and Jay able to talk in this way, they would be creating a platform from which to confide in each other about this problem they are having with each other. They would be creating a moment of intimacy in the act of talking about their alienation. Knowing the facts about pursuit and distance could help create such a platform.

So a good way for partners to handle pursuit and distance is to be able to talk about it afterward. When they have mastered that, they might then go to the next step and try to have such conversations beforehand. Here's an idealized example of how Paula and Jay could have done this:

PAULA: I really want to talk right now, but I'm trying to resist the urge because I know that you need to study.

Instead of talking to Jay (or trying not to talk), Paula is telling him about her *wish* to talk.

JAY: Yes, I do, and especially tonight. I'm worried about math.

Instead of skirting around the problem, which is what Paula and Jay usually do, they are talking directly. Jay gets to explain that he really needs to study and Paula gets to hear what's on his mind.

PAULA: Oh? What's happening there?

JAY: I totally blew the midterm. I'm worried I'm going to fail.

Hearing Jay express his concerns makes Paula feel more included in his life. As a result, she feels more content to do things on her own. In fact, she becomes so engrossed reading movie reviews on the Internet that Jay has to tear her away when, after closing his math books, he suggests they go for a pizza.

This brief interchange means a lot to Jay, also. It's important to him to be able to tell Paula his worries about school. It makes him feel closer to her. That's why he wants to take her out for a pizza.

To the extent that partners learn to accept pursuit and distance as a commonplace event rather than as something awful and unacceptable, they'd be better able to think about, talk about, and deal with this occupational hazard of being a couple.

Chapter 17
Bypassing and Nonbypassing

Partners need a way to deal with the common situation in which one gets caught up in a fantasy while the other is left behind in reality. When Polly thinks of having a party, she thinks of:

- The chance to experiment with exotic new recipes
- Sparkling conversation
- Everyone having a great time
- The chance to invite friends whom she hasn't seen for months
- The chance, finally, to use the new serving platter she got last Christmas
- The chance to introduce her neighborhood friends to her work buddies—she's sure they'll really get along
- The chance to introduce her best friend, Maggie to the interesting new single man at work—she's sure they'll really hit it off
- Everyone noticing what a great decorating job she and Mike did on their living room

And thinking about a party this way—as something wonderful—Polly really wants to have one. She suggests the idea to Mike. When Mike thinks of a party, however, he thinks of:

- The expense
- Cleaning up the mess afterward
- People feeling left out and resentful because they weren't invited

- His neighborhood friends not getting along with his work buddies
- People noticing what a lousy job he did wallpapering the bathroom
- Forgetting people's names when he tries to introduce them
- Strained conversation; no one quite knowing what to say
- Food spills leaving stains that won't come out on the rug
- People leaving early because they're bored
- People having such a good time that they stay till six in the morning
- Eating leftovers for a week

And thinking about it this way, Mike doesn't want to have a party.

MIKE: A party's the last thing we need right now. We just finished redecorating.

POLLY: That's exactly why we do need it: to celebrate and to show what a great job we did.

MIKE: Yes, but after all that work, I need a rest.

POLLY: Rest later. After all that work, we should show it off while it's all sparkly and fresh.

MIKE: You're forgetting all the effort it will take: the shopping, the invitations.

POLLY: What effort? It'll be fun.

MIKE: And the cleaning? Will the cleaning be fun? And the expense? Did you see our credit card bills this month?

POLLY: Oh pooh! Do you always have to be such a spoilsport?

MIKE: No way. I'm just being realistic. Wasn't it *you* who said "Remind me never to throw another party?" Okay, I'm reminding you.

POLLY: Oh, I didn't really mean it. I was just frustrated that time. You remember. We couldn't find the table leaf, we forgot the charcoal, and I couldn't get the turkey into the oven. But I got over it, and we had a blast.

As this exchange demonstrates, there are at least two ways to think about a party:

- You can go into *fantasy overdrive.* You can be like Polly and get caught up in a dream about how wonderful it will be.
- Or you can go into *reverse.* You can be like Mike and think of all the problems.

What's interesting is that Mike wouldn't inevitably have been against a party. He might even have gotten into the spirit of it. For this to have happened, however, he would have needed Polly to appreciate how he felt, as in this exchange:

POLLY: Yeah, I see your point. A party is a lot of work. I keep forgetting how much work it is—the invitations, the cleanup, *everything* you said. I know it's ridiculous to want it so much. It's just that the idea of it really turns me on.

Hearing this—having Polly acknowledge the truth in what he is saying—Mike might now begin to feel more like joining the fantasy.

MIKE: Well, what the hell. Another two hundred dollars isn't going to sink us. And maybe it would be fun to show off a little.

Or the opposite might occur. Seeing that Mike has come around— not only has he agreed to the party, but he even thinks it's a good idea—Polly might now begin to realize that she had been over glamorizing it. The fact that they are no longer arguing (she no longer feels the need to defend herself) makes it possible for Polly to consider what Mike has said:

POLLY: You know, now I'm not sure. All that time, money, and effort, and truthfully, I'm always a little disappointed. Sometimes more than a little.

In reacting to an idea, one partner may go on fantasy overdrive, and the other may go into reverse. How the partners talk about these different ways of reacting can intensify or reduce their conflict about it.

Three Instances of Fantasy Overdrive

Most people would want to be like Polly. It's more fun to have a positive attitude than a negative one. And it's more fun to deal with a problem by going into fantasy overdrive (becoming enthusiastic) than it is to withdraw, fight, or become depressed, which is what many people do.

But let's go back earlier in the day to see what led up to this conversation. Polly was getting ready to go out and do some weeding when she and Mike had the following exchange:

POLLY: How come you don't help in the yard anymore?

MIKE: Do you think I want to go out and get dirty and sweaty just to get nagged? Because that's what happens. You don't like the way I prune.

POLLY: Oh, come on. I've never criticized your pruning.

MIKE: Oh yeah? What about last fall with the roses?

POLLY: I was just giving you a few pointers.

MIKE: Pointers or orders? Anyway, since when are *you* the expert? I've got my own way of pruning.

POLLY: Hacking at my rose bush with a pair of clippers is hardly a "way of pruning."

MIKE: You see? You *don't* like the way I prune

POLLY: Well, I didn't like your hacking my roses.

MIKE: Hacking? You call what I do hacking? And what do you mean *your* roses? It was my idea to plant them, so it ought to be up to me how to take care of them.

POLLY: Well, in that case, they have all my sympathy. They'll need it.

MIKE: And you have all mine because you're not going to get me out there again.

POLLY: At least the roses will be safe.

When Polly comes in from the yard, she and Mike don't speak for an hour. And when they finally do talk, they are hesitant and tense with each other. They don't want to start another fight.

So that was the atmosphere in which Polly went into fantasy over-drive and suggested that they throw a party. She ignored the tension between them and pretended that they were getting along so well that they might even want to collaborate on a big event.

Although Polly was discouraged when Mike rejected the idea, a little later she went into fantasy overdrive again. She approached Mike with a handful of travel brochures. Her hope—although she was not thinking of it in this way at the time—was to patch things up by musing about fabulous vacations they might take together.

While Polly was thinking of having a great time getting away with Mike, doing exciting things, really getting along, and making love in quaint and exotic places, Mike was thinking of jetlag, boring guided tours, getting on one another's nerves, arguing about what to see, and making love in uncomfortable and unfamiliar beds.

Sensing that Mike was not sharing her enthusiasm about a vacation either, Polly gathered up her brochures and put them away.

A few hours later, Polly went into the bedroom where Mike was reading and started caressing him. Her hope—although she was not thinking of it in this way at the time—was to patch things up through sex. She was thinking how handsome he was and how sexually giving they could be to one another.

And, again, Mike went into reverse. "What makes her think I'd be interested in sex? he said to himself. First she criticizes me, then she doesn't talk to me, then we quarrel about having a party and going on a trip."

"In response to touch," Bernard Apfelbaum writes, "there is one kind of person for whom all worries and grudges are suddenly forgotten; for another kind of person worries and grudges are just as suddenly remembered."

Apfelbaum refers to the first type of person as a "bypasser" and the second as a "nonbypasser."

- Bypassers can enjoy sex despite what is going on in the relationship. They are somehow able to overlook the fact that, for instance, they haven't exchanged a civil word with their partners all day.
- Nonbypassers can't enjoy sex because they can't overlook what's going on in the relationship. The thought of physical intimacy with their partners just makes them more aware of the lack of emotional intimacy.

The ideas of bypassing and nonbypassing can be applied not only to sex, but to any activity.

Bypasser-Nonbypasser Conflicts

Bypassing and nonbypassing are mutually incompatible ways of dealing with problems.

- The bypasser's way to solve a problem is to stop talking about it, because that just makes it worse, and to trip off into fantasy.
- The nonbypasser can't trip off into fantasy. In order to solve a problem, he or she has to try to talk about it, even though talking about it might make things worse.

So when Polly, the bypasser, deals with the problem by approaching Mike for sex (she has the fantasy of their having great sex to compensate for the problems of the day), Mike, the nonbypasser, deals with it by trying to talk.

MIKE: What makes you think I'd be interested in sex? We've been fighting all day. And when we weren't fighting, we weren't talking. And then, when we did begin to talk, you started

pressuring me about having a party and going on a trip. And
I'm still smarting over what you said about my pruning.

And having said all that, Mike now feels a little better and a little more
like having sex. The chance to state feelings and make complaints
can have a powerful affection-reviving and love-reviving effect.

But while Mike now feels more like having sex, Polly now feels
less like having it. It's hard for Polly to think of how handsome Mike
is and how sexually giving they could be to one another when he's
making these complaints.

POLLY: Why did you have to bring all that up and ruin the mood? I
don't even feel like sex anymore.

So here's the problem of bypasser-nonbypasser conflicts: what each
partner needs to improve the mood ruins the mood for the other.
Nonbypassers maintain their feeling of love by talking about their
problems. Bypassers maintain their feeling of love by *not* talking
about their problems. In a bypasser-nonbypasser conflict, each partner's way of staying in love interferes with the other's way of doing
so.

Bypassers such as Polly can't understand why their nonbypassing
partners can't "relax a little," "take things as they come," "put aside
their problems," and "stop having to talk about everything." They
don't see why it would cost their partners so much to do the very
little they require to keep the fantasy of intimacy going: an "I love
you" once in a while, a hug, a card, or a willingness to have sex or
muse about romantic vacations. They are forced to conclude that
their partners must *want* to frustrate them.

Nonbypassers such as Mike can't understand how their bypassing
partners can possibly *want* to have sex or muse about romantic vacations given the problems between them. They don't see why it would
cost their partners so much to do the very little they require: to talk
about their problems. Getting things off their chests is so relieving
to them that they can't understand why their partners don't experience the same relief.

Although Polly is generally the bypasser and Mike is generally the nonbypasser, at times they reverse roles. Mike loves fishing, and Polly hates it. If, among the vacation plans Polly had suggested to Mike, she had included fly casting, Mike would have immediately gone into fantasy overdrive. He'd have forgotten about the disagreeableness of the day, and, appreciating Polly's willingness to consider such a trip, he'd begin thinking how wonderful it would be—just the two of them alone on the river with all that trout. Polly would never suggest fly casting, of course, since just the thought of fishing makes her want to yawn.

So what do you do if you're trying to deal with a particular problem by bypassing while your partner is trying to do so by nonbypassing? First, you'll need to appreciate that you and your partner are adopting contrasting strategies in dealing with a difficult problem:

- The bypasser, having given up on the possibility of dealing with the problem by talking about it, shifts into fantasy overdrive.
- The nonbypasser, having given up on the possibility of dealing with the problem by shifting into fantasy overdrive, tries to talk about it.

And now it's easy to see how bypassing and nonbypassing relate to pursuit and distance, the other major pattern talked about in this section of the book:

- Pursuit and distance refer to readiness to engage: the pursuer engages, and the distancer doesn't.
- Bypassing and nonbypassing refer to what the pursuer is trying to engage the partner in. The bypasser tries to engage the partner in a fantasy. The nonbypasser tries to engage the partner in talking.

So, depending on who is trying to engage whom in what, either the bypasser or the nonbypasser can be the pursuer.

Recognizing bypassing and nonbypassing as understandable, although alternative, strategies for dealing with difficult problems may enable partners to feel less accusing toward themselves and each other for adopting them.

Polly and Mike could even have talked about their alternative strategies, although since it is talking, it's something that the nonbypasser (Mike) is more likely to want to do:

MIKE: I don't like your not wanting to talk about our problems, but I must admit that you're right that talking can make things worse. In fact, in some ways I wish I could do what you do and forget our problems and just imagine feeling good about one another.

POLLY: I don't like your not wanting to have sex (or plan a party or muse about vacations), but it is true that we haven't said a civil word to one another all day. And the fact that *I'm* caught up in a fantasy about sex (or about a party or about romantic vacations) doesn't mean that *you* have to be.

It's clear that Polly and Mike would have an easier time dealing with the situation if they were to think and talk about it in this non-accusing way.

Part VII

COMPROMISING AND FANTASIZING

Chapter 18
Discovering the Hidden Compromises

Everyone hopes that relationships are based on love. While the honeymoon feeling doesn't last, it is thought that over time a deeper less intense love develops. And this deeper love lasts until death do us part. And the rough edges mellow; the characteristics of our partner that used to be so annoying are now endearing to us. And we find ourselves wanting to please our partner and do things with and for our partner. And we find ourselves wanting to remain faithful. We're so in love that we don't even think about having affairs.

But, back in the real world, everyone is afraid that relationships are based, instead, on obligation. Being in a relationship, we believe, is having to give when you want to receive. It's being reassuring when you feel like ignoring. It's being faithful when you want to give into temptation. It's work. It's going to a ballgame when you want to go to a flower show. It's going to a flower show when you want to go to a ballgame. In short, it's doing things you don't want to do in order to make the other person happy.

Many people seem resigned to the duty view and are skeptical about the love view. We tell ourselves to avoid romantic fantasies and unrealistic expectations and to recognize that a relationship requires compromise, hard work, commitment, and sacrifice: "You think that a relationship is glamour, romance, and sex. It's not. It's diapers, washing the floor, and 'Sorry, I've got a headache tonight'."

In the following chapter, I discuss the love view. I show that romantic fantasies create problems, but so does trying not to have them.

In this chapter, I discuss the duty view. I show that failing to make compromises can cause problems, but so can making them. I show in particular:

1. People make compromises so quickly and so automatically that they are often unaware of doing so.
2. The boredom and devitalization that can creep into a couple's relationship are unrecognized consequences of the continuous flow of compromises and accommodations.
3. What appears to be a partner's unwillingness to compromise may actually be reactions to unrecognized compromises that he or she is already making.
4. Compromises are hidden gambles. People gamble that they will be able to make compromises without becoming too resentful. Sometimes the gamble pays off, and sometimes it doesn't.
5. Beneath the emphasis placed on the automatic need to compromise is the belief that people are basically selfish; they have to be weaned from the childish joys of always getting their way.

Not compromising can ruin relationships. But so can compromising.

Already Existing Hidden Compromises

One danger with the common view that partners should always try harder to make compromises is that problems often arise from the hidden ways in which they are already compromising. Here is an example:

Joyce and Claire are a couple who have lived together for five years. They are in their early thirties. Joyce seems unreasonable and uncompromising because she's unresponsive to Claire's needs for affection. When Claire comes into the kitchen for a hug, Joyce turns away. When Claire persists, Joyce becomes impatient:

JOYCE: Can't you see I'm stirring the soup?

CLAIRE: These days you're always stirring the soup, about to walk the dog, or whatever.

What might seem like unresponsiveness to Claire's needs is a consequence of Joyce's dedication to them. Claire's presence in the kitchen
is a nuisance because Joyce is already so busy trying to fulfill Claire's
needs, or at least what she thinks are Claire's needs. Claire has never
been much of a cook, so one of the special things that Joyce does for
her is to prepare all of the meals. And she does so even though she
goes to school and has a full-time job. For Joyce, Claire's coming into
the kitchen for a hug is simply another demand on her time.

Both partners feel that Joyce is being cold and selfish in failing to
give Claire a hug when she wants one. They think that people have
to extend themselves a little if a relationship is to work out.

An alternative view is that people may appear selfish and uncompromising because of the hidden ways in which they are already
compromising. Joyce comes to Claire later that evening and says:

JOYCE: Hey, I feel bad about pushing you away earlier.

What makes this the beginning of a conversation rather than an
argument is that Joyce isn't criticizing Claire's behavior. Instead, she
is criticizing her own, which leads Claire to criticize *her* own.

CLAIRE: Yeah, well, my timing was off. You had your hands full right
then.

By talking about their own contributions to the fight and not their
partner's, Joyce and Claire are keeping the discussion from turning
back into the fight.

JOYCE: I was working on that shrimp curry you love. But if I'm
going to push you away like that, it defeats the whole
purpose.

CLAIRE: (*hesitantly*) Dare we consider the possibility of my fixing
dinner sometimes?

JOYCE: But you work hard at the hospital. You deserve to come
home to a good meal.

CLAIRE: Well, maybe I deserve it, but what I'd like is to see you relaxing in the living room rather than working as my unpaid personal chef.

Claire is trying to help Joyce stop compromising—to become less concerned with what she thinks are Claire's needs. If Joyce were to stop compromising, she might be able to give Claire what she really wants. Claire would rather have a hug from a relaxed partner than a big meal from a tense one.

A Chain of Compromises

People make compromises so quickly and so automatically that they are often unaware of doing so. Martha and James are a married couple in their mid-thirties. Martha goes to a local college and works part time as a nurse. James is a general contractor.

On the way home from her job one day, Martha finds herself daydreaming about a vacation in Italy. Since she knows that James is worried about money and would immediately veto such a trip, she quickly dismisses the idea and, instead, thinks of getting tickets to an Italian opera. No, she thinks, he doesn't like opera, so she dismisses this idea too and, instead, imagines them having dinner at an Italian restaurant. Oh, but it's Wednesday; since she knows that James doesn't like to eat out in the middle of the week, she finally decides to order a pizza.

Martha hasn't even talked to James yet, and she's already made three compromises.

When James says that he doesn't feel like a pizza, Martha throws a tantrum and then sulks. James can't figure out what's gotten into her. And Martha doesn't know what's gotten into her either. Compromises are made so quickly and so automatically that people often forget they've made them. James (and Martha too) now see her as a selfish, unreasonable, and uncompromising person who gets upset if she doesn't immediately get what she wants.

What James doesn't know, and what Martha herself has forgotten, is that she isn't getting *anything* she wants. She started out with a dream of Italy, but was willing to make do with the delivery of a pizza. And James won't even go along with that.

Martha's tantrum, which both of them attribute to her demanding, uncompromising attitude, is the result of compromises she has made with James that he knows nothing about. He's unaware of all that was riding on the pizza.

Even so, James's saying no to pizza is a surprise. He usually looks for any opportunity to satisfy his pizza craving. In substituting his favorite food for a trip to Italy, Martha is only asking for something that she has every reason to believe James would love.

James's saying no to pizza turns out to be a consequence of unspoken compromises of his own. Since he is worried about money, he has been wanting to suggest that Martha quit school and get a full-time job. He hasn't suggested this, however, since he knows how important school is to her. He thinks it's small-minded of him to begrudge her an education, and he doesn't want to be seen as a man who stands in his wife's way. So, instead, he's considered making the more modest request of asking her to cut down on her expenses. But he doesn't do this either. In the past when he's asked Martha to spend less, she has felt falsely accused of being a spend-thrift and has become upset. So, instead, James decides on the still more modest plan of cutting down on luxuries such as restaurants, movies, and sending out for pizza. He doesn't tell Martha about any of this, however, since he thinks she won't like hearing it; she already thinks he's too concerned about money.

Martha and James need a conversation in which they sort out what has happened. Here is an idealized picture of how such a conversation might go:

MARTHA: I don't even like pizza that much—you're the pizza-lover around here—so I don't understand why I got so upset.

Since Martha isn't blaming James, he doesn't have to defend himself:

JAMES: Yes, it killed me to say no. But counting the tip and the tax, do you know how much it would have come to?

Now that the issue of money has come up, things could get sticky. James could say something like, "You always spend too much" or "It's hard making ends meet when you don't bring in your share," which would immediately transform the conversation into an argument.

But, instead, James says:

JAMES: I'm worrying about money again, and I thought it might help if we cut out all the extras right now. Alas, little did I know that the first thing to go would be my beloved pie.

MARTHA: Well, maybe you'll feel better when you hear how much I saved us today. I started out daydreaming about two weeks in Italy. But I know that's totally out of the question, so I decided to make do with a night at the opera. But opera tickets are so crazy expensive, so I shifted to dinner at *La Strada*. But then I pictured the check after the zabaglione and stopped that fantasy dead in its tracks. Thus, the pizza. You didn't realize all that was riding on a few anchovies.

Hearing how Martha had compromised and how much thought and effort it has taken, James now feels like doing the same.

JAMES: Well, what the hell. Let's get that pizza—or, better yet, maybe *La Strada* has a last-minute cancellation. We can start saving money tomorrow.

The problem, it now becomes clear, is that Martha and James had been deprived of the opportunity to state what they really wanted and to discover what the other really wanted. And they had been deprived of the feeling of goodwill that would enable them to want to do things for their partner and to actually enjoy compromising.

Compromises are Hidden Gambles

People often think that compromising (putting themselves out a little) is easy to do. All it takes, they believe, is a little maturity and the willingness to think of someone besides themselves. It's not going to kill a person to skip tennis and, instead, stay home with the kids so his or her partner can go swimming. And it's not going to hurt a person to go occasionally to the kind of movie the other likes to see. People make accommodations all the time. Compromising is not hard, they think. It's no big deal.

We don't ordinarily think of it this way but compromises are gambles. In compromising, people force themselves to do things that they otherwise wouldn't want to do. If the accommodation or sacrifice turns out to be more difficult and unpleasant than anticipated and to have less of a payoff, the person may rebel and become angry or withdrawn. The gamble is that people will be able to get the benefits of compromising (pleasing the partner and cementing the relationship) without becoming resentful and without withdrawing.

James takes Martha to the restaurant and, a few months later, offers to get tickets to *La Bohème* for her birthday. He thinks he owes it to her, even though he doesn't much care for that kind of music—or the suit, or the tie, or the parking. But Martha makes so many compromises for him. She doesn't particularly like baseball, for example, but she recently suggested that they go to a game when the Red Sox come to town.

But even before the curtain rises, James realizes he has made a mistake. He wonders, "How did I get myself into this? It hasn't even begun and already I want to go home. I've got to get out of here, but I can't think how. Maybe there'll be an earthquake, and the stage will collapse. Bad thought, bad thought. I just wish they'd get it started and get it over with."

James gets through it to the end. On the way home, when Martha criticizes him for driving too fast, he blows up:

JAMES: I've just spent three hours bored to tears in order to give you a treat we can't afford, and all you can say is, "You're driving too fast." Of course I'm driving too fast. I'm trying to get home and take off my tie and get these hysterical arias out of my head.

Martha is immediately sorry they ever went to the opera. She is sorry she was even born. And she's upset with James for being so nasty. She spits out her response:

MARTHA: Well, don't give it a minute more thought. We never have
to go again.

A month later, at the baseball game, Martha realizes that *she* has
made a mistake She let's out a great sigh and thinks, "I can't believe
it's just the second inning. It seems like we've been here for years.
It's clouding up. Maybe it'll rain, and we can go home. I'm hungry.
Where's the guy with the hotdogs? Just my luck if the game goes into
extra innings. I'm really thirsty now."

Martha makes it to the end. On the way home, James says to her:
"You seem quiet. Is something wrong?"

"No. I'm just a little tired," she answers.

This is a classic exchange of partners when they sense that something's amiss but don't quite know what it is or how to talk about
it.

James and Martha's calculated risks didn't work out. James didn't
realize the extent to which he would hate the opera, and Martha
didn't realize the extent to which she would hate the baseball game.
But their gambles could have worked out. Other gambles of a similar
nature had, at times, worked out in the past:

The previous winter, as a special favor to James, Martha agreed to
go skiing with him. The fact that she had such low expectations—she
hadn't the slightest hope that she'd enjoy any part of the trip—
allowed her to relax and kind of enjoy it. James was so pleased that
Martha had come along with him and, in addition, that she seemed
to be in such good spirits about it, that he felt like doing something special for her. He suggested they go dancing, something she
had always loved but had pretty much had to abandon. And just
as Martha had gotten caught up in skiing, James got caught up in
dancing. He found her enthusiasm contagious. And he was touched
by how touched she was at his suggesting it. She was more affectionate than she had been in years, and later that evening they had
the greatest sex ever.

What allows people to force themselves to do things they don't
really want to do and still have it come out all right? Much depends
on how much of a sacrifice it is. Dancing turned out to be much
more pleasant than James had anticipated, and the opera turned out

to be much less pleasant. Skiing turned out to be better than Martha had anticipated, and the ballgame a lot worse.

Chance plays an important role. Whatever chance James had for enjoying the opera—and there was some—was completely destroyed by the fact that his best friend had phoned just before they left and offered him boxing tickets for that very evening. So going to the opera meant he had to give up the fights. Furthermore, traffic crawled, parking was hard to find, and the theater was overheated. To top it all off, Martha wasn't nearly as grateful for his sacrifice as he had expected. The gamble, which James didn't even know he was making, was that all parts of the universe would collude in his favor.

People differ in how they react when their gambles fail and when they realize that they have committed themselves to something they really can't stand:

1. Some immediately un-commit themselves. James, for example, might have announced to Martha that even though the opera hadn't started, he hated it already, and that he would meet her in the bar next door when it was over. Martha was unlikely to be very happy about this. And James himself might have felt bad about letting her down. On the other hand, he would no longer have felt trapped.

2. Some, as James did, force themselves to go through with the activity and express their resentment afterwards. This usually makes both partners regret that they ever came up with the idea.

3. Some, as Martha did, force themselves to go through with the activity and don't express any resentment. The common result is a subtle withdrawal, which in some ways can be even more disturbing to the relationship.

People who know that their efforts to compromise are gambles will be better able to recover from those that don't work out. Here's the idealized conversation that James and Martha might have had at the opera. James would turn to Martha:

JAMES: I know you're not going to like hearing this, but I made a big mistake in coming here. It might have worked if Sam hadn't called with tickets to the fights, if the traffic hadn't been so bad, and if we didn't have to park a million miles away, where the dead walk by night. Who knows if the car's going to be in one piece when we get out? I feel really bad about this. Here I'm trying to do something really great on your birthday, and I'm screwing it up already. And I feel even worse that I'm starting to blame you when it was my idea to do this in the first place.

If Martha were to respond angrily, they might have a whispery fight right there and then. After their fight, however, and depending on whether Martha and James felt they had gotten their points across, interesting and unexpected things might have happened:

- The opportunity to say how much he hated the opera, to describe how everything had gone wrong, and to have his feelings acknowledged may have enabled James to stop hating it. He may have now been content to stay.
- And the chance to express her resentment about James having taken her to the opera and then abandoning her may have enabled Martha to feel at least partly okay about his waiting across the street.

Selfishness

The issue of compromise is important because of its connection with selfishness. Selfishness is one of those terms—dependent and controlling are others—that bring an end to useful thinking. When we use such terms to describe people, it means that we have shifted from thinking to judging. We have stopped trying to understand their behavior and have slipped into reproaching them for it. The sense of reproach is clear when we look at what we mean when we say that people are selfish. We think of them as spoiled, self-centered, narcissistic, interested only in their personal pleasure, unwilling to compromise, unable to imagine how others might feel, and getting too much out of their self-indulgent behavior to be willing to give it up. If we were to look at their plight rather than stand back in judgment of them, we would see that they could more accurately be described as *deprived*. They are deprived of the major source of personal pleasure and the ultimate form of selfishness: having someone whom they feel so close to that they care dearly how he or she feels.

The issue of "selfishness" is a complex one that requires a full-scale debate.

- Representing the proposition that people are basically selfish and have to learn to compromise, we have Lucy, Judy's upstairs neighbor, who, as you may remember, uses the character-flaws explanation. She's the natural person to represent the position that people are basically selfish, since selfishness is a major character flaw that looms large in her vocabulary.
- Representing the position that people who seem selfish are actually deprived is Joe, one of the passengers in Tom's car, who, as you may remember, uses the unrecognized-feelings explanation. He insists that behavior that we generally see as childish, primitive, and selfish can be tracked back to an understandable adult feeling.

LUCY: Let's face it. If people are going to work out even a halfway decent relationship, they have to learn to suppress their selfish wishes, extend themselves, and compromise every inch of the way.

JOE: But it's all that suppressing, extending, and compromising that causes many of these problems. Joyce's effort to extend herself and do something special for Claire (make dinner for her every night) backfired because it made her unavailable to Claire in more important ways. Instead of feeling loved, Claire felt rejected. And James's suppressing his wish to complain about the opera led to his tantrum on the way home.

LUCY: Well, let's talk about James. There are lots of things that he could have done besides suppress his anger and have a tantrum. If he didn't like the singing, he could have focused on parts that he *did* like—the costumes or the sets, for instance. Or he could have spent the time mentally going over his schedule for the week. Or he could have just enjoyed the fact that he was pleasing Martha and making up for all the things that she had done for him over the years.

JOE: Well yeah, those are good things to try, and, as it happens, James tried them all. Unfortunately, he was even less a costume person than he was an opera lover. And when he tried to use the time to go over his schedule, the loud music kept him from concentrating. And when he tried to focus on the pleasure of doing something for Martha, he kept coming back to his displeasure in feeling trapped.

LUCY: Well, he obviously didn't try hard enough. The world is full of people who are so busy satisfying their own needs that they can't find the time to make their relationship work.

JOE: You're forgetting that selfishness isn't necessarily the fun thing it's cracked up to be. I realize, Lucy, that this differs from your belief that there's so much pleasure in it that people practically have to go into detox. But, if you think about it, selfishness (pushing people out of the way and grabbing what you want) is a second-rate satisfaction. It's a fallback position. It's what people do when they feel cheated, mistreated, frustrated, disappointed, starved, desperate, lonely, or bored. It's what people do when they don't value, or have temporarily lost the sense of the value of, the relationships with those they then end up bullying. It's the result of a relationship that's not going well.

LUCY: But let's be honest here. We'd all be selfish if we thought we could get away with it. At least children are up front about it. They make it clear that they want to get things rather than to give them. They say "gimme, gimme, gimme." That's what children say, and that's exactly what they mean.

JOE: But children *do* want to give. In fact it's hard sometimes to keep them from doing so. They're always bringing you things, trying to help you, trying to do things for you. Children are like everyone else. They like to get things, and they like to give them.

LUCY: Well, you're right. But the "getting" comes naturally. And the "giving"? Well, that's only because their parents have guilt-tripped and bribed them into it. But let's look at a grownup who has thrown all that aside. Let's look at the husband who plops in front of the TV and expects his wife to bring him the paper, a drink, and all his other props. And then he watches only his programs, never hers. His only unmet need is that there's not a button on the remote that can shut her off when she asks for a little affection or conversation. Would you call that "giving" and "getting" or just plain selfishness?

JOE: If it's selfishness, he's doing a pretty poor job of it. Turning a partner into a servant is like buying a Ferrari and then using it to haul trash. There are much better things to do with a partner. A partner can be somebody to get excited about, to share daydreams with, to enjoy taking care of as well as to enjoy being taken care of by, to talk things over with, to enjoy giving things to and getting things from, and to feel in it together with. This man is getting none of these things. In other words, he may seem self-indulgent, but in reality he's deprived.

Conclusion

When you think about it, the people whom we generally see as "selfish" because they exploit their partners leave untouched and untapped the major sources of satisfaction that are available in a relationship.

There are better ways to be selfish than most people realize. And these better ways involve collaboration.

And what would such "collaboration" look like? I've been talking about it all along, of course. It's the kind of interaction that becomes possible when partners adopt non-accusing forms of thinking, which allow them to:

- Build upon (rather than have to defend against) what the other says
- Develop a shared nonjudgmental vantage point for looking at their relationship
- Use their problems as clues

Chapter 19
Using Fantasies as Clues

People have fantasy wishes, and they have them all the time. They hope, for example, that their partners will automatically and spontaneously:

- Perform particularly thoughtful or caring acts (surprise them with a special dessert, get up with the kids on Saturday mornings, do the vacuuming without being asked) that will really make them feel loved and satisfied rather than taken for granted
- Engage in sex more enthusiastically, more frequently, with greater abandon, or be willing to engage in a particular sexual act that will really make them feel loved and satisfied
- Share a particular interest of theirs that is especially important to them (tennis, camping, gardening, and, yes, even opera) rather than saying no or participating grudgingly
- Take care of tasks that seem particularly burdensome at the moment (putting away the baby's toys or trying to get through to the repair shop for the third time)
- Greet them at the end of a bad day with the kind of love and reassurance that will make it all seem worthwhile
- Share their good mood rather than bring them down
- Snap them out of their bad mood rather than bring them down further

- Or, since everybody's fantasies are different, share their bad mood instead of trying to jolly them out of it

SKEPTIC: People who have such fantasy hopes are just asking for trouble.

WILE: If so, we're all asking for trouble, because we all have such hopes.

Recovering Overlooked Fantasies

Everyone knows about the hazards of fantasy expectations:

- People who expect the honeymoon feeling to last throughout the marriage may end up with lots of marriages (and lots of honeymoons).
- People who wait for the perfect partner to come along may end up with no partner at all.
- People who expect their partners to know what they want and how they feel without being told will likely end up continually disappointed.
- People who believe that they and their partners should want to spend all their time together may end up wanting to spend very little time together.
- People who believe that partners who truly love each other never exchange cross words may end up exchanging practically no words.

Few people are aware, however, of the hazards of trying *not* to have fantasies. In fact, this is the great hidden hazard in couple relationships.

Loretta is an eighth-grade teacher. Her husband, Fred, manages a bakery. They have been married twelve years and have three children. It's Loretta's fortieth birthday, and she insists that she doesn't want a party. So Fred arranges a celebration for just the two of them. He takes her to a hot springs for a sauna and massage, which has always been a special treat for her. Then he surprises her with dinner at her favorite restaurant. When they get home, he opens a bottle of fancy champagne, and gives her a special gift: a sexy nightgown. And, just in case she thinks the nightgown is more for his enjoyment than hers, he also gives her the flannel pajamas she liked in the catalog.

But something goes wrong right away for Loretta. The sauna and massage don't feel as good as she remembers them. The lighting in the restaurant just seems dark instead of romantic. And when they get home, champagne, nightgown, and pajamas notwithstanding, Loretta just feels sad.

Loretta's problem is a fantasy wish she doesn't know how to deal with. On the way to the hot springs, she realized that she really wanted a party after all. And she hoped that Fred had ignored her instructions and had secretly arranged one for her.

She imagined her friends coming from all over the country. People would even write songs for the occasion. The party would last till three in the morning, everybody having too good a time to go home. And she would be at the center of it all, feeling so close to everyone and so grateful to Fred.

That's how she wanted to turn forty. And that's why she felt dissatisfied at the hot springs and impatient at the restaurant. And that's why she was disappointed when they got home, and there was no crowd of friends springing out at her and yelling "surprise." She was disappointed, and she was angry. She was angry because she felt that Fred didn't want to give her a party. She felt that he had been secretly relieved when she had told him she didn't want one.

> **SKEPTIC:** Loretta's not going to get much sympathy from me. It's egotistical for her to want such a fuss made over her fortieth birthday. And, at forty, it's childish of her to get angry at Fred because he couldn't read her mind. Talk about unrealistic expectations.

> **WILE:** But everyone has unrealistic expectations, and everyone has them all the time. The wish to be given a surprise party is a particularly common one.

> **SKEPTIC:** Maybe so. But Loretta doesn't just expect Fred to know she wants a party. She expects him to know she wants one even though she tells him she *doesn't*. People

like that are doomed to disappointment, and they
deserve it when they get it.

WILE: Yeah, that's what Loretta believes too, and that's the
problem. Her self-criticism and embarrassment about
her fantasy prevent her from confiding in Fred about
it. And that's too bad, because it could be a significant
relief if she were able after dinner to tell him how she
felt:

LORETTA: I know it's totally unfair of me, but I had the magical
hope that you might have arranged a party as a surprise even
though I told you not to.

A surprise party would have been nice. But the lack of one—the
disappointment of Loretta's fantasy wish—is not her major problem.
Disappointment is an everyday, even an hourly, event. People are
used to being disappointed, and they learn to take it in stride. Loretta's major problem is her shame about having such a fantasy wish and
the disconnection she feels from Fred because she is unable to talk
with him about it. Confiding in him about it could be a good way to
deal with this embarrassment and disconnection.

Loretta needs a new way of looking at this fantasy wish. She needs
to be able to say to herself:

1. My wish for a surprise party is an ordinary wish and not a selfish
    one. Everyone has wishes like this whether they like it or not.
    It's the human condition.
2. It's okay to change my mind. The fact that I told Fred a month
    ago that I didn't want a party doesn't mean that it's illegal for
    me to want one sometime later.
3. True, if I were to tell Fred about my fantasy wish, he might feel
    criticized for not fulfilling it. I'll do my best to make it clear
    that I'm not criticizing him.

People would be less embarrassed by their fantasies if they could see
them as inevitable accompaniments to life. Where they had been
saying, "What's wrong with me that I'm having this fantasy?" they

would now be able to say, "Amazing! I never would have predicted *this* fantasy showing up."

Finding Fantasies in Unexpected Places

SKEPTIC: I'm not convinced that fantasies are so inevitable. Maybe Loretta has them, but lots of people don't. For instance, I'll bet a person like Fred doesn't have them.

WILE: Oh, but he does. His are just harder to notice. At the same time Loretta was hoping for a surprise birthday party, Fred was having a fantasy of his own.

At first, Fred planned Loretta's birthday celebration dutifully, because a husband is supposed to do something special for his wife on her birthday and because Loretta would be hurt and angry if he didn't. He was relieved that Loretta didn't want a party, because that would have required a lot of time and effort.

But then Fred began to get into the spirit of things. He found himself wanting to feel close to Loretta and make her birthday really memorable. He phoned the resort to make an appointment for Loretta with the masseuse she had been so happy with the last time she was there. He stopped by the restaurant and ordered a special dish—burgundy duck—that required four days' advance notice. And he searched all over town for a gift that would really please her. And he thought he had found it: the nightgown.

Fred imagined how delighted Loretta would be coming home after the special massage and the special burgundy duck and then opening the special gift while sipping the special champagne. Tears would come to her eyes. She would throw her arms around him and want to make love right then and there, on the bed of shredded gift wrap.

But Loretta didn't react the way he hoped. The massage was just okay, maybe a little rough. She was impatient during dinner because the service seemed too slow. And as for the nightgown—well, it was lucky he thought of the flannel pajamas.

When Loretta's fantasy wishes were disappointed, she was clearly upset, although she had difficulty telling Fred what it was about. When Fred's fantasy wishes were disappointed, he just shrugged a little. He didn't seem distressed. He just seemed the same old Fred. His fantasy wishes developed, collapsed, and disappeared without a trace. No one would have known that they had existed. And he had almost no memory of them himself, although a subtle, almost undetectable sadness crept into his feelings toward Loretta.

How could Fred have been rescued from this situation? Had he felt more comfortable with his fantasy wish, he might have been able to tell Loretta about it:

LORETTA: You have to admit it; you wouldn't have wanted the hassle of a party.

FRED: Well okay, sure. I *was* relieved when you said you didn't want one. But I was still trying to make things special. That's why I planned all the other stuff, like, did you notice the label on the champagne?

Fred's willingness to admit that he did not originally want a party puts Loretta in a conciliatory mood, in which she is able now to attend to what he *was* trying to do for her.

LORETTA: I feel bad now. I was so busy hoping that you'd read my mind about the party that I didn't really appreciate how much you did.

Loretta's willingness to acknowledge what Fred was trying to do puts him in a conciliatory frame of mind in which he's able to attend to what she wanted him to do.

FRED: I should have been able to figure out that you really wanted a party. Or, at least I could have checked it out with you again to make sure you hadn't changed your mind.

Fred's willingness to suggest that he should have figured it out makes Loretta feel like reassuring him that he couldn't have.

LORETTA: Yes, but by then it would have been too late. All our friends would have already made plans. And, anyway, how could you be sure I wouldn't just say, "Hey, didn't I tell you no party?"

Loretta and Fred are in a positive cycle in which each makes a conciliatory comment in response to the other doing the same.

To a great many couples being able to talk this way is more important than having or not having a birthday party.

Half-expressed Fantasy Wishes

Feeling embarrassed or self-critical about their fantasy wishes, people withhold them. Or, as in the following example, they blurt them out and then get stuck defending them. Arthur and Charlotte are a couple in their thirties. Arthur is struggling to start a consulting business. Charlotte quit her job as a high school music teacher to take care of their three young children. She supplements their income by giving piano lessons. While driving to the store, Arthur and Charlotte pass a couple on bicycles.

ARTHUR: (*blurting out his fantasy wish*) Why don't we buy bicycles?

CHARLOTTE: Do you think we'd really use them?

ARTHUR: Why do you immediately put down every idea I have?

CHARLOTTE: Because they're always so impractical.

ARTHUR: Buying bikes *isn't* impractical. We'd save money on gas.

CHARLOTTE: Sure, when it's not raining or too cold, or the rare times we don't have groceries or kids.

ARTHUR: Okay, okay. You're so logical. You take the fun out of everything.

> **SKEPTIC:** I can't get very interested in this couple. Arthur is clearly irresponsible. And he's immature. He has to have everything that strikes his fancy.
>
> **WILE:** But Arthur isn't really expecting to get these bikes. He

and Charlotte got into an argument so quickly that they never had a chance to realize that he actually agrees with her. He knows it doesn't make any sense to get these bikes. If he had told her the whole story, it would have come out this way:

ARTHUR: I know we don't have the money, and we probably wouldn't even use them that much, but seeing that couple on their bikes makes me wish we could be like them. I feel so burdened down by the struggle to get the business going, and I'm so worried about money that I wish we could just ride off together and forget it all.

To which Charlotte might have answered:

CHARLOTTE: Yeah, me too. And I know just the perfect place for it too. In fact, why don't we actually go there today and rent bikes? We have two hours before we have to pick up the kids.

And with this suggestion, Charlotte would be joining Arthur in his fantasy and turning it into a reality.

The problem with Arthur's original statement ("Why don't we buy bicycles?") is that he doesn't make it clear that he knows his plan is impractical. Charlotte is stuck having to do it. And then Arthur is stuck having to defend his fantasy. His spirited idea, a potential contribution to their relationship, has been transformed into a problem.

Charlotte and Arthur could solve the problem at any point if one of them recognized his "Let's buy bicycles" as a wish, rather than as something that he really expects them to do. Here is Arthur doing just that:

ARTHUR: Wait a minute. Why am I defending this crazy idea? Of course we don't have the money to get them or the time to use them. I was just tripping out on how wonderful it would be if we could.

Here is what Charlotte might say if she recognized Arthur's "Let's buy bicycles" as just a wish:

CHARLOTTE: Wait a minute. Maybe you were just playing with the idea of buying bikes, and I jumped in too quickly.

Skillfully Tracking Down Fantasy Wishes

Couple life is a succession of half-experienced, half-stated, half-fulfilled, easily lost, and quickly forgotten fantasies. I recommend developing skill in tracking them down and talking about them.

Let's go back to Karen and Joseph, the partners who greeted one another at the door at the end of a difficult day (Chapters 13 and 14).

- On the way home from work, Joseph had the fantasy wish that Karen would somehow magically know that he has had a hard day. She'd meet him at the door with an extra spicy Bloody Mary, have the newspaper put back together for him, keep the kids reasonably civilized, and bring his dinner to him while he watched the news. Later, she'd give him a back rub and listen with loving concern as he told her the troubles of his day, followed by …
- And Karen had her own fantasy. She imagined that Joseph would somehow magically know that her day was sheer domestic misery. He'd bring home a really great DVD, listen with rapt attention as she explained all that had gone wrong, and insist that she sit down and relax while he took care of the kids and made dinner. Later, he'd suggest that they go away for the weekend, just the two of them, and he'd arrange the babysitting.

But as soon as Joseph walks through the door, both partners' fantasy hopes are crushed. Each discovers that the fantasy rescuer is the one who needs rescuing.

SKEPTIC: Why doesn't that surprise me? It's pretty unrealistic

to expect your partner to forget his or her own
problems and immediately start taking care of you.

WILE: True, but it wouldn't take much—just a kind word, and
a chance to express their frustrations—to brighten up
Karen and Joseph's view of the world. People generally
make do with just a fraction of the fulfillment they wish
for.

SKEPTIC: I still think it's wrong for people to expect others to
take care of them. Doesn't maturity mean being able to
take care of yourself?

WILE: Karen and Joseph agree with you. And that's why they
were unable to talk about their wishes. Rather than
telling Karen about his fantasies, Joseph just presented
himself at the door with the vague, half-conscious hope
that Karen would spontaneously start fulfilling them.
And Karen didn't express her wishes either. She simply
listed all the things that had gone wrong that day,
hoping that Joseph would figure out that she needed
comforting. And then, when they saw that their fantasy
wishes weren't going to be fulfilled, they immediately
forgot them.

SKEPTIC: That's just as well, don't you think? I can't imagine
what else they could do with them. They certainly
couldn't talk about them. How can you tell your partner
about such nonsense without feeling ridiculous?

WILE: Well, how about admitting that you feel ridiculous?
Joseph could say:

JOSEPH: I know it's unreasonable for me to even think this, but
I was hoping that somehow you would magically know I
had a horrible day and you would just make all the bad
stuff disappear. You know, greet me with a whole arsenal of
goodies—a drink, some peace and quiet, all of it.

If Joseph had stated it this way—that is, as a wish that he knew was ridiculous, rather than as something that he really expected Karen to do and that he blamed her for not doing—Karen would have been less likely to feel attacked and might have responded sympathetically:

KAREN: I'd love to have done that for you, but the way my day went, first the flat tire and then the dog eating a whole stick of butter—you have no idea how fast it went through him—I needed some comforting myself.

> **SKEPTIC:** So, what's your point? Karen and Joseph are making pretty speeches, but nothing has really changed.

> **WILE:** Well, it may seem as if nothing has changed. Neither partner's fantasies are getting fulfilled, and it looks like they're not going to be. Each is too much in need of comfort to offer it to the other. But Joseph and Karen are doing something that partners rarely do. They are talking as if:

- It's okay to have outrageous, unfulfillable fantasies
- It's possible to talk about your fantasies without having to accuse your partner of not fulfilling them
- It's possible to listen to your partner's fantasies without having to feel responsible for fulfilling them

I'm suggesting this alternative way of looking at fantasies. As it is now, they're seen, on the one hand, as something that you shouldn't be having and, on the other hand, as something that your partner should be fulfilling. No one ever has the luxury of simply having them listened to and understood.

Karen and Joseph wouldn't have their fantasies of DVDs and backrubs fulfilled. What they would get, however, is help from each other in feeling that it's okay to have those wishes. And with such help, they wouldn't have had to withdraw. Instead, they might have been able to commiserate about their bad luck in having a bad day at the same time so that neither was able to help the other. After a day of alienating experiences like this one, a moment of shared commiseration can go a long way.

So that's how it's possible to become skillful in tracking down and talking about fantasy wishes. Three things are required:

1. The idea that, when something's not quite right between you and your partner, unrecognized fantasies may be hiding in the shadows too embarrassed to come out (People who are on the lookout for such hidden fantasies will be at an advantage in finding them.)
2. The belief that it's okay to have such fantasy wishes
3. The ability to talk about your fantasies in a way that doesn't make your partner defensive—that is, making clear that you see them as just that (fantasies) and that you don't really expect your partner to fulfill them

Using Fantasies as Clues

Once you are able to notice your fantasies, you are ready for the next step, which is using them as clues. Let's go back to Katie's fantasy, which I discussed in Chapter 11.

Katie thinks longingly back on the early days of the relationship, when she and Burt used to party, dance, and stay up all night talking and making love.

Daydreaming about the excitement she felt early in their marriage reveals Katie's concern about its absence now.

Just as pearls are clues to the existence of grains of sand in oysters, fantasies are clues to the existence of wishes and disappointments in people. And the nature of these fantasies reveals the nature of their wishes and disappointments.

But people hardly ever think to use their fantasies as clues. Instead, they spring into action. That's what Katie does. She finds Burt and makes a suggestion:

KATIE: Let's go rowing on the lake tonight.

Her hope is to recapture some of the old romantic feeling. She doesn't tell Burt that she has been missing the intimacy that they had early in their relationship and that she hopes a romantic activity they use to share might bring it back. She simply says, "Let's go rowing."

Katie's having a positive fantasy. She hopes an evening in the moonlight will revive their romance. Burt's having a negative fantasy. He thinks the same activity will show how *un*romantic they've become. So he says:

BURT: Sounds okay to me, but let's talk about it later.

Burt hopes Katie will forget about it. She doesn't forget about it; neither does she bring it up again. She just feels another degree sadder.

Actually, there isn't anything necessarily wrong with springing into action. I do it all the time, and I get a lot out of it. And Katie and Burt could possibly have gotten a lot out of it, too. If Burt had agreed to go rowing, the two of them might have been able to recapture some of the old spirit.

Springing into action is a problem only when people limit themselves to it. I recommend springing into action *and* talking about the underlying fantasies.

Two weeks later, Katie does try to talk about these fantasies. Unfortunately, as typically happens with feelings that have been held back, when they do emerge, they do so as accusations, which triggers a negative cycle.

KATIE: Why is it that we never stay up all night talking anymore or go to parties or go dancing or even make love the way we use to? (*She is implying that he is the one who doesn't want to do these things.*)

Burt responds as people generally do when they feel accused. He defends himself. He responds with reasons rather than feelings.

BURT: You know I have to get up early to go to work. We were in school back then, and we could sleep till noon.

The battle lines have been drawn. Katie answers that they both had morning classes, so they couldn't have slept till noon. Burt says that they had only one class in the morning, one day a week, and that they did so sleep till noon. The discussion gets stuck on their schedule twenty-five years ago, and Katie never does get her point across about missing the romantic feeling they used to have about each other. She comes away depressed that Burt won't listen to her. And secretly she worries that she's too demanding.

Katie's mistake is stating her fantasy as a complaint rather than as a wish. Actually, there's nothing wrong with stating a fantasy as a complaint. At least, let's hope there's not, because that's what we all do. It's difficult to resist slipping into accusation when feeling awkward, uncertain, or frustrated. And people often feel that way about their fantasies.

Stating a fantasy as a complaint is a problem only when that's all you do. I recommend making the complaint, perhaps having the argument that may result, and then coming back later and using the fantasy as a clue. That's what Katie does. She goes to Burt later.

KATIE: I don't know what got into me. Just because I want to go out on the lake doesn't mean that you have to. And at our age who even wants to stay up all night making love?

BURT: Actually, that part of it did kind of appeal to me.

KATIE: Hmm. Why doesn't that surprise me? Well, I didn't say exactly what we'd do when we were in that rowboat.

BURT: (*smiling*) Oh, maybe I was too quick to say no to the boat.

For a moment, Katie and Burt have regained that old spirit. This is how they used to talk.

KATIE: (*continuing*) I don't even know what got me thinking about the lake … Well, actually, maybe I do. I've been missing the old spark—you know, how it was when we used to do things like that.

BURT: Those were good times.

KATIE: I felt a lot closer to you then ... though, I don't know, I feel pretty close to you right now.

Katie feels close right now because she's just confided what's on her mind, which is that she hadn't been feeling close. That's what Katie's fantasy is about. She had been daydreaming about periods of special intimacy in the past because she missed feeling intimate right now. And she got the intimacy back—at least for the moment—by confiding what was on her mind.

Intimacy is the result of talking; it is hearing what's on your partner's mind and telling your partner what's on yours, even—no, particularly—if what's on your mind is that you don't feel intimate.

Clues We Never Use

The ideal is for partners to use their fantasies as clues. But that's hard to do. When have you ever heard anyone say anything like the following?

- "I've been thinking about how we used to stay up all night talking and making love, and that must mean I'm feeling what I usually feel when I have that fantasy: distant from you."
- "I've been thinking all day about the time we took off all our clothes and went swimming in that lake in the mountains—so it must mean I'm feeling what I usually feel when I have that fantasy: that things haven't been feeling special enough between us."
- "Lately I've been imagining living alone in a cabin in the woods. What could that mean but that I've agreed to do more things with you (shopping, skiing, that cooking class) than I really want to do."
- "I've been thinking again about that affair you had ten years ago, so it must mean that I'm feeling ignored by you."
- "I've been thinking about my former boyfriend, so it must mean that I'm feeling taken for granted."

- "I've been wishing that you would greet me at the door in
a particularly warm, loving, sexy, and charming way (or
tell me how much you care for me, or come over and give
me a hug, or suddenly feel all turned on by me and want
to have mad, passionate sex), so it must mean that I'm
feeling neglected."

People don't talk about their fantasies. And while it's a shame that
they don't, it's also understandable.

If a woman told her husband that she had been looking forward
to being greeted at the door by a charming, masterful, and rescuing
man rather than the depressed, grumpy, and withdrawn person that
she usually found, he is likely to get upset. And if he answers that
he had been looking forward to being greeted by a warm, loving,
comforting, and rescuing woman rather than the complaining,
frazzled, ill-tempered person he usually found, she is likely to get
upset.

But even if they were to say these things, all is not lost. What is left
for these partners—and it is a very considerable compensation—is to
commiserate with one another. Husband and wife may agree that it
is a shame neither is able to give the love and caring the other wants
because, among other reasons, at the moment both need to be loved
and cared for themselves.

Partners can comfort each other regarding the human condition—the fact that many of our most important needs and wishes
remain unfulfilled.

Fortunately, it's an irony of the human condition that the very act
of sharing unfulfilled fantasies may go a long way toward fulfilling
them. A man who has spend half the day at the unemployment
office—standing on long lines, feeling ignored by the very staff that
are paid to help him, being criticized for not accepting dishwashing
jobs—reacts by imagining being affirmed at home at least to the same
degree that he felt humiliated earlier. He thus comes home with a
rather extravagant fantasy of how his wife might express this affir-
mation. It might take no more than a kind word from her, however,
and a chance to talk about the frustrations of the day, to interrupt
his view of the world as cold and indifferent and to substitute a more

benign one. He might no longer need his fantasy expectation to be fulfilled; it would in a sense have been fulfilled.

It is not difficult to understand how this might happen. People often respond to frustrations in the sphere of reality by imagining exquisite gratifications in the sphere of fantasy. It might take no more than a fragment of real satisfaction—a kind word from the person you're closest to—to make fantasy satisfaction no longer necessary.

In summary, fantasies are:

- Inevitable accompaniments to life (Everybody has them.)
- Compensations for momentary frustrations and deprivations (As such they provide clues to the existence of these frustrations and deprivations.)
- *Exaggerated* compensations (They aren't necessarily to be taken literally. A man starving out in the wild fantasizes, not about a sandwich and a cup of coffee, but about an orgy of food—a Roman feast. But a real sandwich does the job and, oh yes, the coffee.)

SKEPTIC: I'll tell you *my* fantasy.

WILE: Yeah, what?

SKEPTIC: That I get to win one of the arguments we've been having.

WILE: That truly is a fantasy, since this is my book. If you want to win an argument, you'll have to write your own book.

Part VIII

CONCLUSION: A NEW WAY TO HAVE A RELATIONSHIP

Chapter 20
It's Not What You Do
But What You Know

I have always disliked the kind of book that I'm now writing—books that promise, for example, "ten ways to a better relationship." How can relationship problems that reflect longstanding personal difficulties possibly be resolved by advice such as "be tactful," "learn to compromise," "listen to your partner," "avoid unrealistic expectations," "never go to bed still angry," and so on?

I now believe that there are, indeed "ten ways to a better relationship." Or, as I would prefer to put it, there are ten (or, actually, forty-two) things to *know* that can help you work out your problems. What I think partners need to know, however, differs from what is generally suggested.

- We're told in these books to compromise. But we've already compromised—and that's part of the problem.
- We're told that it's important to have a positive attitude (that is, to expect the best), and it is. But it's also important to have a negative attitude (that is, to expect the worst).
- We're told we shouldn't take our fantasy-based expectations seriously. In fact, we need to take them much more seriously.
- We're told that problems come from blaming our partners. But problems also come from trying *not* to blame our partners.
- We're told that dependency is a childish quality we need

to outgrow. But dependency is an adult skill we need to develop.

- We're told that intimacy comes from doing things together. But intimacy comes from talking together about whatever we do and whatever we think.

My objection to the ideas in certain self-help books is not that they offer quick solutions but that the quick solutions they offer may contribute to the problem. Partners are often *already* reproaching themselves and each other for *not* having a more positive attitude, being more independent, more willing to compromise, and so on—and such self-reproach is much of the problem. Self-help books too often teach people how to be better at hating themselves.

So I've developed my own list of useful things for partners to know. Here, collected from the rest of the book, are the ideas partners need if they are to work out a satisfying relationship.

SKEPTIC: Oh no. I feel another list coming up!

A Hidden Rationality

1. Behavior that appears on the surface to be inappropriate, irrational, childish, or pathological has a hidden rationality—and in terms of the present and not just the past. Behavior that *is* about the past may also be about the present. A partner's special sensitivities from childhood may enable him or her to detect subtle difficulties that are actually occurring in the present relationship. A wife's childhood-based special sensitivity to being ignored (she feels rejected by her mother) can enable her to detect the subtle ways in which she is actually being ignored by her husband now.

Makeshift Solutions

2. When people are unable to think or talk effectively about their problems, they engage in makeshift solutions that often lead to

worse problems. At the same time, makeshift solutions sometimes work and are the major way we solve our problems. A man brings home a DVD in hopes that watching it with his wife will draw them closer together, which it might. But it might also have the opposite effect. Sitting there silently watching it together might just make him more aware of how truly distant they have become.

Cultural Slogans

3. A great deal of our thinking is self-propaganda—attempts to talk ourselves into or out of our feelings. We employ culturally sanctioned complaints or slogans as a way of justifying hard-to-justify feelings and wishes.

Problems

4. A relationship problem is really two problems: (a) the problem itself, and (b) how you talk (or don't talk) about it. How you talk or don't talk about a problem is often the major part of the problem.

5. Certain relationship problems are unsolvable, at least for the moment. Accordingly, the best way to deal with them is to establish an ongoing way of talking about them and to develop skill in recovering from them.

6. We're told that it's important to have a positive attitude, and it is: "If you expect problems," we're told, "you'll find them." But it's also important to have a negative attitude: "If you expect problems," I suggest, "you'll be better prepared to deal with them."

7. No one ever begins a relationship in such a way (it's seen as much too unromantic) but there is value, when choosing a long-term partner, in realizing that you will inevitably be choosing a particular set of irresolvable problems that you'll be grappling with for the next ten, twenty, or fifty years. What people don't like about their partners may be the other side of what they

do like. In fact, a relationship is, in some sense, the attempt to work out the negative side effects of what attracts you to your partner in the first place.

8. Problems can be used as clues to hidden feelings; that is, they can be turned to advantage. A man criticizes his wife for being a compulsive housekeeper when he feels she's ignoring him. He thinks he shouldn't feel upset about her not greeting him at the door, but he does feel justified in complaining about her fastidiousness. Ideally, this husband could use his sudden preoccupation with his wife's housekeeping as a clue to the fact that he just felt slighted by her.

9. Problems are the result of conversations we fail to have. If this husband had been able to talk about feeling slighted, and if his wife had responded compassionately, he might find himself no longer wanting to criticize her housekeeping, at least not as much. People get upset and start doing provocative things or acting crazy when they are unable to express what they need to say.

Intimacy

10. Intimacy comes from telling your partner the main things on your mind and hearing the main things on your partner's mind. It's talking about what you're feeling even if what you're feeling is that you miss being intimate. The chance to express feelings and make complaints can have a powerful love-reviving and closeness-reviving effect.

Dependency

11. "Dependent" is a ruined concept. Once the term is used, the person so labeled is automatically considered as having a crucial deficit. And that's too bad, because dependency is a skill that needs to be developed rather than a deficit that needs to be overcome. Dependency is too important a task to be left to children.

The Curative Power of Relationships

12. One of the major purposes of relationships is to cure. Despite what you might have been told, you *can* expect your relationship to solve your problems, fill the gaps in your personality, and help you love yourself.

Conversational Booby Traps

13. Almost all of us repeatedly give advice or offer solutions when, instead, our partners just want us to appreciate how they feel. The way to deal with this problem is to recognize such unwanted advice or fixing as a common error, become skillful at recognizing it when it occurs, and develop a non-blaming way of talking about it when it does.

14. When you are bored by what your partner says, it's easy to conclude that your partner is "just boring" or that you are "just self-centered" or that the two of you are "just incompatible." These nightmare ideas keep you from realizing that your partner may be boring as a result of his or her efforts *not* to be boring or because he or she is leaving out the most important parts—feelings. And you may be bored because of your inability to talk about being bored.

Using Communication Errors as Clues

15. We are told to make "I statements" rather than "you statements." But you statements are clues to hidden I statements. You statements indicate that something needs to be talked about; I statements provide the means to do it.

16. We are told not to say "always" or "never." But people say always and never when they feel they aren't getting their points across. It's a means of emphasis and an expression of frustration.

17. We are told to listen to our partners and not interrupt them. But we have a hard time listening when, as often happens, we feel un-listened-to by our partner. We are left with a difficult

choice: to interrupt, which squelches the other person, or not to interrupt, which squelches us.

18. We are told not to speculate about our partners' feelings, but to talk only about our own. But mind reading—reading our partner's mind—might reveal what's on our mind and, as such, might be a useful clue to what we are feeling. The statement, "Why are you so angry at me?" might mean "I'm worried that you're angry. I've been working late so many nights in a row, and I'm worried that you might be upset about it. Are you?" Mind reading is often an expression of our feelings—particularly of worry or fear—put in the form of assertions about our partner's feelings.

19. We are told that when we talk about difficult issues we should stick to the topic and avoid digging up grievances from the past. But we're *not* going to stick to the topic if doing so puts us at a disadvantage in the fight. And we *are* going to dig up grievances from the past if that's what it takes to find a clear example of what we are trying to show is happening in more subtle ways now.

20. We are told not to name-call and not to get bogged down arguing about irrelevant issues. But we name-call because we are feeling so frustrated, hurt, stung, put upon, or un-listened-to that we are willing to resort to almost anything—even to statements that will make our partners even less likely to listen to us. And we argue about irrelevant issues because we are so upset with our partners that we don't want to agree with them about anything.

21. We are told not to dump out stored-up complaints. But if we don't dump them out, they might never get out at all. And it's important that these complaints be brought to the surface so that they can be talked about.

Fighting

22. Partners may either express anger, which leads to fighting, or suppress it, which leads to boredom, loss of love, *and* fighting.

People withdraw in order not to fight, and they fight as a reac
tion to withdrawal.

23. What you are saying may be more accusatory than you realize. Accusing turns your partner into someone who can't listen. Listening to your partner turns him or her into someone who might listen.

24. Fights become irresolvable when, as often happens, neither partner is able to get across what he or she needs to say. Partner A has no interest in hearing what Partner B has to say until Partner B listens to what Partner A has to say. But that won't happen because Partner B has no interest in hearing what Partner A has to say until Partner A listens to what Partner B has to say.

25. The belief that you are having a discussion when you are really having an argument has given talking a bad name. Thinking they're "only talking" when they're actually fighting, people come away all the more convinced that talking just makes matters worse.

26. It's difficult to have a fight and a conversation at the same time (although we continually try to do it), and it's necessary to have the fight first. Although a fight is the wrong climate in which to work out any issues, it's often only during a fight that we ever bring up these issues. Fights are, thus, both pathways and obstacles to conversations. After the fight is the time to discuss the issues revealed by the fight.

27. The initial statements of held-back complaints are exaggerated and inaccurate. The dust may need to settle before you'll be able to find out how angry your partner really is and what he or she is actually angry about.

28. Your partner is more likely to listen to you if you report your anger (that is, say that you are angry) rather than unload it (say angry things). And your partner is even more likely to listen to you if you report the hurt or disappointment that underlies your anger.

29. One way to get your partner to listen to you is to express the ways in which you agree with what he or she has just said and go

on from there to make your point. Talking about your partner's contribution to the fight is likely to rekindle the fight.

Pursuit and Distance

30.   In each couple, one partner typically wants to do a particular thing (talk, spend time together, have sex) at least slightly more than the other does. Soon, the first person (the "pursuer") is seen by both as always wanting to do that thing, and the second person (the "distancer") is seen as never wanting to do it.

31.   Both the pursuer and the distancer are partly right. The pursuer is right, for example, that it's important to be able to talk about their problems, whereas the distancer is right that, at the moment, they have no way to do so that doesn't just lead to a fight.

32.   The common advice given to partners in a pursuer-distancer interaction is that the pursuer should stop pursuing, and the distancer should stop withdrawing. But the pursuer can't stop pursuing, and the distancer can't stop withdrawing. Furthermore, the pursuer is already spending most of his or her time trying not to pursue (and that's part of the problem), and the distancer is already making futile attempts not to withdraw.

33.   Everyone knows that pursuers are deprived. That's why they pursue: to try to get what they're missing. But no one realizes that distancers are just as deprived. While the pursuer may be deprived, for example, of having a partner who looks forward to spending time with him or her, the distancer is deprived of having a partner he or she wants to spend time with. In addition, in pursuer-distancer relationships, both partners lose part of themselves: distancers lose the part that might want to engage with, talk to, and be affectionate toward their partners; pursuers lose the part that might otherwise have prompted them to do things on their own.

34.   The best way to deal with pursuit and distance or, for that matter, any of the other troublesome couple patterns, is to

recognize their inevitability and develop a joint perspective from which to view them.

Bypassing and Nonbypassing

35.   In a bypasser-nonbypasser conflict, the bypasser gets caught up in fantasy while the nonbypasser is left behind in reality. Bypassers and nonbypassers have mutually incompatible ways of solving problems. The bypasser's way is to stop talking about it (because that just makes matters worse) and to trip out into an idealized version of reality. The nonbypasser's way is to try to talk about it (even though talking about it might make matters worse) because he or she can't trip off in fantasy. For the nonbypasser, love requires an ability to complain. For the bypasser, love requires not being complained about.

Compromising

36.   People make compromises so quickly and so automatically that they are often unaware of doing it. People may become uncompromising because of the hidden compromises that they are already making. The boredom and devitalization that creep into relationships are consequences of the continuous flow of unrecognized compromises and accommodations.

37.   Compromises are calculated risks that people don't even realize they are making. The risk is that they will be able to get away with doing something they really don't want to do without becoming so resentful that they either start a fight or withdraw.

Fantasies

38.   Fantasies are inevitable accompaniments to life. Everybody has them. They are compensations for life's frustrations and depri-

vations. As such, they provide clues to the nature/existence of these frustrations and deprivations.

39. Fantasies are seen, on the one hand, as something that you shouldn't be having and, on the other hand, as something that your partner should be fulfilling. People rarely have the luxury to be able just to have their fantasies—and to learn from them—without having to do anything about them.

40. Problems arise when one partner's fantasy musings are mistakenly heard by the partner as something that he or she actually intends for them to do. While walking in their neighborhood, a man says to his wife, "Look, that house is for sale. What do you think of our putting a bid on it?" The wife, not realizing that he's only fantasizing about the house, says, "Are you crazy? We can't afford that. We'd be in hock for the rest of our lives." The husband, angered by her tone, stubbornly argues that they can *so* afford it. They get into a fight in which the wife gets stuck pointing out reality, and the husband gets stuck defending the fantasy, when, actually, they agree: both would like the house, and both know they can't afford it.

Ideas Are Dangerous

And there is a further idea that people need to have. This idea, which challenges all the other ideas, is that ideas can themselves be dangerous. They become dangerous when they turn into *shoulds*. For example, the important idea that "anger is natural" can quickly turn into the rule that people should express anger. Whereas before people criticized each other (and themselves) for expressing anger; now the criticism is for failing to express it. "You shouldn't hold onto your anger," they say, "You should let it all out."

This tendency to turn ideas into rules seems characteristic of human thinking. Constance Apfelbaum talks about "a reflex-like conversion of insight into moral imperative as a habit of human consciousness," by which she means that ideas that originally have the effect of liberating us can themselves become imprisoning.

- When "nice" women were rescued from the Victorian belief that sex for a woman was no more than an unpleasant duty, they then felt duty-bound to enjoy sex.
- When women were freed from the pre-women's movement belief that their only place was at home as wife and mother, they then felt duty-bound to have careers.
- When men were allowed to shed the macho image, they then felt duty-bound to have feelings.

Closing the door on one rule may result merely in opening it to another. The "Human Potential" or "Growth" movement was founded on an important insight—that certain widely accepted and longstanding social virtues (politeness, propriety, and dutifulness)— had serious drawbacks. Specifically, these virtues led to superficial relationships and unnecessary emotional barriers. But what began as a liberating idea—people opening up to each other—turned into a new pressure: they now felt *required* to express deep feelings and have meaningful conversations.

So here is idea number 41:

41. Ideas that have the potential to free people (including all the ideas on this list) can turn into rules that further oppress them.

But Can Ideas Really Help?

SKEPTIC: You're saying that ideas are powerful and dangerous. But if you ask me they're weak, ineffectual, and beside the point. People talk *ad nauseam* and I've yet to see any good come out of it.

WILE: Yes, a lot of talking *is* beside the point—or, worse, counterproductive. One of my objectives in the book is to distinguish the kind of talking and thinking that is helpful from that which is not. Take a look at my list. You'll have to admit that the ideas on it are useful.

SKEPTIC: I'll admit nothing. But even if some of them are useful, how realistic is it to expect that any of them will make a difference—or that a reader will even remember them? There are so many, and most of them go against what we've always been taught.

WILE: Sadly, you're right. I have difficulty remembering them, and I wrote the book. But I know a couple who have just read this book and can explain it better than I can. Sybil and Gus are in their early forties and have been living together for ten years. Sybil is a dietician at a private hospital, and Gus is an architect in a large firm. My book happens to be open and sitting on the kitchen table right in front of them.

Gus is telling Sybil about a new underground bowling alley that he and Ben, a colleague in his firm, are building in the new shopping center. He is deep into the part about "reinforced arches," "ceiling joists," and "tensile strength," when he sees Sybil stifling a yawn.

Gus is about to do what he usually does when Sybil seems bored: blurt out "Well, if you're not interested, forget it" and immediately leave the room. But before he can do this, his gaze falls on this book and he reads:

IDEA NUMBER 14: Your partner may be boring as a result of his or her efforts *not* to be boring or because he or she is leaving out the most important parts—feelings.

GUS: Oh, so you want to hear about my feelings? I'll tell you about my feelings. I've been royally screwed. They shouldn't have let Ben anywhere near the project. I came up with the design, and then they give the project to him to oversee. He's letting the contractors get away with murder. I go crazy when I think of all the things that could go wrong later.

Sybil is no longer bored. Instead, she's upset.

SYBIL: You've got to go to your boss first thing tomorrow and tell him. Better yet, call him right now. Here's the phone.

Gus had wanted Sybil's interest, but not this! She senses that her comment isn't going over well, but she doesn't know why. And Gus doesn't know, either. He thinks he should be appreciating her interest, not resenting it.

So they grab the book and frantically look for something that might help them figure out what is happening. And they find it.

> **IDEA NUMBER 13:** Almost all of us repeatedly give advice or offer solutions when, instead, our partners just want us to appreciate how they feel.

SYBIL: How embarrassing! You probably just want me to listen, and here I am telling you what to do.

GUS: Right, I already feel overloaded.

SYBIL: I can believe it! Just hearing about it overloads me. Ben is the boss's nephew, isn't he?

GUS: That's probably why he got the job.

SYBIL: I can't stand how they pulled it right out from under you. That's why I wanted you to phone right away—because I felt so helpless.

Sybil came on strong because she was unable to tell Gus how painfully frustrated she felt on his behalf, which she recognizes as another idea in the book. She reads:

> **IDEA NUMBER 9:** People get upset and start doing provocative things when they're unable to express what they need to say.

SYBIL: You know, it's funny, but if I'd been able to say all this, maybe I wouldn't have had to tell you to call your boss.

GUS: Yes, you wouldn't have. That's because I'd be thinking of doing it myself. You'd have helped me realize how helpless I feel about it.

Sybil and Gus are able to have this conversation because they read the book and had it lying open on the table. Without the book, Gus would be getting in his car and driving too fast trying to cool down, and Sybil would be sitting in the kitchen fighting off the strongest urge for a cigarette she'd had since giving up smoking ten years ago.

But how realistic is it to expect Sybil and Gus to have such a conversation even with the book so readily available? It's hard to imagine anyone thinking that fast, being so articulate, and having all the ideas they need exactly when they need them.

Fortunately, Sybil and Gus wouldn't have to have the whole conversation. Even just a fraction of it could make a big difference.

And they wouldn't have to have the conversation right away. Suppose Gus hadn't glanced at the book and, instead, had run out of the house and into his car. Even while that upset, he might suddenly realize that Sybil was bored because he hadn't told her how he felt. And he might then come back inside and tried to talk with her about it.

And they wouldn't have to have the conversation all at once. Gus may realize two days later that he was resentful that Sybil hadn't appreciated how he felt. And Sybil may realize three days after that that she'd come on so strong because she felt helpless. They could have a conversation bit by bit over the course of days as the information slowly came out.

In fact, they wouldn't have to have the conversation at all. Just Gus knowing that he was being boring because he was leaving out his feelings or that Sybil's bossy behavior was the result of her feeling helpless could go a long way in clearing things up. Gus would no longer have to see himself as "just boring." And he'd no longer have to see Sybil as "just selfish" and "just bossy."

We're all used to operating at a severe disadvantage. Just having a little edge, now and again, can make a big difference.

My goal in this book is to do for other important ideas what George Bach, in *The Intimate Enemy* and other books, did for the idea of anger. People came away from his books on couple fighting convinced that the anger that they and their partners feel toward each other is inevitable rather than, as they feared, the sign of a bad relationship. And for some, this new insight remained permanently accessible. My hope is to make the ideas about relationships presented in this book just as familiar, usable, and reliably available to partners.

The ideal in the case of Sybil and Gus would be for them to apply this new knowledge in future situations. But how realistic is this? In a few weeks they might have only a dim memory of what the book was about.

And even if they did remember, they're still likely to slip back into their classic, "real" beliefs that:

- Gus is just boring
- Sybil is too self-involved to care about Gus and his work
- Gus refuses to take Sybil's good advice about how to handle his problems at work
- Sybil just comes on too strong

In other words, Sybil and Gus would have slipped back into their accusing kind of reasoning that blocks useful thinking and talking.

The problem with the forty-one ideas is that they don't stick to your bones. And that brings us to the forty-second and final idea:

42. You're likely to forget the other forty-one. These ideas are so difficult to remember because they go against what we've always been taught.

But just being aware of this danger—that is, knowing that we're likely to forget these ideas—may enable us to prepare for the forgetting to happen and to feel less upset about it when it does.

And remembering that we won't remember is the most crucial idea of all. That's because the ultimate goal in a couple relationship is the creation by partners of a joint platform from which to view their inevitable lapses into accusatory or self-accusatory thinking in which they forget everything useful they know.

> **SKEPTIC:** That's the weakest, least ambitious, most anticlimactic "ultimate goal" I've ever heard! If that's the best you've got to offer, I might as well stick to suppressing my complaints, avoiding fights, using

self-restraint, maintaining a positive attitude, making compromises, avoiding unrealistic expectations, and just trying to get along.

WILE: But imagine if you had suppressed complaints, avoided fights, and used self-restraint while reading this book. It wouldn't have been nearly as much fun. You wouldn't have gotten as much out of it. And you might have stopped reading it halfway through.

SKEPTIC: Maybe.

WILE: And without your comments, this book wouldn't have been as much fun for me, either. I wouldn't have gotten as much out of it. And I might have stopped writing it halfway through.

SKEPTIC: Well, I'm touched.

WILE: So, in couple relationships, the more of your thoughts, feelings, complaints, wishes, fantasies, disappointments, resentments—everything—you can include in your relationship, the more you'll get out of it, and the less you'll want to end it halfway through.